EMPOWERING OUR MILITARY CONSCIENCE

Military and Defence Ethics

Series Editors

Don Carrick – Project Director of the Military Ethics Education Network based in the Institute of Applied Ethics at the University of Hull.

James Connelly – Professor of Politics and International Studies, Director of the Institute of Applied Ethics, and Project Leader of the Military Ethics Education Network at the University of Hull.

Paul Robinson – Professor in Public and International Affairs at the University of Ottawa.

George Lucas – Professor of Philosophy and Director of Navy and National Programs in the Stockdale Center for Ethical Leadership at the US Naval Academy, Annapolis M, USA.

There is an urgent and growing need for all those involved in matters of national defence – from policy makers to armaments manufacturers to members of the armed forces – to behave, and to be seen to behave, ethically. The ethical dimensions of making decisions and taking action in the defence arena are the subject of intense and ongoing media interest and public scrutiny. It is vital that all those involved be given the benefit of the finest possible advice and support. Such advice is best sought from those who have great practical experience or theoretical wisdom (or both) in their particular field and publication of their work in this series will ensure that it is readily accessible to all who need it.

Also in the series

Kantian Thinking about Military Ethics
By J. Carl Ficarrotta
ISBN: 978-0-7546-7992-9

Ethics Education for Irregular Warfare
Edited by Don Carrick, James Connelly and Paul Robinson
ISBN: 978-0-7546-7700-0

Empowering Our Military Conscience

Transforming Just War Theory and Military Moral Education

Edited by

ROGER WERTHEIMER
Agnes Scott College, USA

ASHGATE

Published by
Ashgate Publishing Limited
Wey Court East
Union Road
Farnham
Surrey, GU9 7PT
England

Ashgate Publishing Company
Suite 420
101 Cherry Street
Burlington
VT 05401-4405
USA

www.ashgate.com

British Library Cataloguing in Publication Data
 Empowering our military conscience : transforming just war
   theory and military moral education. -- (Military and
   defence ethics)
   1. Just war doctrine. 2. Military ethics. 3. Military
   ethics--Study and teaching.
   I. Series II. Wertheimer, Roger.
   172.4'2-dc22

Library of Congress Cataloging-in-Publication Data
Empowering our military conscience : transforming just war theory and military moral
education / edited by Roger Wertheimer.
     p. cm. -- (Military and defence ethics)
 Includes bibliographical references and index.
 ISBN 978-0-7546-7894-6 (hbk) -- ISBN 978-0-7546-9765-7 (ebook)
 1. Military education--Moral and ethical aspects--United States. 2. Military education--
Moral and ethical aspects. 3. Conscience--United States. 4. Conscience. 5. Military ethics-
-United States. 6. Military ethics. 7. Just war doctrine. 8. Moral education--United States.
9. Moral education. 10. War--Moral and ethical aspects. I. Wertheimer, Roger.
   U408.3.E48 2009
   172'.42--dc22   2009032350

ISBN: 9780754678946 (hbk)
ISBN: 9780754697657 (ebk)

Mixed Sources
Product group from well-managed
forests and other controlled sources
www.fsc.org Cert no. SA-COC-1565
© 1996 Forest Stewardship Council
FSC

Printed and bound in Great Britain by
MPG Books Group, UK

Contents

Notes on the Contributors   *vii*
Preface   *ix*
Acknowledgments   *xi*

Introduction: A Great Awakening
    Roger Wertheimer   1

PART I   JUS AD BELLUM

1   The Triumph of Just War Theory (and the Dangers of Success)   15
    Michael Walzer

2   "Methodological Anarchy": Arguing about Preventive War   33
    George R. Lucas, Jr.

3   Crossing Borders to Fight Injustice: The Ethics of Humanitarian
    Intervention   57
    Richard W. Miller

PART II   JUS IN BELLO

4   The Proper Role of Intention in Military Decision Making   77
    T.M. Scanlon

5   Ethics for Calamities: How Strict is the Moral Rule Against
    Targeting Non-combatants?   93
    Jeffrey Reiman

6   Invincible Ignorance, Moral Equality, and Professional
    Obligation   107
    Richard Schoonhoven

PART III   JUS ANTE BELLUM

7   The Moral Singularity of Military Professionalism   133
         Roger Wertheimer

8   The Morality of Military Ethics Education   159
         Roger Wertheimer

Index   *197*

Notes on the Contributors

George R. Lucas, Jr. is Professor of Philosophy and Director of Navy and National Programs in the Vice Admiral James B. Stockdale Center for Ethical Leadership at the United States Naval Academy (Annapolis, MD). He is also Visiting Professor of Ethics at the Naval Postgraduate School (Monterey, CA), and Senior Research Associate in the Center for Ethics Research at the French Military Academy (Saint-Cyr). He has taught at Emory University, Georgetown University, and served as Chair of the Department of Philosophy at Santa Clara University, and also as Assistant Director in the Division of Research Programs in the National Endowment for the Humanities. He was a Fulbright Fellow in Belgium in 1989, and held a fellowship from the American Council of Learned Societies in 1983. Lucas is author of five books, over 60 journal articles, translations, and book reviews. He has also edited several collections of articles in systematic philosophy, the history of philosophy, and ethics, including *Perspectives on Humanitarian Intervention* (University of California, 2001), and *Anthropologists in Arms: The Ethics of Military Anthropology* (Alta Mira, 2009).

Richard W. Miller is Professor of Philosophy at Cornell. His writings, in social and political philosophy, ethics, epistemology, the philosophy of science and aesthetics, include many articles and four books, *Analyzing Marx* (1984), *Fact and Method* (1987), *Moral Differences* (1992), and *Globalizing Justice* (2010).

Jeffrey Reiman is the William Fraser McDowell Professor of Philosophy at American University in Washington, D.C. and is the author of *In Defense of Political Philosophy* (1972), *Justice and Modern Moral Philosophy* (1990), *Critical Moral Liberalism: Theory and Practice* (1997), *The Death Penalty: For and Against* (with Louis P. Pojman, 1998), *Abortion and the Ways We Value Human Life* (1999), *The Rich Get Richer and the Poor Get Prison: Ideology, Class, and Criminal Justice* (9th edition, 2010), and more than 60 articles in philosophy and criminal justice journals and anthologies. He is co-editor (with Paul Leighton) of the anthologies *Criminal Justice Ethics* (2001) and *The Rich Get Richer and the Poor Get Prison: A Reader* (2010).

T.M. Scanlon was educated at Princeton, Oxford, and Harvard, where he received his Ph.D. in 1968. He taught philosophy at Princeton from 1966 until 1984 and then moved to Harvard, where he is now Alford Professor of Natural Religion, Moral Philosophy, and Civil Polity. Scanlon was one of the founding editors of the journal, *Philosophy & Public Affairs*, and most of his publications have been in moral and political philosophy. In his 1982 article, "Contractualism and Utilitarianism", he defended a "contractualist" theory, according to which an action is morally wrong if any principle that permitted it could reasonably be rejected. This theory is further developed in his book, *What We Owe to Each Other* (Harvard University Press, 1999). His most recent book is *Moral Dimensions: Permissibility, Meaning, Blame.*

Richard Schoonhoven is Associate Professor of Philosophy at the United States Military Academy (West Point). He received his B.A. from UC Berkeley and his Ph.D. from the University of Michigan. His doctoral dissertation was *Explaining Causation: Toward a Humean Theory of Scientific Explanation and Causation* (2000), and he continues to write on topics at the intersection of philosophy of science and metaphysics, as well as on issues regarding the morality of war.

Michael Walzer taught at Princeton, Harvard, and since 1980 has been at the Institute for Advanced Study in Princeton. He has published over 25 books including *The Revolution of the Saints* (1965), *Obligations* (1970), *Just and Unjust Wars* (1977), *Spheres of Justice* (1983), *Interpretation and Social Criticism* (1987), *What It Means to be an American* (1992), *On Toleration* (1997, translated into 15 languages), and *Arguing About War* (2004). He is currently working on the toleration and accommodation of "difference" in all its forms and also on a collaborative, multi-volume work, *The Jewish Political Tradition.*

Roger Wertheimer studied at Brandeis and Harvard, receiving Harvard's Carrier Prize for the outstanding philosophy doctoral dissertation (1969). He has worked as a Deputy Sheriff, Guggenheim Fellow, psychotherapist, entrepreneur, and philosophy professor at schools such as Tufts, Carnegie-Mellon, Irvine, CUNY, Houston, Cincinnati, Portland, and the U.S. Naval Academy, where he was Distinguished Chair of Ethics (2001-2003). He has authored *The Significance of Sense* (1972) and essays in philosophy of language, metaphysics, and issues within theoretical or applied ethics or about their relation.

Preface

This book presumes and promotes two ideas. First, while what is popularly called Just War Theory (JWT) has long been widely recognized to encompass the two subjects of *jus ad bellum* (the propriety of going to war, of warring at all) and *jus in bello* (the propriety of conduct within war), and now recognizes the subject of *jus post bellum* (the propriety of the treatment of a defeated people), there is a fourth area meriting inclusion: *jus ante bellum*, a key part of which is *jus in disciplina bellica*, the ethics of educating for warfare. The Ashgate series in which this volume appears and the pages of military journals in recent years evidence an emerging recognition of the existence and importance of this field. Its questions have long been with us waiting to be asked.

Second, what militaries now call Professional Military Ethics Education (PMEE) must transmit the ethos of military professionalism. That is a definitional truth, like: Triangles must have three angles. It's also a consequential historical fact, a peculiarity of the context in which questions about military ethics education are now framed and considered. Today, such education must accommodate and advance something called Professional Military Education (PME). Our military culture has a near two century heritage of insistently conceiving of its officers as "professionals". This self-conception is now so engrained that our military has little capacity and less patience for considering alternative conceptions of the proper ends and means of military education—about ethics or anything else. So, assessments of PMEE policies and programs are bootless without a proper understanding of military professionalism.

These two ideas motivate the whole work but they are referenced or operative only in the Introduction and Part III (Jus Ante Bellum). The Introduction explains how the chapters of Part I (Jus ad Bellum) and Part II (Jus In Bello) serve the aims of this book.

Roger Wertheimer

Acknowledgments

The chapter by Michael Walzer is a substantial revision by him for this volume of an essay of the same title, based upon a lecture given at both the U.S. Naval Academy and Georgetown University, and originally published in the journal, *Social Research* (vol. 69, no. 4: winter, 2002; pp. 925-44). The editor is grateful to the editor of *Social Research*, Professor Arien Mack, for permission to publish Dr. Walzer's revisions in this volume.

Introduction:
A Great Awakening

Roger Wertheimer

All it is is think

CWO Hugh Thompson
USNA William C. Stutt Ethics Lecture, Fall 2003

Near 20 years ago a committee of the United States Senate directed its federal military academies to submit their students to a college credit course in ethics before commissioning them as officers. Hitherto, academy ethics course requirements had been imposed or lifted as each superintendent saw fit. Provoked by the antics of an Annapolis graduate and his prevarication in their chambers, our elected representatives saw fit to impose the requirement by Congressional mandate.

The mandate and courses are matters of public record, not state secrets, but public knowledge of them is nil. Their significance is not appreciated, not considered. No reckoning is made of what these matters tell us about the culture of this nation and the culture of its military. It takes a peculiar mindset, an historically novel house of assumptions and hopes, for a society to respond to the misbehavior of a military officer by compelling his successors to study the most intellectually cultivated thinking on ethics and the proper conduct of the managers of its means of killing masses of persons. This is, I believe, the sole Congressionally enjoined course at our service academies—or anywhere. That students may refer to it as "the Ollie North course" with some degree of cynicism is not surprising or dispiriting.

This book testifies to that mandate's significance. So the book owes much to the escapades of Lt. Col. Oliver North, USMC (ret.), and appreciates his most enduring contribution to the nation he served so daringly and thoughtlessly. The new requirement rejuvenated ethics education at his alma mater, the U.S. Naval Academy (USNA), where it had been rather moribund, unlike the U.S. Military Academy (USMA) and the U.S. Air Force Academy (USAFA). These institutions share a central mission of instilling character and central assumptions of how to execute it. Character instillation has always been mostly by various modes of indoctrination, not education: training and exhortation, not intellectual challenges and critical thought. The fate of Philosophy and Ethical Theory had waxed and waned over the years, each school having its own history.[1] At USNA, with the

---

1 Throughout this volume, the term "philosophy" refers primarily to the process and product of dialectical thought in the Socratic tradition typified by this collection. The

mandated introduction of a mandated course and the institutional focus on this new intellectual component, other of the character development programs became more educational, less inculcational, more analytic, critical, thoughtful and thought provoking. The other academies have trended alike.

To advise and aid its efforts, USNA instituted a position, the Distinguished Chair in Ethics (DCE), which was, I believe, without precedent. It was an academic faculty position, a visiting professorship (effectively for two years) in the Ethics Section, yet its prime function was neither teaching nor scholarly research, but instead advising the Academy's Superintendent (College President), the Commandant (Dean of Students), and the Provost/Academic Dean regarding USNA's very various efforts at enhancing the moral character of midshipmen. The DCE was funded with a private, alumni donation. Taxpayer support of this mission was insufficient.

The advising extended to overseeing the academy's diverse Ethics Across the Curriculum (EAC) activities. Advisory competence was presumed to come from applying an expertise in moral reasoning and its instruction at civilian institutions to the knowledge acquired as participant-observer in USNA's ethics and character education programs, sitting on Academy executive boards and team-teaching the core ethics course with three to five civilian Ph.D.s and some 30 senior military officers, from Marine Majors to retired Fleet Admirals. The DCE's understanding of his client's needs was regularly facilitated and encouraged with frank personal conversations and sponsored on-site inspections of the comparable programs at USMA and USAFA. I met less suspiciousness than when I advised a law enforcement agency decades prior. (Per usual, suspicions peak in middle management.) The absence of clearance for classified matters of national security did not thwart relevant inquiries.

The DCE was designed to be a position of influence, not window-dressing for outsiders. In USNA's military organizational flow chart the DCE was one of about eight persons reporting directly to the commanding officer, the Superintendent, a 3-star admiral. The only other faculty member with that access was the DCE's counterpart, with whom he shared a secretary, the Distinguished Chair in Leadership, a retired 3- or 4-star admiral.

I was honored to be the last holder of this visiting chair. The DCE was terminated when its mission was largely accomplished. USNA ethics education had been vitalized. The Ethics Section was staffed with (just barely) enough Philosophy Ph.D.s. The core course had evolved and stabilized. Retaining a plushly paid and supported DCE became a luxury for an academy facing brutal budget cuts (some 25 percent) for an indefinite future due to America's "war on terror" (a term rolling some Admirals' eyes.)

---

ruminations of a Marcus Aurelieus and comparable thoughtful warriors are not disdained, just not discussed. So too for prophetic teachings, preachings and parables presented without reasoned argument.

As overseer of the Academy's EAC programs, the DCE directed a lecture series, inviting outside philosophy professors to give informal brown bag talks open to the USNA faculty and staff—and often attended by the Superintendent himself. (Faculty at civilian schools with 4000+ students can report how commonly they see their President at comparable events.) Midshipmen were welcome but their schedules allow scant options.

Many of these monthly talks were original contributions to scholarly philosophical thought as intellectually impressive as any presented at Harvard or Oxford. Many of our nation's most esteemed moral philosophers came happily, despite an honorarium well below the going rate at civilian schools. Many talks were on topics not distinctively military. Enough of the best had enough specific military focus to publish a collection with topical coherence. Another talk I helped arrange that called for inclusion was the Fall 2002 guest lecture in the military ethics course by Michael Walzer, the pre-eminent theorist in the field.

Serendipitously, the selections make a neat structure of six essays, each a substantial contribution to the literature of so-called *Just War Theory* (JWT), with three in Part I on *jus ad bellum* (the propriety of going to war, engaging in war at all) and three in Part II on *jus in bello* (the propriety of military conduct within a war). Part I presents competing conceptions of the intellectual and political history of JWT, and competing conceptions of basic principles and their application to America's main recent military ventures. Collectively they shred their government's two favorite rationalizations for invading Iraq. The chapters of Part II finely analyze and compellingly challenge three pillars of current *jus in bello* orthodoxy.

The lead essay, Michael Walzer's "The Triumph of Just War Theory (and the Dangers of Success)", is a brief intellectual and political history of JWT focusing on *jus ad bellum*. His contribution is something of a retrospective on his *Just and Unjust Wars* (1977), which took JWT from the cloisters of religious and legal theorists and made it a cottage industry in secular, civilian, academic political philosophy. Such thinking entered the academies with the intellectualization of moral education there. Cadets and midshipmen had long been taught the laws of war. Now they studied the best moral theorizing about those laws and debates questioning their onerous restrictions. Walzer's book became the only text on JWT the military academies (independently) required in all the required ethics courses. In his USNA talk, as usual, Walzer's historical analysis is at the service of his political analysis, in this case, on the principles regarding preemptive and preventive wars, and their import for the impending U.S. invasion of Iraq (at that time, some four months away) and the "Bush doctrine".

George R. Lucas, Jr.'s "Methodological Anarchy: Arguing about Preventive War" looks at JWT and its history afresh, also with an eye toward evaluating the Bush doctrine. He sees Walzer working in a distinctive, modern tributary, departing in important respects from older streams of thought, with a distinctive style of analysis and a more restricted, defensive attitude than the original, Catholic tradition supported. Walzer's historical account describes an evolution with great continuities in the content of JWT and great shifts in its political influence. Lucas emphasizes the contrasts in the content and methods among distinct and often insular traditions of JWT. On this view, the term, "Just War Theory", may now be a misnomer. The actual referent of that name is no longer (if it ever was) a relatively unified theory but a topic around which families of argument have contended, with various distinctive doctrines, concepts, methodologies and frameworks. For Lucas, this renders suspect any claims about what JWT says on controversial issues like preventive and preemptive war. This volume well illustrates Lucas' point. Its critiques of core principles of JWT orthodoxy are all in-house proposals for reform of JWT. Neither individually nor collectively do they present a repudiation of any doctrine with authoritative claim to the title, "Just War Theory". With this complex history as backdrop, Lucas analyzes our concept of *vigilante* and insightfully applies it to America's invasion of Iraq, and a remarkable recent trend of cases.

Richard Miller's "Crossing Borders to Fight Injustice: The Ethics of Humanitarian Intervention" critically examines the most common rationale for U.S. military action in recent years and likely the foreseeable future: "humanitarian intervention". Combining a richly informed historical understanding with careful normative analysis, Miller advances leagues beyond the vague generalizations typical of *jus ad bellum* discussions, and identifies considerations of sufficient plausibility and specificity to frame deliberations about engaging in humanitarian intervention. This is JWT brought down to earth: "applied ethics" applying no ethical theory, but instead skills, best acquired by studying ethical theory, in locating and formulating the essential structure of a complex moral controversy. Miller operates without a net, without reference to any "theory", and lets his readers' good sense see the good sense in some *jus ad bellum* principles with a specificity that limits self-serving interpretation.

These three chapters about deciding to war are tied to past events, but are in no danger of being "dated" or out of date. Their depth ensures their enduring interest.

The other three talks were directed against three principles currently assumed crucial for *jus in bello*: (1) A differentiation of the class of legitimate military targets from a protected class of things not permissibly subject to military attacks; (2) A prohibition of *intentionally* harming members of the protected class that permits harming them unintentionally, even if knowingly, by otherwise permissible acts; (3) A restriction of the responsibility of combatants to compliance with the rules of *jus in bello*, and absolution of their responsibility for their contribution to a heinous activity, their nation's violation of *jus ad bellum*, and its terrible consequences.

Much JWT thinking departs from St. Thomas Aquinas' dicta, while his Doctrine of Double Effect (DDE) still skews *jus in bello* thinking, legal and moral, about military targeting. Applied to war, the DDE assumes a differentiation of legitimate military targets—enemy combatants and the materials essential to their activity (e.g., facilities for producing, transporting or storing munitions)—from illegitimate military targets: non-combatants (most civilians, military clergy and medical personnel, POWs, etc.) and their means of survival. The DDE flatly condemns all intentional harming of non-combatants, and then licenses any military to incinerate, suffocate or dismember any number of noncombatant bodies, just so long as it was *unintentional*, and even when it was as foreseeable as sunrise, but only when the horrific wreckage is "proportionate" according to some incomprehensible comparison with the target's morally mystifying "military value".

T.M Scanlon's "The Proper Role of Intention in Military Decision Making" distinguishes our multiple conceptions of intentionality and explains why intentions have, at most, only an incidental relevance to the moral permissibility of military targeting. Military strategists and tacticians may come away from this highly abstract contribution worrying whether it has any practical import. The question, if not the worry, is appropriate, for Scanlon is not out to reform, but to make systematic sense of, the case by case moral judgments most reasonable people already accept. The practical import here, as in much moral theorizing, is that a refined theoretical understanding lessens our liability to fall into errors, confusion, indecision, or self-deception or to fall for propaganda and self-serving rationalizations when confronting novel or complex controversies. Scanlon argues that the moral discriminations we already make are incompatible with the DDE. The pattern of our "gut" judgments is best explained by our operating, consciously or not, more reasonably, more sensitively to everyone's legitimate interests, and without confusing an action's moral quality with the moral qualities of the agent's motivation. Scanlon's analysis tells against a venerable dogma of *jus in bello*, and equally against the equally venerable dogma of *jus ad bellum* that however much our circumstances cry us to war, however many millions more suffer if we don't war, however compelling the moral reasons for going to war, we must not war unless these are the reasons that will us to war. (Nations need be wary of guidance from those more concerned with sin than international justice.)

Jeffrey Reiman's answer to his title question, "Ethics for Calamities: How Strict is the Moral Rule Against Targeting Non-combatants?" is a trenchant criticism of the traditional conception of military discrimination presupposed by the DDE. Reiman shares many of Scanlon's intuitive doubts about the moral significance of intentionality, but his own primary target is the moral significance of the combatant-noncombatant distinction sanctioned by the current laws of war. The conventions determining combatant and noncombatant status have notorious incongruities, and Reiman is hardly the first to notice various obvious paradoxical features of the orthodoxy here. Reiman goes deeper and proposes a novel restructuring of principles to register our untutored responses to warfare's scale of manmade suffering. He boldly yet cautiously defends some radical conclusions that many readers may recoil from, while many others greet gladly for their sensitivity to their own moral sensibilities.

Richard Schoonhoven's "Invincible Ignorance, Moral Equality, and Professional Obligation" critiques the modern assumption that deems war a moral singularity and walls off issues of *jus in bello* from those of *jus ad bellum* and made war a moral singularity. Outside warfare, unless excused by extraordinary coercion, duress or the like, people are held accountable, morally and legally, for their contribution to a wrongful infliction of great suffering. Following Walzer's *Just and Unjust Wars* which would have us "collectivize" responsibility for warring, current JWT orthodoxy (excepting Catholicism's Augustinian tradition) regards all combatants as "moral equals" in the sense that, however just or unjust the cause a combatant serves, every combatant is, morally, equally entitled to harm (kill, injure, imprison) enemy combatants by any means *jus in bello* precepts permit. This amazing modern moral notion says, in essence, that no conscience can justifiably object to military service in any of its nation's wars, for combatants are exempt from all moral responsibility for such service. Nothing remotely like this alleged disappearance of accountability is needed to justify current war conventions prohibiting harsh treatment of all captive enemy combatants. Nor is there historical evidence of this notion explaining why nations all around this planet, whatever their cultural heritage, commit themselves to these conventions. Unalloyed considerations of national self-interest are plenty obvious and powerful enough to explain and justify every nation's signature. Schoonhoven step by step dismantles this principle's standard rationale, which exculpates all combatants by attributing to them an "invincible ignorance" of the justice of their nation's cause. He does not pretend to prove that combatants are morally complicit in the horrendous injustices abetted by their serving their nation. Suffice that Schoonhoven leaves us wondering how we could honestly justify denying this.

A collection of these six contributions would merit publication on its own as a prime candidate for the central text in a college course on JWT. I know of no other single work that can compel such a thorough, fundamental, multifaceted rethinking of JWT. We might all profit if it were read by the world's opinion makers and decision makers.

That these were all invited talks at the Naval Academy of the world's mightiest military makes their publication all the more valuable. They are illuminating historical documents, evidence of a matter of great global interest. They exemplify the efforts of the American military to sharpen and strengthen the moral sense of its officers by confronting them with the most intellectually challenging moral and political thinking on military matters currently available. That two of the six authors are regular, full-time academy professors is further evidence of the quality the academies' moral education programs sometimes attain.

Before my stint as DCE, I, like most civilians, assumed that military ethics education is, as it generally had been, the installation of rigid habits of thought and action, solid skills and stolid character. Of course, unlike their enlisted subordinates, commanders need substantial skills of analysis and innovation, but any questioning of first principles is uncalled for—or so it had been thought and still is by most civilians, and many in the military.

This book documents, celebrates and anxiously reflects upon a Great Awakening, an untrumpeted intellectual and moral liberation within America's military. That military still wants its personnel to be imbued with common core values and principles. But now the organization, or at least enough of its leadership, recognizes that its forces cannot function well unless their officers have the capacities for independent, critical thought developed by a liberal arts education that explores and questions the central pillars of its culture, including its most fundamental moral assumptions. This realization has much the same roots as the recognition, expressed by the Chairman of the Joint Chiefs of Staff, that conditions of the modern world "place a premium on our [military's] ability to foster innovation in our" military personnel.[2]

Publication of these chapters is overdue. Actions of American military personnel at Abu Ghraib, Guantanamo, Haditha, Hamandiyah—and rumors of many more— have shocked the conscience of world opinion like never before, and set off a great surge of concern, sweeping across the United States and around the world, about the ethics education of American military personnel. A global concern with the moral character of America's military personnel is understandable and justifiable. Regrettably, the anxious babbling has rumbled self-righteously along unchecked by any inkling of the transformation in American military moral education over the last two decades. This nation, its allies and its enemies, all ought to learn of the admirable efforts that have been made, starting long before the invasion of Iraq, to armor the conscience of America's military officers with the world's most advanced weapons of ethical reasoning. Every nation has reason to join this book in celebrating this military's strivings to make the quality of moral thought in its academies as good as it gets anywhere.

Publication of these contributions is needed to provide interested parties everywhere, not the fleeting comfort of vague assurances, but a vivid, first-hand sense of the character and quality of ethics education at America's military academies. It matters mightily that what USNA wanted and got were talks of utmost critical acuity and intellectual rigor, not sermons or pep talks reciting official doctrine. My guess is that it would (rightly) mean little to most people to be told that our future officers read a few bits and pieces from the classics (Aristotle, Kant, etc.) It might mean lots to lots of people to read and wrestle with the kind of current, intellectually daunting, counter-establishment, moral and political critiques this military has its present and prospective leaders consider and come to terms with.

The academies must contend with the reality that most citizens suppose (with none but anecdotal evidence) that the old ways are wisest, that service personnel are best kept on paths straight and narrow just by firm discipline and ritual reaffirmations of moral platitudes. Many people, like the many entering these military academies, are blissfully certain that they already know perfectly well what is right and what is wrong, and they see no value in—indeed no possibility of—further *education* in such matters. For that mindset it is unimaginable how officers could benefit from confronting arguments of the gauge, caliber, and penetrating power of these essays. In fact, as officers often come to appreciate (after the course or after the academy), they desperately need to learn that there

---

2   "Joint Vision 2020", U.S. Printing Office, Washington, DC, 2000.

really are moral arguments markedly more mature than anything they meet in the media, officer clubs, or church.

The audience for these talks are persons of demonstrably superior intelligence who could recognize that what they were being exposed to is a lot of stuff the likes of which they had not seen before, with an unfamiliar density of abstraction, nuanced qualifications, novel distinctions, close argument and counter-argument. Whether any in the audience was persuaded by any of the reasoning is immaterial. While much of the character training at the academies has a definite doctrinal agenda, what drives much of the compulsory ethics course, and the whole EAC lecture series (and this volume deriving from it) is not any doctrinal agenda. (No guiding animus against JWT orthodoxy lurks here.) The audience is properly empowered even when struggling to grasp the subtleties of the more abstract essays. They can still see that their difficulties in following the argument lie with themselves. This is all fairly jargon-free reasoning, but the ratio of argument to assertion is high, and the language is taut, precise, without fluff. It is reasoning that *compel*s respect, even if not concurrence. These contributions show their audience what Socrates showed his: that another human being may very well have thought through some moral matter more skillfully, imaginatively and insightfully than they had or could have on their own, and come to other conclusions. Appreciating that unnerving fact is the first step toward a proper humility about one's capacities as a leader, a decision maker, a moral judge and a human being.

These chapters are one indicia of our military's enlightenment. Another indicia is the creation of the DCE position. America's citizenry would do well to reflect upon the fact that our military turned to academic ethical theorists, with no ties to the military or reliance on allegedly revealed truths, to guide its efforts to cultivate its officers' moral thought and character. Many professed patriots, who avow profound fealty to and fondness for their nation while forsaking its founding principles, would call for the academies to trust chaplains and Holy Scripture to give whatever moral guidance is needed.

Still another indicia of our military's intellectual liberation. Many a patriot would suffer a slacked jaw on learning of their defense force's hiring me, of all people, for DCE despite both the FBI dossier on the 1968 return of my draft card in protest of the Vietnam War, and the taste for acidic irony, alien to academese and militarese alike, indulged in my writings More, USNA hired me despite my showing no signs of mellowing but instead, during my interview, bluntly voicing skepticism of the contents, structure and staffing of what I had seen of USNA's core ethics course. Still more startling (my marveling remains), the academy leadership I worked for evidently welcomed my ungenerous assessments, and sure seemed to take my advice seriously by acting on it with greater than random frequency, sometimes despite influential opposition. All this testifies to the intellectual and moral seriousness of my employers, not to any talents I may have.

Yet, predictably, the enlightenment of America's military remains a work in progress, and sometimes in regress. Though not in headlong retreat, the advances have sometimes given ground. There is a characteristic military mindset, distinctive habits of thought and feeling, favored by the organizational imperatives of the military. Those imperatives make uniformity a priority and motivate mechanisms encouraging and entrenching the mindset. Revising core cultural assumptions or encouraging the questioning of them is bound to engender resistance from many of the multi-million members of the Department of Defense (DoD) and its service branches—and disconnects among its enormous complex of offices, policies and practices. The enlightenment exhibited and nurtured by the academies is partial even there. Outside their walls, the reigning mindset continues, knowingly or unthinkingly, to subvert it. However dismaying, it is hardly surprising to hear official organs broadcast "Stormin" Norman Schwarzkopf's sorry simplification: "The truth of the matter is that you always know the right thing to do. The hard part is doing it." That conviction, with its evident certainty, so natural for military minds, is a dagger at the heart of the ethics education programs this volume celebrates.

As DCE teaching in USNA's core ethics course, I needed to acquire a deep understanding of JWT. As DCE advising USNA's leaders on all aspects of its efforts at developing moral character, I needed to acquire a deep understanding of Professional Military Ethics Education (PMEE). Some results of my efforts comprise the two chapters of this volume's Part III. My ambitions there are multiple. One main aim of Part III is to chart or create connections between JWT and PMEE that neither has much noticed. The first chapter, "The Moral Singularity of Military Professionalism" (MSMP), aims (1) to contribute to JWT as traditionally conceived by considering Schoonhoven's topic of combatant moral equality from the perspective of the ethos of military professionalism, rather than the Schoonhoven-Walzer academic ethicists' perspective, and (2) to understand military professionalism as the Enlightenment's response to the peculiar "moral precariousness" inherent in warrior work that Walzer's conception of moral equality responds to improperly. The understanding of that ethos developed in MSMP is fitted for the needs of PMEE, which is the subject of the next chapter, "The Morality of Military Ethics Education" (MMEE). These two chapters are joined by a continuing dominant focus on the interplay within military professionalism of distinct, legitimate, basic imperatives (principles, goals, values). MMEE finds the PMEE of American academies negotiating various competing demands, most commonly between the organizational imperative of maximization of military proficiency and the Enlightenment call for respect for persons. These conflicts are inherent in the transformed military moral education exemplified by the contributions of Parts I and II. I wish for these chapters to be understood, taken together, as reconceiving the reach of JWT.

Philosophical geniuses as far apart as Plato, Rousseau, Kant, and Dewey have appreciated that abstract moral theorizing is a feckless enterprise when detached from any mechanism for cultivating decision makers' capacities and dispositions to translate philosophy into conduct. This is especially pertinent to theorizing about the ethics of warfare. In this case the absence of an educational mechanism can be a grave injustice.

A nation has the responsibility for training and licensing its own military personnel, especially its leadership. The government is derelict if it doesn't do what it can to adequately equip them morally as well as materially, physically, intellectually, and emotionally. As MMEE explains in greater detail, to let loose upon the world commanders of military power ill-prepared to properly appreciate the moral aspects of their fateful decisions is to put in peril their fellow citizens and military subordinates, other nations, and the commanders themselves.

MMEE is an early foray into the field of *jus in disciplina bellica*. It ranges widely and often rapidly over assorted subjects, in part just to convey some sense of this field's scope and the diversity of its issues. Like the contributions by my fellow contemporary academic ethical theorists, it is written with a style of thought unnatural to military minds, however much they may profitably appreciate it. A profession of radical action does not normally reward a mindset of perpetual questioning and open-ended disputation about starting assumptions and first principles. (That is one of this chapter's topics.)

Unlike the other contributions, much of this final chapter's questioning of fond assumptions might be mistaken for belittlement of America's military or its academies. That would be a grievous misreading. The message is that conflicts within PMEE manifested in our academies (and much of our military) are not conflicts between good and evil, but clashes between competing legitimate aims and interests we are stuck with. They are elemental, not optional. Frequently I question or criticize current responses to these clashes. I have zero interest in assessing or laying blame, and a dominant interest in making plain why the conflicts resist neat resolution. One main conclusion is that, if there be any fault to find in the military regarding this matter, it is a failure to have properly considered the questions raised—a complaint uncomfortably made when the client pays you precisely for your presumed expertise in raising such questions.

This last point alludes to a further peculiarity of the chapter. It is written with the purposes and perspective of a hired applied ethicist, an advisory/consultant profession with its own peculiar, controversial rights and responsibilities, but without, perhaps forever, any officially recognized code of ethics.[3] Still further peculiarities come with the peculiar nature of the client (a Navy and Marine Corps of hitherto unimaginable power) and the proclivities of the advisor, a poster child of the 1960s, long suspicious of his nation's military might and moral sense, and convinced that no better use is to be made of whatever skills he has than assisting this military's PMEE mission.

This last chapter's questioning cuts closer to home for some intended readers. Its edges are more liable to scrape some sensibilities. The chapter's purpose, like that of the DCE's office, is not to congratulate or flatter, but to provide knowledgeable,

---

3   See my "Applying Ethical Theory: Caveats from a Case Study", in D. Rosenthal and F. Shehadi, eds, *Applied Ethics and Ethical Theory*, Utah, 1988, 229-55, and "Socratic Scepticism", *Metaphilosophy*, Oct., 1993 (24,4), 344-62, reprinted in E. Winkler and J. Kuhns, eds, *Applied Ethics*, Blackwell, 1993.

candid, if sometimes unkind, assessment of assorted contentious matters. The intent is not to belittle this military's efforts—except as a means to prodding it to do better. Yet, human intentions are inherently open to multiple, equally accurate or reasonable descriptions. My intent risks seeming threatening for my report aims to put our military on alert that it is woefully unprepared for the battles of ideas it is destined to contend with in the years ahead. Our military risks making moral errors and, error or no, risks public embarrassment (and its command of respect in its ranks and in national and international opinion) by its incomprehension of its unresolved internal moral conflicts. The history of messengers bearing bad news is not cheering.

My harsh appraisals will likely evoke more outraged howls from flag-draped politicos and pundits than from the military leaders I came to respect and admire, who might understandably resent some remarks. I can only hope they all come to see that I can best serve this nation's military by speaking most credibly to those who share some of my anxieties about America's militaristic past and present unprecedented military predominance. Such readers (and some canny commanders) would rightly be more suspicious of a kinder, gentler, more respectful report.

PART I
Jus ad Bellum

Chapter 1

The Triumph of Just War Theory
(and the Dangers of Success)

Michael Walzer

Section I

Some political theories die and go to heaven; some, I hope, die and go to hell. But some have a long life in this world, a history most often of service to the powers-that-be, but also, sometimes, an oppositionist history. The theory of just war began in the service of the powers. At least, that is how I interpret Augustine's achievement: he replaced the radical refusal of Christian pacifists with the active ministry of the Christian soldier. Now pious Christians could fight on behalf of the worldly city, for the sake of imperial peace (in this case, literally, *pax Romana*); but they had to fight justly, only for the sake of peace, and always, Augustine insisted, with a downcast demeanor, without anger or lust.[1] Seen from the perspective of primitive Christianity, this account of just war was simply an excuse, a way of making war morally and religiously possible. And that was indeed the function of the theory. But its defenders would have said, and I am inclined to agree, that it made war possible in a world where war was, sometimes, necessary.

From the beginning, the theory had a critical edge: soldiers (or, at least, their officers) were supposed to refuse to fight in wars of conquest and to oppose or abstain from the standard military practices of rape and pillage after the battle was won. But just war was a worldly theory, in every sense of that term, and it continued to serve worldly interests against Christian radicalism. It is important to note, though, that Christian radicalism had more than one version: it could be expressed in a pacifist rejection of war, but it could also be expressed in war itself, in the religiously driven crusade. Augustine opposed the first of these; following in Aquinas's footsteps, Catholic theologians and philosophers set themselves more and more firmly against the second. The classic statement comes in the sixteenth century from the Spanish Dominican, Francisco de Vitoria: "Difference of religion cannot be a cause of just war." For centuries, from the time of the Crusades to the religious wars of the Reformation years, many of the priests and preachers of Christian Europe, many lords and barons (and even a few kings), had been committed to the legitimacy of using military force against unbelievers: they

---

1   Augustine's argument on just war can be found in 1962, pp. 162-83; modern readers will need a commentary: see Dean, 1963, pp. 134-71.

had their own version of *jihad.* Vitoria claimed, by contrast, that "the sole and only just cause for waging war is when harm has been inflicted."[2] Just war was an argument of the religious center against pacifists, on the one side, and holy warriors, on the other, and because of its enemies (and even though its proponents were theologians), it took shape as a secular theory—which is simply another way of describing its worldliness.

So the rulers of this world embraced the theory, and did not fight a single war without describing it, or hiring intellectuals to describe it, as a war for peace and justice. Most often, of course, this description was hypocritical: the tribute that vice pays to virtue. But the need to pay the tribute opens those who pay it to the criticism of the virtuous. I mean, of the brave and virtuous, of whom there have been only a few (but one could also say: at least a few). I will cite one heroic moment, from the history of the academic world: sometime around 1520, the faculty of the University of Salamanca met in solemn assembly and voted that the Spanish conquest of Central America was a violation of natural law and an unjust war.[3] I haven't been able to find out anything about the subsequent fate of the good professors. Certainly, there were not many moments like that one, but what happened at Salamanca suggests that just war theory never lost its critical edge. The theory provided worldly reasons for going to war, but the reasons were limited--and they had to be worldly. Converting the Aztecs to Christianity was not a just cause; nor was seizing the gold of the Americas or enslaving its inhabitants.

Writers like Grotius and Pufendorf incorporated just war theory into international law, but the rise of the modern state and the legal (and philosophical) acceptance of state sovereignty, pushed the theory into the background. Now the political foreground was occupied by people we can think of as Machiavellian princes, hard men and sometimes women, driven by "reason of state," who did what (they said) they had to do. Worldly prudence triumphed over worldly justice; realism over what was increasingly disparaged as naive idealism. The princes of the world continued to defend their wars, using the language of international law, which was also, at least in part, the language of just war. But the defenses were marginal to the enterprise, and I suspect that it was the least important of the state's intellectuals who put them forward. States claimed a right to fight whenever their rulers deemed it necessary, and the rulers took sovereignty to mean that no-one could judge their decisions. They not only fought when they wanted; they fought how they wanted, returning to the old Roman maxim that held war to be a lawless activity: *inter arma silent leges*—which, again, was taken to mean that there was no law above or beyond the decrees of the state; conventional restraints on the conduct of war

---

2   See Vitoria, 1991, pp. 302-4, and for commentary, Johnson, 1975, pp. 150-71.

3   See Boswell (1952, p. 129), quoting Dr. Johnson: "'I love the University of Salamanca, for when the Spaniards were in doubt as to the lawfulness of conquering America, the University of Salamanca gave it as their opinion that it was not lawful.' He spoke this with great emotion..."

could always be overridden for the sake of victory.[4] Arguments about justice were treated as a kind of moralizing, inappropriate to the anarchic conditions of international society. For this world, just war wasn't worldly enough.

In the 1950s and early 1960s, when I was in graduate school, realism was the reigning doctrine in the field of "international relations." The standard reference was not to justice but to interest. Moral argument was against the rules of the discipline as it was commonly practiced, though a few writers defended interest as the new morality.[5] There were many political scientists in those years who preened themselves as modern Machiavellis and dreamed of whispering in the ear of the prince; and a certain number of them, enough to stimulate the ambition of the others, actually got to whisper. They practiced being cool and tough-minded; they taught the princes, who didn't always need to be taught, how to get results through the calculated application of force. Results were understood in terms of "the national interest," which was the objectively determined sum of power and wealth here and now plus the probability of future power and wealth. More of both was almost always taken to be better; only a few writers argued for the acceptance of prudential limits; moral limits were, as I remember those years, never discussed. Just war theory was relegated to religion departments, theological seminaries, and a few Catholic universities. And even in those places, isolated though they were from the political world, the theory was pressed toward realist positions; perhaps for the sake of self-preservation, its advocates surrendered something of its critical edge.

Vietnam changed all this, although it took a while for the change to register at the theoretical level. What happened first happened in the realm of practice. The war became a subject of political debate; it was widely opposed, mostly by people on the left. These were people heavily influenced by Marxism; they also spoke a language of interest; they shared with the princes and professors of American politics a disdain for moralizing. And yet the experience of the war pressed them toward moral argument. Of course, the war in their eyes was radically imprudent; it couldn't be won; its costs, even if Americans thought only of themselves, were much too high; it was an imperialist adventure unwise even for the imperialists; it set the US against the cause of national liberation, which would alienate us from the Third World (and significant parts of the First). But these claims failed utterly to express the feelings of most of the war's opponents, feelings that had to do with the systematic exposure of Vietnamese civilians to the violence of American war making. Almost against its will, the left fell into morality. All of us in the anti-war camp suddenly began talking the language of just war—though we didn't know that that was what we were doing.

---

4   With some hesitation, I cite my own discussion of military necessity (and the references there to more sympathetic treatments): Walzer, 1977, pp. 144-51, 239-42, 251-5.

5   The best discussion of the realists is Smith, 1986; chapter 6, on Hans Morganthau, is especially relevant to my argument here.

It may seem odd to recall the 1960s in this way, since today the left seems all-too-quick to make moral arguments, even absolutist moral arguments. But this description of the contemporary left seems to me mistaken. A certain kind of politicized, instrumental, and highly selective moralizing is indeed increasingly common among leftist writers, but this is not serious moral argument. It is not what we learned, or ought to have learned, from the Vietnam years. What happened then was that people on the left, and many others too, looked for a common moral language. And what was most available was the language of just war. We were, all of us, a bit rusty, unaccustomed to speaking in public about morality. The realist ascendancy had robbed us of the very words that we needed, which we slowly reclaimed: aggression, intervention, just cause, self-defense, non-combatant immunity, proportionality, prisoners of war, civilians, double effect, terrorism, war crimes, and so on. And we came to understand that these words had meanings; of course, they could be used instrumentally; that's always true of political and moral terms; but if we attended to their meanings, we found ourselves involved in a discussion that had its own structure. Like characters in a novel, concepts in a theory shape the narrative or the argument in which they figure.

Once the war was over, just war became an academic subject; now political scientists and philosophers discovered the theory; it was written about in the journals and taught in the universities—and also in the (American) military academies and war colleges. A small group of Vietnam veterans played a major role in making the discipline of morality central to the military curriculum.[6] They had bad memories. They welcomed just war theory precisely because it was in their eyes a critical theory. It is, in fact, doubly critical—of war's occasions and its conduct. I suspect that the veterans were most concerned with the second of these. It wasn't only that they wanted to avoid anything like the My Lai massacre in future wars; they wanted, like professional soldiers everywhere, to distinguish their profession from mere butchery. And because of their Vietnam experience, they believed that this had to be done systematically; it required not only a code but also a theory. Once upon a time, I suppose, aristocratic honor had grounded the military code; in a more democratic and egalitarian age, the code had to be defended with arguments.

And so we argued. The discussions and debates were wide-ranging even if, once the war was over, they were mostly academic. It is easy to forget how large the academic world is in the United States: there are millions of students and tens of thousands of professors. So a lot of people were involved, future citizens and army officers, and the theory was mostly presented, though this presentation was also disputed, as a manual for wartime criticism. Our cases and examples were drawn from Vietnam and were framed so as to invite criticism (the debate over nuclear deterrence was also carried on, in part, in the language of just war, but this was a highly technical debate and engaged far fewer people than did Vietnam). Here

---

6   Anthony Hartle is one of those veterans, who eventually wrote his own book on the ethics of war: 1989.

was a war that we should never have fought, and that we fought badly, brutally, as if there were no moral limits. So it became, retrospectively, an occasion for drawing a line—and for committing ourselves to the moral casuistry necessary to determine the precise location of the line. Ever since Pascal's brilliant denunciation, casuistry has had a bad name among moral philosophers; it is commonly taken to be excessively permissive, not so much an application as a relaxation of the moral rules. When we looked back at the Vietnamese cases, however, we were more likely to deny permission than to grant it, insisting again and again that what had been done should not have been done.

But there was another feature of Vietnam that gave the moral critique of the war special force: it was a war that we lost, and the brutality with which we fought the war almost certainly contributed to our defeat. In a war for "hearts and minds," rather than for land and resources, justice turns out to be a key to victory. So just war theory looked once again like the worldly doctrine that it is. And here, I think, is the deepest cause of the theory's contemporary triumph: there are now reasons of state for fighting justly. One might almost say that justice has become a military necessity.

There were probably earlier wars in which the deliberate killing of civilians, and also the common military carelessness about killing civilians, proved to be counterproductive. The Boer War is a likely example. But for us, Vietnam was the first war in which the practical value of *jus in bello* became apparent. To be sure, the "Vietnam syndrome" is generally taken to reflect a different lesson: that we should not fight wars that are unpopular at home and to which we are unwilling to commit the resources necessary for victory. But there was in fact another lesson, connected to but not the same as the "syndrome": that we should not fight wars about whose justice we are doubtful, and that once we are engaged we have to fight justly so as not to antagonize the civilian population, whose political support is necessary to a military victory. In Vietnam, the relevant civilians were the Vietnamese themselves; we lost the war when we lost their "hearts and minds." But this idea about the need for civilian support has turned out to be both variable and expansive: modern warfare requires the support of different civilian populations, extending beyond the population immediately at risk. Still, a moral regard for civilians at risk is critically important in winning wider support for the war ... for any modern war. I will call this the usefulness of morality. Its wide acknowledgement is something radically new in military history.

Hence the odd spectacle of George Bush (the elder), during the Gulf war, talking like a just war theorist.[7] Well, not quite: for Bush's speeches and press conferences displayed an old American tendency, which his son has inherited, to confuse just wars and crusades, as if a war can only be just when the forces of good are arrayed against the forces of evil. But Bush also seemed to understand—and this was a constant theme of American military spokesmen—that war is properly a war of

---

7   See the documents collected in Sifry and Cerf, 1991, pp. 197-352, which include Bush's speeches and a wide range of other opinions.

armies, a combat between combatants, from which the civilian population should be shielded. I don't believe that the bombing of Iraq in 1991 met just war standards; shielding civilians would certainly have excluded the destruction of electricity networks and water purification plants. Urban infrastructure, even if it is necessary to modern war making, is also necessary to civilian existence in a modern city, and it is morally defined by this second feature.[8] Still, American strategy in the Gulf war was the result of a compromise between what justice would have required and the unrestrained bombing of previous wars; taken overall, targeting was far more limited and selective than it had been, for example, in Korea or Vietnam. The reasons for the limits were complicated: in part, they reflected a commitment to the Iraqi people (which turned out not to be very strong), in the hope that the Iraqis would repudiate the war and overthrow the regime that began it; in part, they reflected the political necessities of the coalition that made the war possible. Those necessities were shaped in turn by the media coverage of the war—that is, by the immediate access of the media to the battle and of people the world over to the media. Bush and his generals believed that these people would not tolerate a slaughter of civilians, and they were probably right (though what it might mean for them not to tolerate something was and is unclear). Hence, though many of the countries whose support was crucial to the war's success were not democracies, bombing policy was dictated in important ways by the democracies.

This will continue to be true: the media are omnipresent, and the whole world is watching. War has to be different in these circumstances. But does this mean that it has to be more just or only that it has to look more just, that it has to be described, a little more persuasively than in the past, in the language of justice? The triumph of just war theory is clear enough; it is amazing how readily military spokesmen during the Kosovo and Afghanistan wars used its categories, telling a causal story that justified the war and providing accounts of the battles that emphasized the restraint with which they were being fought. The arguments (and rationalizations) of the past were very different; they commonly came from outside the armed forces—from clerics, lawyers, and professors, not from generals—and they commonly lacked specificity and detail. But what does the use of these categories, these just and moral words, signify?

Perhaps naively, I am inclined to say that justice has become, in all Western countries, one of the tests that any proposed military strategy or tactic has to meet—only one of the tests and not the most important one, but this still gives just war theory a place and standing that it never had before. It is easier now than it ever was to imagine a general saying, "No, we can't do that; it would cause too many civilian deaths; we have to find another way." I am not sure that there are many generals who talk like that, but imagine for a moment that there are; imagine that strategies are evaluated morally as well as militarily; that civilian deaths are minimized; that new technologies are designed to avoid or limit collateral damage,

---

8   I made the case against attacks on infrastructural targets immediately after the war (but others made it earlier) in DeCosse, 1992, pp. 12-13.

and that these technologies are actually effective in achieving their intended purpose. Moral theory has been incorporated into war making as a real constraint on when and how wars are fought. This picture is, remember, imaginary, but it is also partly true; and it makes for a far more interesting argument than the more standard claim that the triumph of just war is pure hypocrisy. The triumph is real: what then is left for theorists and philosophers to do?

This question is sufficiently present in our consciousness so that one can watch people trying to respond. There are two responses that I want to describe and criticize. The first comes from what might be called the postmodern left, which doesn't claim that affirmations of justice are hypocritical, since hypocrisy implies standards, but rather that there are no standards, no possible objective use of the categories of just war theory.[9] Politicians and generals who adopt the categories are deluding themselves—though no more so than the theorists who developed the categories in the first place. Maybe new technologies kill fewer people, but there is no point in arguing about who those people are and whether or not killing them is justified. No agreement about justice, or about guilt or innocence, is possible. This view is summed up in a line that speaks to our immediate situation: "One man's terrorist is another man's freedom fighter." On this view, there is nothing for theorists and philosophers to do but choose sides, and there is no theory or principle that can guide their choice. But this is an impossible position, for it holds that we can't recognize and condemn the murder of innocent people.

A second response is to take the moral need to recognize and condemn very seriously and then to raise the theoretical ante—that is, to strengthen the constraints that justice imposes on warfare. For theorists who pride themselves on living, so to speak, at the critical edge, this is an obvious and understandable response. For many years, we have used the theory of just war to criticize American military actions, and now it has been taken over by the generals and is being used to explain and justify those actions. Obviously, we must resist. The easiest way to resist is to make noncombatant immunity into a stronger and stronger rule, until it is something like an absolute rule: all killing of civilians is (something close to) murder; therefore any war that leads to the killing of civilians is unjust; therefore every war is unjust. So pacifism re-emerges from the very heart of the theory that was originally meant to replace it. This is the strategy adopted, most recently, by many opponents of the Afghanistan war. The protest marches on American campuses featured banners proclaiming, "Stop the Bombing!" and the argument for stopping was very simple (and obviously true): bombing endangers and kills civilians. The marchers didn't seem to feel that anything more had to be said.

Since I believe that war is still, sometimes, necessary, this seems to me a bad argument and, more generally, a bad response to the triumph of just war theory. It sustains the critical role of the theory vis-à-vis war generally, but it denies the theory the critical role it has always claimed, which is internal to the business of

---

9   Stanley Fish's op-ed piece in the *New York Times*, October 15, 2001, provides an example of the post-modernist argument in its most intelligent version.

war and which requires critics to attend closely to what soldiers try to do and what they try not to do. The refusal to make distinctions of this kind, to pay attention to strategic and tactical choices, suggests a doctrine of radical suspicion. This is the radicalism of people who do not expect to exercise power or use force, ever, and who are not prepared to make the judgments that this exercise and use require. By contrast, just war theory, even when it demands a strong critique of particular acts of war, is the doctrine of people who do expect to exercise power and use force. We might think of it as a doctrine of radical responsibility, because it holds political and military leaders responsible, first of all, for the well-being of their own people, but also for the well-being of innocent men and women on the other side. Its proponents set themselves against those who won't think realistically about the defense of the country they live in and also against those who refuse to recognize the humanity of their opponents. They insist that there are things that it is morally impermissible to do even to the enemy. They also insist, however, that fighting itself can't be morally impermissible. A just war is meant to be, and has to be, a war that it is possible to fight.

But there is another danger posed by the triumph of just war theory—not the radical relativism and the near absolutism that I have just described, but rather a certain softening of the critical mind, a truce between theorists and soldiers. If intellectuals are often awed and silenced by political leaders who invite them to dinner, how much more so by generals who talk their language? And if the generals are actually fighting just wars, if *inter arma* the laws speak, what point is there in anything we can say? In fact, however, our role hasn't changed all that much. We still have to insist that war is a morally dubious and difficult activity. Even if we (in the West) have fought just wars in the Gulf, in Kosovo, and in Afghanistan, that is no guarantee, not even a useful indication, that our next war will be just. And even if the recognition of noncombatant immunity has become militarily necessary, it still comes into conflict with other, more pressing, necessities. Justice still needs to be defended; decisions about when and how to fight require constant scrutiny, exactly as they always have.

At the same time, we have to extend our account of "when and how" to cover the new strategies, the new technologies, and the new politics of a global age. Old ideas may not fit the emerging reality: the "war against terrorism," to take the most current example, requires a kind of international cooperation that is as radically undeveloped in theory as it is in practice. We should welcome military officers into the theoretical argument; they will make it a better argument than it would be if no one but professors took an interest. But we can't leave the argument to them. As the old saying goes, war is too important to be left to the generals; just war even more so. The ongoing critique of war-making is a centrally important democratic activity.

Section II

Let me, then, suggest two issues, raised by our most recent wars, that require the critical edge of justice.

First, risk-free war making. I have heard it said that this is a necessary feature of humanitarian interventions like the Kosovo war: soldiers defending humanity, in contrast to soldiers defending their own country and their fellow-citizens, will not risk their lives; or, their political leaders will not dare to ask them to risk their lives. Hence the rescue of people in desperate trouble, the objects of massacre or ethnic cleansing, is only possible if risk-free war is possible.[10] But, obviously, it is possible: wars can be fought from a great distance with bombs and missiles aimed very precisely (compared with the radical imprecision of such weapons only a few decades ago) at the forces carrying out the killings and deportations. And the technicians/soldiers aiming these weapons are, in all the recent cases, largely invulnerable to counter-attack. There is no principle of just war theory that bars this kind of warfare. So long as they can aim accurately at military targets, soldiers have every right to fight from a safe distance. And what commander, committed to his own soldiers, would not choose to fight in this way whenever he could? In his reflections on rebellion, Albert Camus argues that one cannot kill unless one is prepared to die.[11] But that argument doesn't seem to apply to soldiers in battle, where the whole point is to kill while avoiding getting killed. And yet there is a wider sense in which Camus is right.

Just war theorists have only recently begun to address this question, which now has some urgency. Massacre and ethnic cleansing commonly take place on the ground. The awful work might be done with bombs and poison gas delivered from the air, but in Bosnia, Kosovo, Rwanda, East Timor, and Sierra Leone, the weapons were rifles, machetes, and clubs; the killing and terrorizing of the population was carried out from close up. And a risk-free intervention undertaken from far away—especially if it promises to be effective in the long run—is likely to cause an immediate speed-up on the ground. This can be stopped only if the intervention itself shifts to the ground, and this shift seems to me morally necessary. The aim of the intervention, after all, is to rescue people in trouble, and fighting on the ground, in the case as I have described it, is what rescue requires. But then it is no longer risk-free. Why would anyone undertake it?

In fact, risks of this sort are a common feature of *jus in bello*, and while there are many examples of soldiers unwilling to accept them, there are also many examples of their acceptance. The principle is this: when it is our action that puts

---

10   This argument was made by several participants in a conference on humanitarian intervention held at the Zentrum fur interdisziplinare Forschung at Bielefeld University in Germany, January 2002.

11   "A life is paid for by another life, and from these two sacrifices springs the promise of a value." Camus, 1956, p. 169. See also the argument in Act I of *The Just Assassins*, Camus, 1958, especially pp. 246-7.

innocent people at risk, even if the action is justified, we are bound to do what we can to reduce those risks, even if this involves risks to our own soldiers. If we are bombing military targets in a just war, and there are civilians living near these targets, we have to adjust our bombing policy—by flying at lower altitudes, say—so as to minimize the risks we impose on civilians. Of course, it is legitimate to balance the risks; we can't require our pilots to fly suicidal missions. They have to be, as Camus suggests, prepared to die, but that is consistent with taking measures to safeguard their lives. How the balance gets worked out is something that has to be debated in each case. But what isn't permissible, it seems to me, is what NATO did in the Kosovo war, where its leaders declared in advance that they would not send ground forces into battle, whatever happened inside Kosovo once the air war began. Responsibility for the intensified Serbian campaign against Kosovar civilians, which was the immediate consequence of the air war, belongs no doubt to the Serbian government and army. They were to blame. But this was at the same time a foreseeable result of our action, and insofar as we did nothing to prepare for this result, or to deal with it, we were blameworthy too. We imposed risks on others and refused to accept them for ourselves, even when that acceptance was necessary to help the others.[12]

The second issue has to do with war's endings. On the standard view, a just war (precisely because it is not a crusade) should end with the restoration of the status quo ante. The paradigm case is a war of aggression, which ends justly when the aggressor has been defeated, his attack repulsed, the old boundaries restored. Perhaps this is not quite enough for a just conclusion: many just war theorists would argue (as I have) for the trial and punishment of the political leaders who launched the aggression; there are good reasons to aim for that, but not if it extends the war and increases its costs. Beyond that, the victim state might deserve reparations from the aggressor state, so that the damage inflicted on it can be repaired—a more extensive understanding of restoration, but restoration still. And, finally, the peace treaty should probably include new security arrangements, of a sort that didn't exist before the war, so that the status quo will be more stable in the future. But that is as far as the rights of the victims go; the theory as it was commonly understood did not extend to any radical reconstitution of the enemy state, and international law, with its assumptions about sovereignty, would have regarded any imposed change of regime as a new act of aggression. What happened after World War II in both Germany and Japan was something quite new in the history of war, and the legitimacy of occupation and political reconstitution is still debated, even by theorists and lawyers who regard the treatment of the Nazi regime, at least, as justified. Thus, as the Gulf war drew to a close in 1991, there was little readiness to march on Baghdad and replace the government of Saddam Hussein, despite the denunciation of that government in the lead-up to the war as Nazi-like in character. There were, of course, both military and geo-

---

12   For arguments in favor of using ground forces in Kosovo, see Buckley, 2000, pp. 293-4, 333-5, 342.

political arguments against continuing the war once the attack on Kuwait had been repulsed, but there was also an argument from justice: that even if Iraq "needed" a new government, that need could only be met by the Iraqi people themselves. A government imposed by foreign armies would never be accepted as the product of, or the future agent of, self-determination.[13]

The World War II examples, however, argue against this last claim. If the imposed government is democratic and moves quickly to open up the political arena and to organize elections, it may erase the memory of its own imposition (hence the difference between the western and eastern regimes in post-war Germany). In any case, humanitarian intervention radically shifts the argument about endings, because now the war is from the beginning an effort to change the regime that is responsible for the inhumanity. This can be done by supporting secession, as the Indian government did in what is now Bangladesh; or by expelling a dictator, as the Tanzanians did to Uganda's Idi Amin; or by creating a new government, as the Vietnamese did in Cambodia. In East Timor, more recently, the UN organized a referendum on secession and then worked to set up a new government. Had there been, as there should have been, an intervention in Rwanda, it would certainly have aimed at replacing the Hutu Power regime. Justice would have required the replacement. But what kind of justice is this? Who are its agents, and what rules govern their actions?

As the Rwandan example suggests, most states don't want to take on this kind of responsibility, and when they do take it on, for whatever political reasons, they don't want to submit themselves to a set of moral rules. In Cambodia, the Vietnamese shut down the killing fields, which was certainly a good thing to do, but they then went on to set up a satellite government, keyed to their own interests, which never won legitimacy either within or outside of Cambodia and brought no closure to the country's internal conflicts. Legitimacy and closure are the two criteria against which we can test war's endings. Both of them are likely to require, in almost all the humanitarian intervention cases, something more than the restoration of the status quo ante—which gave rise, after all, to the crisis that prompted the intervention. Legitimacy and closure, however, are hard tests to meet. The problems have to do in part with strategic interests, as in the Vietnamese/Cambodian case. But material interests also figure in a major way: remaking a government is an expensive business; it requires a significant commitment of resources—and the benefits are largely speculative and nonmaterial. In fact, we can still point to the usefulness of morality in cases like these. A successful and extended intervention brings benefits of an important kind: not only gratitude and friendship, but an increment of peace and stability in a world where the insufficiency of both is costly—and not only to its immediate victims. Still, any particular country will always have good reasons

---

13   Bush's statement on stopping the American advance, and his declaration of victory, can be found in Sifry and Cerf, 1991, pp. 449-51; arguments for and against stopping can be found in DeCosse, 1992, pp. 13-14, 29-32.

to refuse to bear the costs of these benefits; or it will take on the burden, and then find reasons to perform badly. So we still need justice's critical edge.

The argument about endings is similar to the argument about risk: once we have acted in ways that have significant negative consequences for other people (even if there are also positive consequences), we can't just walk away. Imagine a humanitarian intervention that ends with the massacres stopped and the murderous regime overthrown; but the country is devastated, the economy in ruins, the people hungry and afraid; there is neither law nor order nor any effective authority. The forces that intervened did well, but they are not finished. How can this be? Is it the price of doing well that you acquire responsibilities to do well again...and again? The work of the virtuous is never finished. It doesn't seem fair. But in the real world, not only of international politics, but also of ordinary morality, this is the ways things work (though virtue, of course, is not so easy to find). Consider the Afghan/Russian war: the American government intervened in a major way, fighting by proxy, and eventually won a big victory: the Russians were forced to withdraw. This was the last battle of the cold war. The American intervention was undoubtedly driven by geo-political and strategic motives; the conviction that the Afghan struggle was a war of national liberation against a repressive regime may have played a part in motivating the people who carried it out, but the allies they found in Afghanistan had a very restricted idea of liberation.[14] When the war was over, Afghanistan was left in a state of anarchy and ruin. At that point, the Americans walked away and were certainly wrong, politically and morally wrong, to do so; the Russians withdrew and were right to do so. We had acted (relatively) well, that is, in support of what was probably the vast majority of the Afghan people, and yet we were bound to continue acting well; the Russians had acted badly and were off the hook; even if they owed the Afghan people material aid (reparations), no one wanted them engaged again in Afghani affairs. This sounds anomalous, and yet I think it is an accurate account of the distribution of responsibility. But we need a better understanding of how this works and why it works the way it does, a theory of justice-in-endings that engages the actual experience of humanitarian (and other) interventions—so that countries fighting in wars like these know what their responsibilities will be if they win. It would also help if there was, what there isn't yet, an international agency that could stipulate and even enforce these responsibilities.

Section III

The Iraq war of 2003 provides another example of the triumph of just war theory and also of the dangers of success—for the debate about the war was largely cast in just war terms, by both opponents and supporters. Writing before the war, I

---

14   Artyom Borovik,1990, provides a useful, though highly personal, account of the Russian war in Afghanistan; for an academic history, see Goodson, 2001.

attempted to deploy the critical resources of the theory in qualified opposition. I attach here, as a kind of appendix, the argument that I made in the fall of 2002—with occasional comments interpolated in parentheses.

Without access to US intelligence data, it is hard to judge whether the Bush administration is threatening a war that it would be right to fight (as things turned out, access wouldn't have helped; it would have led to exactly the inaccurate assumptions that I go on to make). But democratic arguments are often carried on with inadequate or incomplete information. So I propose to make some common sense stipulations and then join the argument. These are the stipulations: first, the Iraqis have developed chemical and biological weapons and are trying to develop nuclear weapons; second, our government isn't certain about how close they are to having a usable nuclear weapon, but as of this moment they don't have one; third, Iraq has used chemical weapons in the past, though only on its own territory, during the war with Iran and in efforts to repress the Kurds; and fourth, the Iraqi regime is sufficiently brutal internally and hostile externally—to some of its neighbors and to the US—so that we can't rule out its readiness to use such weapons again and more widely or to use nuclear weapons if and when it develops them; we also can't rule out, though there is as yet no evidence for, the transfer of weapons of mass destruction from the Iraqi military or secret services to terrorist groups.

If these stipulations are plausible today, they have been plausible for a long time. They suggest how wrong it was to allow the first UN inspection system to collapse. There was a just and necessary war waiting to be fought back in the 1990s when Saddam was playing hide and seek with the inspectors. That would have been an internationalist war, a war of enforcement, and its justice would have derived, first, from the justice of the UN resolutions it was enforcing and, second, from its likely outcome, the strengthening of the UN and the global legal order. Both these points are critically important in thinking about what we are doing today.

Though Iraq did not use weapons of mass destruction in the Gulf war of 1991, the peace agreement imposed after the war, which was authorized and, in part, implemented by the UN, included restrictions on the development and deployment of such weapons. As an aggressor state, Iraq was subjected to a set of constraints designed to make future aggression impossible. Imagine it as a state on parole, deprived of full sovereignty because of its previous behavior. This was a just outcome of the Gulf War, and the inspection system was its central feature.

Once the inspectors were in place, they revealed to the world how hard Saddam's government had been working on a variety of horrific weapons and how far along some of the work was. For a while, at least, the inspections seemed to be effective; a number of facilities and large quantities of dangerous materials were discovered and destroyed. But memory is short in political life, and commitments and coalitions are fragile. The urgencies of the war and its immediate aftermath receded, and some of Iraq's old trading partners, France and Russia most importantly, began to renew their ties. By the middle 1990s, Saddam felt that he could safely test the will of the UN and the coalition of 1991, and so he began delaying the inspections or denying the inspectors access to the sites they wanted to visit. And he was right: there was no will to enforce the inspection system—not at the UN, which passed many resolutions but did nothing else, not in Europe, and not in the Clinton administration. The US was prepared to use its air power to maintain the "no-fly zones" in the north and south, but was not prepared for a larger war.

I believe that had there been a readiness to use force in 1995 or 1996, a readiness visible on the ground, it would not have been necessary to do so. But if it had been necessary, it would certainly have been justified. The justification would not have worked in the usual way, by reference to aggression, but rather by reference to the violation of the 1991 ceasefire agreement. The agreement should have been enforced. Indeed, the failure to enforce it, the failure to fight, or to be ready to fight, a just war when justice required war, is the most important cause of the harsh dilemma we face today (the most important cause, indeed, of the war we finally fought).

If the inspectors had been forcibly supported, their employer, the UN, would be much stronger than it currently is, and it would have been very difficult, as a result, for the US or anyone else to talk about going to war without reference to the UN's decision-making procedures. But the failure of the 1990s is not easy to rectify, and it doesn't help to pretend that the UN is an effective agent of global law and order when it isn't. Many states insist that they support the renewal of the inspection system, but so long as they are unwilling to use force on its behalf, their support is suspect. They profess to be defending the international rule of law, but how can the law "rule" when there is no law enforcement? When the Bush administration worried in September, 2002 that the return of the inspectors would be, in Vice President Cheney's words, "false comfort," it was reflecting a general belief, shared by Saddam, that our European allies, and the UN as a whole, would never agree to fight. And, indeed, until September, probably because they were reluctant to face the enforcement question, the Europeans were not seriously trying to renew the inspection system. UN negotiators dithered with Iraqi negotiators, in a diplomatic dance that seems to have been designed for delay and ultimate failure.

Delay is dangerous because once Iraq has weapons of mass destruction and effective delivery systems, the threat to use force would be far less plausible than it is now. But so far as we know, Iraq doesn't have such weapons yet. If the administration thinks that Iraq is already a nuclear power, or is literally on the verge of becoming one, then the months of threatening war rather than fighting it would seem to represent, from its perspective, something like criminal negligence. If there is even a little time before Iraq gets the bomb, then a coercive system of UN inspections is surely the right thing to aim at—immensely preferable to the "pre-emptive" war that many people in Washington seem so eager to fight.

In a speech at West Point in June, 2002, President Bush made his case for the necessity and justice of pre-emptive war, and provided at the same time a useful example of why we have to be a little uneasy about the "triumph" of just war theory. For in the absence of evidence suggesting not only the existence of Iraqi weapons but also their imminent use, pre-emption is not an accurate description of what the president was threatening. No one expected an imminent Iraqi attack at that time or subsequently—so, strictly speaking, there was nothing to pre-empt. The war that was being discussed was preventive, not pre-emptive, which means that it was designed to respond to a more distant threat. The general argument for preventive war is very old; in its classic form it has to do with the balance of power. "Right now," says the prime minister of country X, "the balance is stable; each of the competing states feels that its power is sufficient to deter the others from attacking. But country Y, our historic rival across the river, is actively and urgently at work, developing new weapons, preparing a mass mobilization, and if this work is allowed to continue, the balance will shift, and our deterrent power will no longer be effective. The only solution is to attack now, while we still can."

International lawyers and just war theorists have never looked with favor on this argument because the danger to which it alludes is not only distant but speculative, whereas the costs of a preventive war are near, certain, and usually terrible. The distant dangers, after all, might be avoided by diplomacy; or the military work of the other side might be matched by work on this side; or country X might look for alliances with states possessing the deterrent power that it lacks. Whether or not war is properly the last resort, there seems no sufficient reason for making it the first.

But perhaps we need to reopen the question of preventive war: the old argument did not take weapons of mass destruction into account—or delivery systems that allow no time for arguments about how to respond. Perhaps the gulf between pre-emption and prevention has now narrowed, so that there is little strategic, and therefore little moral, difference between them. The Israeli attack on the Iraqi nuclear reactor in 1981 is sometimes invoked an as example of a justified preventive attack that was also, in a sense, pre-emptive: the Iraqi threat was not imminent, but an immediate attack was the only possible action against it. Once the reactor was in operation, an attack would have endangered civilians living many miles around it. So it was a question of now or never. Or better: a single bombing raid could be effective now, but never again; afterwards, only a full-scale war could have prevented the Iraqi acquisition of nuclear weapons. But if this very limited argument for preventive war applied to Israel in 1981, it does not apply to the US in 2002. Iraq, after all, was already formally at war with Israel, and its hostility was visible and threatening. And no one was offering the Israelis a UN inspection system. In fact, the "now or never" argument of 1981 would seem to strengthen the case for doing everything we can do now, short of war, to make the inspections work. The first UN inspectors supervised the destruction of facilities and materials that it would have been dangerous to bomb from the air. There is still time for them to do that again.

For a long time, the president and his advisors have seemed determined to avoid inspection, partly because they don't think that it would work, and also because they have larger ambitions—not just the disarmament of Iraq but also its political transformation. And however effective they were, the inspectors will not overthrow the regime of Saddam Hussein—though their work would certainly help to weaken the regime.

In any case, change of regime is not commonly accepted as a justification for war—and, except in extreme cases, it shouldn't be. The precedents are not encouraging: Guatemala, the Dominican Republic, Iran, and Chile on our side; Hungary and Czechoslovakia twice, on the Russian side: all these reflect the bad old days of cold war "spheres of influence" and ideologically driven military or clandestine interventions. Regime change can sometimes be the *consequence* of a just war--when the defeated rulers are moral monsters, like the Nazis in World War Two. And humanitarian interventions to stop massacre and ethnic cleansing can also legitimately result in the installation of a new regime, as described earlier. But once a zone of relative safety was carved out for the Kurds in the north, there was no case to be made for humanitarian intervention in Iraq. The Baghdad regime is brutally repressive and morally repugnant, certainly; but it is not engaged in mass murder or ethnic cleansing; there are governments as bad—well, almost as bad—all over the world. (If there is, one day, a democratic regime in Iraq, this might speak to the question of *jus post bellum*, it would not override the argument here about the decision to go to war, *jus ad bellum*.)

The only reason for targeting Saddam is the belief that he will never give up the pursuit of weapons of mass destruction. But faced with a unified international community, committed to the enforcement of inspection, with soldiers ready to move, Saddam would probably suspend his pursuit—and the suspension would last as long as the commitment did; it's the commitment that is the problem. In any case, many other regimes around the world, including democratic regimes like India's, have developed or are trying to develop these weapons, so how can we be sure that future Iraqi rulers would not resume Saddam's project? If we are interested in the safety of Iraq's neighbors, inspection is probably a more reliable option than regime change.

The right thing to do is what we seemed to be doing when President Bush appeared before the United Nations: re-create the conditions that existed in the mid-1990s for fighting a just war. And we should do this precisely to avoid the war that many people in the Bush administration clearly want to fight. The Europeans could have done the necessary work by themselves much earlier, if they were serious about challenging American unilateralism and defending the rule of law. No government in Baghdad could have resisted a European ultimatum—admit the inspectors by a date certain or else!—so long as the states behind the ultimatum included France and Russia, who have been Iraq's key protectors, and so long as the "or else!" involved both economic and military action. Why didn't the Europeans do this? Bush spoke about a "difficult and defining moment" for the UN, but it is really the Europeans and the Americans who have been tested in recent months. These two needed to agree on a tough and intrusive inspection system—which required an American willingness to let inspections work and a European readiness to make them work. Neither party has looked terribly good: the US talked as if we wanted to take the project of global law and order wholly into our own hands, while the Europeans seemed unwilling to take any part of the project into their own hands.

The real and only argument for war is not that war is the right choice or the best available choice, but that there is no international commitment to actions short of war—coercive inspections and, more generally, the containment of countries like Iraq—which require the threat of war. Germany's prime minister Schroeder made it a point to foreswear that threat as a matter of principle—and yet there cannot be any sort of law and order, either in domestic or international society, without a visible and explicit will to use force if necessary. I think it is fair to say that many influential Europeans, from both the political class and the intelligentsia, prefer a unilateral American war to a European readiness to fight—even if, to quote Shakespeare's Hamlet, "the readiness is all," and war could thereby be avoided.

I have now worked through what I take to be an application of just war theory. But I have dealt only with the occasions of war, not with its conduct. I haven't said anything about how the war with Iraq should be fought, if fighting it could be justified. The theory always has these two parts. It makes military action morally *possible* by limiting its occasions and constraining its conduct. When states act within the limits and constraints, the action is justified, and the theorist of just war has to say exactly that, even if he sounds like an apologist for the powers-that-be. When states act beyond the limits and constraints, when war is unjust or its conduct brutal, he has to say that, even if he is called an enemy of the people. It is important not to get stuck in either mode—defense or critique. Indeed, just war theory requires that we maintain our commitment to both at the same time. In this sense, just war is like good government: there is a deep and permanent tension between the adjective and the noun, but no necessary contradiction between them. When reformers come to power and make government better (less corrupt, say), we have to be able to acknowledge the improvement. And when they hold on to power for too long, and imitate their predecessors, we have to be ready to criticize their behavior. Just war theory isn't an apology for any particular war, and it isn't a renunciation of war itself. It is designed to sustain a constant scrutiny and an immanent critique. We still need that, even when generals sound like theorists, and I am sure that we always will.

References

Augustine, *The Political Writings of St. Augustine*, ed. Henry Paolucci. Chicago: Henry Regnery Company, 1962.

Borovik, Artyom, *The Hidden War: A Russian Jounalist's Account of the Soviet War in Afghanistan*. London: Faber and Faber, 1990.

Boswell, James, *Life of Samuel Johnson LL.D.* Chicago: Encyclopedia Britannica, 1952 (Great Books of the Western World, ed. Robert Maynard Hutchins, vol. 44).

Buckley, William Joseph, *Kosovo: Contending Voices on Balkan Interventions*. Grand Rapids: William B. Eerdmans Publishing Company, 2000.

Camus, Albert, *The Rebel*, trans. Anthony Bower. New York: Vintage, 1956.

Camus, Albert, *Caligula and Three Other Plays*, trans. Stuart Gilbert. New York: Vintage, 1958.

Dean, Herbert A., *The Political and Social Ideas of St. Augustine*. New York: Columbia University Press, 1963.

DeCosse, David E., ed., *But Was It Just? Reflections on the Morality of the Persian Gulf War*. New York: Doubleday, 1992.

Goodson, Larry P., *Afghanistan's Endless War: State Failure, Regional Politics, and the Rise of the Taliban*. Seattle: University of Washington Press, 2001.

Hartle, Anthony E., *Moral Issues in Military Decision Making*. Lawrence: University Press of Kansas, 1989.

Johnson, James Turner, *Ideology, Reason, and the Limitation of War: Religious and Secular Concepts, 1200-1740*. Princeton: Princeton University Press, 1973.

Sifry, Micah L. and Cerf, Christopher, eds, *The Gulf War: History, Documents, Opinions*. New York: Times Books/Random House, 1991.

Smith, Michael Joseph, *Realist Thought from Weber to Kissinger*. Baton Rouge: Louisiana State University Press, 1986.

Vitoria, Francisco de, *Political Writings*, ed. Anthony Pagden and Jeremy Lawrance. Cambridge: Cambridge University Press, 1991.

Walzer, Michael, *Just and Unjust Wars*. New York: Basic Books, 1977.

Chapter 2
"Methodological Anarchy": Arguing about Preventive War

George R. Lucas, Jr.
U.S. Naval Academy (Annapolis)[1]

Rival Modes of Discourse in the Just War Tradition

Within the broad moral and legal framework of what is often termed "just war theory," there are several distinct, yet equally well-established approaches to arguing about the justification of war in specific instances. I am not here referring to debates about, and with, pacifists, opposed in principle to any use of military force for political purposes. That sharp divide in public opinion has shaped the terms of moral discourse about war for centuries. Nor am I referring to debates over the legitimacy of a particular conflict, such as the intervention in March, 2003, of U.S.-led "coalition" forces to effect "regime change" in Iraq. These complex disagreements over both salient facts and governing principles represent honest differences of opinion over which, as Hume remarked, "reasonable persons may be allowed to differ." In *Arguing About War*, Michael Walzer notes that these latter kinds of principled disagreements have almost always characterized public debates about the moral legitimacy of any particular war,[2] and are to be expected when deliberating about so difficult, complex, and important a moral dilemma.

The question I want to consider is this: to what extent do these latter sorts of "principled disagreements" (as Walzer terms them) stem from our different *ways* of arguing about war? When engaging in this argument, for example, many participants in the ensuing debate will rely solely on the language of treaty, tolerated custom, and the so-called "black-letter" or "bright-line" statutes and provisions of existing

---

1   This chapter was orginally delivered at the U.S. Naval Academy and the U.S. Air Force Academy in the spring of 2003, and subsequently revised and delivered as the convocation address for a National Endowment for the Humanities summer institute on "war and morality" held at the U.S. Naval Academy (June 1-25, 2004). I am grateful to other faculty and to the participants in that institute for a number of useful suggestions incorporated in the present draft.

2   Michael Walzer explicitly defends this feature of ambiguity or indeterminateness in just war discourse, while explaining his own retreat from an earlier strong presumption against wars of intervention, in the introduction to his volume of essays on this subject, *Arguing About War* (New Haven, CT: Yale University Press, 2004).

international law when stating their opposition to, or support of a military conflict. Others, by contrast, approach the same argument by invoking philosophical or theological principles that arise as a result of centuries of moral conversation and reflection, within many different cultures, upon the proper limitations to be imposed upon state-sanctioned violence. Some, but not all, of the latter scholars and practitioners argue about specific wars by rehearsing a *list* of concepts or criteria emerging from those historical and cultural conversations, the provisions of which seem to function in some imprecise sense as necessary conditions for the moral justification of any specific war.[3]

In 1979, the eminent Catholic scholar, Brian Hehir, called attention to the underlying tensions between what he termed the "two normative traditions" within the just war tradition, by which he meant his own brand of Catholic moral philosophy, as distinct from contemporary international law.[4] Hehir presciently suggested ways in the then-foreseeable future in which these two distinctive approaches to the justification of force might radically diverge when, for example, moral concerns for basic human rights came into conflict with legal claims of sovereignty and territorial integrity.

Hehir's prescient analysis of this subtle tension during the Cold War finally came to haunt us throughout the acrimonious debates, beginning in the 1990s, concerning the legal versus moral legitimacy of wars of intervention, preemption, or preventive self defense. Offensive (or, at least, non-defensive) conflicts are treated very differently within these two contrasting traditions. International law privileges sovereignty, while morality tends to limit sovereignty on behalf of the more fundamental primacy of basic human rights.

For their part, however, Hehir and his colleagues for many years utterly ignored a *third*, very distinctive way of arguing about war that had, only two years before, made its dramatic appearance in Michael Walzer's magisterial and widely-influential, *Just and Unjust Wars* (New York: Basic Books, 1977). In *Arguing about War*, Walzer recapitulates both the history, and the rise to international influence, of that profound new analysis of what he first described as "the legalist paradigm" in international relations—as well as his current misgivings (on the basis of that

---

3   Though it will now seem astonishing, during the debate leading up to the U.S.-led intervention in Iraq in March, 2003, it was still necessary to remind readers of this fact, as just war discourse was widely neglected and largely unfamiliar at that time. The controversy surrounding that war of preventive intervention (amidst which this essay itself was born) has since sparked an extensive revival of interest in this topic. Some of the most eminent authorities currently recognized in the field (e.g., Larry May, Nancy Sherman) had at that time no prior publications or previous stated interest in this area. Such was the abysmal state into which just war discourse had fallen that it required an attack on U.S. soil and two subsequent and controversial wars to spark this revival.

4   J. Bryan Hehir, "The Ethics of Intervention: Two Normative Traditions," in *Human Rights and U.S. Foreign Policy*, eds Peter G. Brown and Douglas MacLean (Lexington, MA: Lexington Books, 1979), 121-39.

earlier analysis) regarding the legitimacy of either preemptive or preventive war in Iraq.

Despite his use of law-like terminology, Walzer warned readers of *Just and Unjust Wars* that his method of analysis was not confined to the deliberations of lawyers, and was moral rather than legal.[5] Notwithstanding this explicit warning, his work was, for decades afterwards, mistakenly classified as a variation of legal reasoning in international relations. It was widely read and taught by scholars in international relations and international law, far more than it was by scholars and teachers in moral philosophy, presumably on account of his attempts to conceptualize the underlying political and moral consensus enshrined in the treaties, customs, and conventions of international law concerning the resort to force. Notwithstanding, Walzer's approach to moral reasoning was always primarily philosophical rather than legal, although his highly original work neither invoked, nor in the least resembled, the philosophical tradition that Hehir had earlier described.

Instead, the approach that Walzer adopted in this celebrated work was one both familiar to, and widely practiced by moral philosophers working within what is loosely characterized as the "analytic" tradition of philosophy, primarily in English-speaking countries during the past quarter-century. The familiarity and widespread appeal of what is usually termed "applied" ethics or "applied philosophy," however, should not blind us to its comparatively recent historical debut in this wider conversation about war, nor should we overlook its unique and distinctive features as a relatively new form of moral discourse.[6]

Notice, for example, that what Hehir had, in 1979, termed the "two normative traditions" of just war discourse, are both what we might, in turn, describe as *compliance-based*. That is, both forms of just war discourse resolve disputes by appealing to compliance, either with established international laws and customs, or (in the case of philosophy) with lists of necessary conditions arising from a longstanding and authoritative tradition of scholarly discourse over

---

5   See the preface to the first edition of *Just and Unjust Wars* (New York: Basic Books, 1977), xvii-xx, where he suggests that his treatment of the topic will constitute a summary of a moral, and not a purely legal, argument with a lengthy history which it is not his explicit intention to discuss (though he makes reference to this history and its major figures from time to time). Later, in Chapter IV, he describes his choice of the phrase "legalist paradigm" for the underlying conventions of this position, "...since it consistently reflects the conventions of law and order. It does not necessarily reflect the arguments of lawyers, though legal as well as moral debate has its starting point here" (p. 61).

6   While the history of applied ethics has yet to be fully written, it developed as a distinct form of moral analysis primarily in the work of J.L. Austin at Oxford, Elizabeth Anscombe and Bernard Williams at Cambridge, and subsequently Judith Jarvis Thomson at M.I.T. in the late 1950s and 1960s. The field mushroomed with growing interest in moral problems arising in medicine, business, and law in the 1960s and 1970s, spawning a generation of new authorities, journals, research centers, and substantial scholarship in these and other areas of applied philosophy.

many centuries. By contrast, Walzer, and other proponents of applied ethics, invite readers instead to engage directly in a kind of moral casuistry by citing, describing, and analyzing specific historical cases or hypothetical examples, and then testing what might be termed their "pre-theoretic moral intuitions" on the historical cases or hypothetical examples cited. From this procedure, they then elicit more general, action-guiding reasons or governing normative principles that resolve or explain the cases, or lead (as do many of the essays in this volume) to challenging or revising conventional wisdom about the meaning or application of such principles, such as the "principle of double effect."[7] Interestingly, these arguments about war often proceed either as if there were no prior history to the discussion, or as if that prior history were largely irrelevant.[8]

Each distinct mode of reasoning and discourse has its own loyal following of practitioners who argue about war, each in their own way, seldom reaching beyond disciplinary or conceptual boundaries to seriously engage or challenge practitioners of competing modes of discourse, and seldom assuming more than a

---

7   This so-called "analytical" approach to moral reasoning is illustrated in several of the essays in this volume, perhaps nowhere more elegantly than in Tim Scanlon's reassessment of the notion of intentionality and the principle of double effect. Despite its usefulness in sorting out complex conceptual muddles, the analytic philosopher's tendency to rely upon hypothetical thought experiments in lieu of actual cases or historical examples often strikes scholars from other disciplines as unusual in the extreme. This method first came to widespread practice in the 1960s and 1970s in discussing moral dilemmas in medicine, business, journalism, and law. With the exception of Walzer, however, leading philosophers engaged in the new kind of analytical moral casuistry characterizing applied ethics after the conclusion of the Vietnam war largely abandoned a once-lively interest in the moral issues surrounding war and the justifiable uses of military force, in effect ceding this territory to traditional Catholic just war theorists and religious pacifists. As mentioned, however, this situation has changed dramatically in the past few years, as the essays in this volume bear witness.

8   There are two senses of this "ahistorical" approach: one benign, the other perhaps morally objectionable. Walzer, exhibiting the benign form of ahistorical consciousness, is fully cognizant of the historical tradition of just war discourse to which Father Hehir refers, but deliberately makes no use of it. It is not, for him, *authoritative* merely in its own right. Quite appropriately, he relies on reasoned argument in moral discourse, rather than merely the authority of tradition, allowing him to challenge the authority of international law equally as well as the presumed authority of Catholic moral philosophy and theology. Less commendably, the quite recent explosion of interest in just war discourse and renewed interest in topics of war and peace to which I refer above has spawned a cadre of scholars in the field with little prior background or interest, and little willingness to engage the work of those to whom they had left the field as, in their estimation, a kind of intellectual backwater. That sort of "bandwagon" or "celebrity" fascination with what is once again in high fashion strikes this author as cynical, opportunistic, utterly lacking in intellectual sincerity, and thus bordering on a kind of "war profiteering."

superficially critical stance toward the foundational presuppositions and habitual tactics of their own.[9]

It would be hard to imagine getting away with this shoddy practice in other contexts. Especially if we come (as many in the humanities and social sciences do) from disciplines rife with methodological conflicts and deep conceptual divides, we might reasonably expect that proponents of a particular methodology would defend their own stance by enumerating, and perhaps attacking, the perceived inadequacies of their methodological rivals. What we would *not* expect is what in fact we encounter within the broad tradition of just war discourse: namely, *a deafening silence* concerning the existence of multiple and divergent modes of discourse in arguing about war, coupled with an almost universal failure to acknowledge or engage modes of discourse other than one's own.

Borrowing from the late philosopher of science, Paul Feyerabend, I am going to label this condition "methodological anarchy."[10] My question in this chapter is: what are we to make of it? There does quite obviously seem to be a multiplicity of ways of going about the task of evaluating the moral legitimacy of war, even within our own culture, let alone between and among differing cultural traditions. Are they all equally valid? Do they all miraculously converge to the same or similar conclusions in specific instances? And if not, to what extent is the conclusion reached dependent upon the mode of discourse in which the supporting analysis is framed? How might we go about adjudicating disputes about specific wars that rely upon competing modes of discourse, or issue from our *different ways of arguing about war*?

Surprisingly, practitioners of the different varieties of just war discourse *seem utterly unconcerned* by this methodological anarchy, even when, like the historian

---

9   Thus, even more than 25 years after the initial appearance of Walzer's *Just and Unjust Wars*, many practitioners of what we might call the traditional or conventional "Catholic" mode of just war discourse, for example, will still begin their deliberations on just war by rehearsing the provisions of that conceptual scheme with barely a mention of Walzer, let alone of the statutes and provisions of international law. Vice-versa, many specialists in international law refer only to the statutes of that body of law in deliberating about war, often ignoring Walzer, and dismissing the Catholic tradition out of hand (if they mention it at all) as merely sectarian nonsense without relevance or standing in the broader international community.

10   This is a term of art for Feyerabend in his treatment of epistemological dilemmas in the philosophy of science; see *Against Method* (London: Verso, 1975). For Feyerabend, however, "methodological anarchy" is a normative stance: that is, against foundationalism and what he regards as specious claims to rigor, Feyerabend advocates a pluralistic or "anarchistic" approach to the project of understanding the foundations of knowledge-claims in the natural sciences. The problem I am identifying is almost the inverse of this. I am claiming that just war discourse is already methodologically pluralistic in a descriptive sense. I am further decrying the apparent fact that its practitioners often seem oblivious to this feature, and fail even to examine its implications for their deliberations about specific wars.

James Turner Johnson, they do see fit to acknowledge it.[11] This relative lack of attention to methodology is nothing short of astonishing when one considers that the principal participants in the just war debate—philosophers, theologians, political scientists, scholars of law and international relations—are nothing if not hypersensitive to, and overly contentious about, methodological differences in their respective disciplines in all other respects. Likewise these scholars and public authorities are nothing if not famous for their rigorous attention to definitional clarity and logical precision, and for their ruthless and inexorable ability to root out and expose the role of hidden and ungrounded conceptual presuppositions or unstated and unjustified governing methodological assumptions in the arguments of rivals. What, then, are we to make of such intellectual slovenliness, especially regarding a subject otherwise so well-established, and a moral question otherwise so transparently grave?

One response is to claim (as Johnson does, for example) that this methodological anarchy is benign. These multiple approaches to the problem of just war have simply grown up together, evolved or emerged from one another, and co-existed alongside of one another for so long a period that practitioners of each distinct way of arguing about war just don't "see" the others, or recognize the differences, nor do they notice when they inadvertently make a transition from one mode to another, or import the principles and conclusions of one mode of discourse into the

---

11   As a well-respected scholar and historian of the just war tradition, Johnson describes it metaphorically as a "great river with many tributaries." In a recent work, *Morality and Contemporary Warfare* (New Haven, CT: Yale University Press, 1999), Johnson gives careful attention to recognition of the fact of pluralism in the tradition, and notes the many contributors to the discussion, past and present, including Walzer, to whom he pays a great deal of attention and respect. He notes that "there are differences of content and emphasis and tensions among the various approaches encompassed in just war tradition," but concludes merely that we need attend carefully to each scholar's particular way of stating and summarizing the tradition, as well as sustaining a dialogue among them (pp. 22-5). While evidencing a clear preference in his own work for classical *jus ad bellum* discussions, he does not suggest how or why we might wish to evaluate these different approaches comparatively, or give preference to one versus another in contemporary debate. Several distinguished scholars recently invited to address participants at the aforementioned National Endowment for the Humanities summer institute on "war and morality" on occasion acknowledged that there were "several different ways" of going about the moral evaluation of war, but did not bother to enumerate what those were, or what might be the relationship among them, let alone why their own approach might be justified *vis á vis* any of the others. One leading Roman Catholic scholar of just war theory described his approach as stemming from a Christian or Catholic approach to the problem, as distinct from what he respectfully described as "a Jewish tradition of just war discourse represented by Michael Walzer." That seemed to those of us listening as a conflation of Walzer's subsequent explicit studies of Jewish political theory with his stance in *Just and Unjust Wars*, the latter of which does not seem to be culturally specific in any meaningful sense.

conversations from the standpoint of another—and no harm is done, or confusion caused, by this.[12]

Even were this miraculously true in the past, the methodological anarchy of the just war tradition was, I submit, the source of considerable confusion during the past two decades of discussion, initially of the justification of armed military humanitarian interventions during the 1990s, and subsequently during debates over counterinsurgency (COIN) military interventions as a component of the ill-titled "global war on terror" (GWOT) early in the present century. At least some of that confusion stemed, in turn, from the unwitting transport of defining principles and substantive conclusions from one mode of discourse into another in ways which cannot easily be justified. This rendered the analysis of significant contemporary dilemmas like humanitarian military intervention and preventive war even more difficult than they might otherwise be.[13]

We might otherwise reassure ourselves that these multiple ways of arguing about war are merely like different languages, coordinate systems, or conceptual schemes. The words for "apple" and the recipes for "apple pie" appear quite different in English, French, German, or Spanish, but in the end we all recognize the fruit and enjoy the same (or at least highly similar) confections produced from it. The representation and analysis of a certain mathematical relation (such as the equation for a circle or an ellipse) appear quite different in polar than in Cartesian coordinates, but the geometric figure is one and the same, and the underlying relationship between the relevant variables that constitute that figure can be easily translated from one coordinate system to another.

So likewise, on this analogy: scholars in political science and international relations speak one language, moral philosophers speak another, and perhaps theologians a third, but the terms regarding military force and its uses are translatable without confusion, and the substantive conclusions about the justification for resort to military force developed within each can be reasonably shown to converge.

---

12   On this assumption, methodological anarchy would be something akin to David Hume's original account of the "naturalistic fallacy:" an unconscious procedure or a habit of discourse so familiar and so long practiced as to be invisible to its practitioners (at least until Hume problematized it), and constituting a genuine problem only if and when the habit itself leads to confusion, or can't easily and automatically be justified.

13   Despite his personal lack of concern about this problem in other contexts, in *Morality and Contemporary Warfare*, Johnson forcibly decries the effects of what I'm calling "methodological anarchy" which he carefully traces in the evolution of the stance towards war of the American Conference of Catholic Bishops. Their "presumption against war" (or, more accurately, against the use of force in pursuit of justice) in the Bishops' pastoral letter, "The Challenge of Peace" (1983) stems, he suggests, from combining the classical, historical tradition of discourse with explicitly contemporary aspects of international law in a manner which inhibits their ability, a decade later, to frame a coherent argument in favor of military intervention for humanitarian purposes (pp. 12-4, 34-8). That is but one example of the confusion toward which this essay is directed.

Alas, these assurances seem misplaced, and these comforting analogies do not appear to hold when arguing about war. The application of sharply variant methodological approaches in the just war tradition to the analysis of some of the most intractable of the contemporary dilemmas concerning the use of military force yielded sharply variant conclusions about the appropriateness or legitimacy of recourse to military force in those instances. Practices like humanitarian intervention, for example, are almost uniformly proscribed in law and international relations, while the same practices are imposed in some instances as a moral obligation within the classical or theological tradition, and are treated equivocally within the philosopher's framework of moral casuistry.[14] Judgments or action-guiding principles—for example, that the use of military force is justified only for the purpose of self defense—may be deemed correct from the standpoint of one, an error or a mistaken inference within a second, and vague or indeterminate within a third.

Consider the debate about preventive war or "preemptive self defense" prompted by the decision of the Bush administration to invade Iraq in the aftermath of "9/11." One important way to frame the terms of that debate was to cite the black-letter statutes of international law, treaties, and, after World War II, the provisions of the United Nations Charter. This way of arguing about war, the legalist mode of discourse, provided nearly unambiguous support for the view that the war of intervention in Iraq was unjust. International law clearly prohibits the use of military force for any but defensive purposes, even under the most creative interpretations of the concept of "self-defense" or of "collective security" under the provisions of

---

14   This observation regarding the status of humanitarian military intervention in international law is the source of a good deal of misunderstanding. Contrary to widespread belief during the period of the Rwandan genocide, for example, the Genocide Convention of 1948 does not impose obligations, nor establish any substantive procedures for U.N.-member nations regarding the use of military force to aid victims of genocide. A careful reading of the convention shows that it was a product of its time: it aimed to prohibit nations from engaging in genocide, or from sheltering individuals who had participated in genocide. That is, it aimed principally at refusing to grant quarter or safe haven to war criminals, and required nations to assist in their capture and prosecution. Thus, fears about using the "G-word" during the Rwandan crisis, for fear they would obligate armed response, were gravely misplaced. The more recent experience in Darfur, Sudan (in which the "G-word" has been frequently invoked to utterly no avail) demonstrate the dilemma. In the aftermath of the Rwandan tragedy, a dissident U.N. faction, the "International Crisis Group," under the leadership of Australian ambassador-at-large Gareth Evans (an unsuccessful candidate for the Secretary-Generalship awarded instead to Kofi Annan), issued a now widely-cited report addressing these deficiencies and proposing remedies in law and policy. See *The Responsibility to Protect: Report of the International Commission on Intervention and State Sovereignty*, eds, Gareth Evans and Mohamed Shanoun. Brussells (BE: International Crisis Group, 2001) http://www.iciss.ca/pdf/Commission-Report.pdf. See also the summary of the Commission's findings in Evans and Sahnoun (2002). "The Responsibility to Protect," *Foreign Affairs* 81: 6, 99-110.

Article VII of the U.N. Charter. Even when a case for "anticipatory self-defense" can be made under existing law, there is certainly no provision granting the power to an individual nation-state to act unilaterally in the absence of recognition of an imminent threat by other members of the international community. Instead, as I will suggest in Part II below, the most lenient characterization one can offer of such practice from the standpoint of law is "vigilantism."

Classical or "theological" just war theorists had a far more difficult time with the doctrine of preemptive or preventive war. It was certainly not correct to claim, as many mistakenly did at the time,[15] that all wars save wars of self defense are not morally justified, when the historical and textual case, at least, is considerably less clear. What this kind of claim itself preempted was a longstanding debate within that mode of discourse over what constitutes a just cause for war, given that self-defense constitutes the clearest (but not the sole) example of such a just cause. Medieval scholastics like Aquinas, Vitoria, and Suarez invoked an important category of justifiable and sometimes even obligatory use of military force that they termed "bellum offensivum," or offensive war, fought to resist evil, punish wrong-doers, or redress injustice.[16] Vitoria, whose thought has enjoyed a considerable renaissance during the past two decades on account of his extended treatment of these issues, even discussed the legitimacy of wars fought for constabulary purposes to defend human rights, and to effect what we would now term "regime change," all within the context of denouncing his own nation's illicit use of force against indigenous peoples during the Spanish Conquest in the sixteenth century.[17]

---

15   See, for example, the resolution opposing the American-led intervention in Iraq proposed at the time by the American Philosophical Association, which stated: "Both just war theory and international law say that states *may resort to war only in self-defense*" (my emphasis; see http://www.apa.udel.edu/apa/divisions/eastern for the full text of this resolution). Both James Turner Johnson and Jean Bethke Elshtain refused to include their names among the 100 theologians and teachers of Christian ethics whose collective petition, published in several national newspapers on the eve of the second Iraq war, denounced the proposed preemptive war as "a contradiction of just war teachings." The refusal by both eminent scholars of this tradition to endorse this interpretation of it stemmed from their conviction that this sweeping interpretation was seriously inaccurate as a matter of fact. See Jean Bethke Elshtain, "A Just War?" *Boston Sunday Globe* (October 6, 2002), pp. H1,H4.

16   See Gregory Reichberg, "Is There a 'Presumption against War' in Aquinas's Ethics?" *The Thomist*, 66, 3 (2002): 337-67.

17   See Question 3, Articles 4 and 5, of Vitoria's *De Indis* for a discussion of lawful regime change and wars in defense of human rights, respectively: in Vitoria, *Political Writings*, eds Anthony Pagden and Jeremy Lawrance (Cambridge: Cambridge University Press, 1992), 287-8. The general discussion of "offensive war" fought for constabulary purposes against "tyrants, thieves, and robbers" is taken up in Question 1, Article 1 of *De Juri Belli*; 296-8. Vitoria writes, for example:

> [A fifth just cause for war might arise] either on account of the personal tyranny of the barbarians' masters toward their subjects, or because of their tyrannical

All that said, the very different structure of justification in this "classical" or "philosophical" mode of discourse about just war quickly comes into play. Not only does this mode of discourse differ methodologically in its approach to justification from the legal discourse cited above, there is, in addition, a disturbing looseness, ambiguity, and *indeterminateness* in the formulation and interpretation of its individual provisions—just cause, legitimate authority, right intention, last resort, and so forth—each of which presumably constitutes a necessary condition for justification of the use of military force. It is not altogether clear how these criteria are to be applied, or in what order. A great deal of latitude is afforded any individual interpreter of the tradition in applying it to specific cases. In an important historical case, Hugo Grotius deliberately elevated the criterion of "just cause" to a position of primacy over "legitimate authority," largely because he could take for granted (as Thomas and Vitoria could not) what we have come to call the "Westphalian paradigm:" namely, that the ruler of a sovereign nation-state explicitly and unilaterally wielded such authority.

By contrast, sovereignty or "legitimate authority" is principally what is at issue in determining whether non-state actors (or their organizations) possess the moral authority to use force, particularly against non-combatants, as well as whether individual nations (like the U.S.) have the right to pursue or punish such acts of aggression without some kind of broader, international approval. All this is to say that the broad consensus, at a high level abstraction, on the shape of the classical tradition's general presumption against appeals to force rapidly dissolves when one turns to any sort of substantive debate over the meaning or relative priority of its specific provisions.[18]

This is, in turn, because the classical philosophical tradition is *conceptually incomplete*: just war theorists in this tradition seldom state the conditions in a uniform or consistent manner, nor do they necessarily agree on the meaning of the individual conditions, let alone on whether, and to what degree, each condition

---

and oppressive laws against the innocent, such as human sacrifice practiced on innocent men or the killing of [criminals and prisoners] for the purpose of cannibalism. [The Spanish, even without the Pope's consent, may use military force] *in lawful defence of the innocent from unjust death.* [Vitoria's own emphasis.] The barbarians are all our neighbors, and therefore anyone, and especially princes, may defend them from such tyranny and oppression. . . . War may be declared upon [such tyrannical rulers], and the laws of war enforced upon them; and if there is no other means of putting an end [to such practices], *their masters may be changed and new princes set up* [my emphasis].

18   Henry Shue is especially critical of this feature of the classical or philosophical just war tradition, complaining about the mechanical manner in which its criteria are invoked, noting that traditions do not attain or deserve moral authority merely by being traditions, and that the medieval contributors cited above countenanced behaviors that any normal moral agent, then or now, would find reprehensible: "War," in *The Oxford Handbook of Practical Ethics*, ed. Hugh LaFollette (Oxford: Oxford University Press, 2003), esp. pp. 736-8.

must be satisfied.[19] Specific conclusions, however, depend importantly on the order and the priority of the principles cited, as well as upon what each of these criteria *mean* in substantive application.[20] The conclusions regarding the moral justification of a specific conflict may also depend upon which specific criteria—for example, "public declaration," or Suarez's requirement of fighting just wars only through "just means"—are included or excluded from various lists, as well as the degree to which each criterion must be satisfied. Hence, it is probably misleading to refer to this classical tradition of moral reflection as a "theory," as many of its practitioners are wont to do. The classical tradition lacks the order, coherence, and precision normally associated with the interlocking elements of a "theory." Properly regarded, it is merely a mode of normative discourse, a philosophical tradition of reflection on the moral constraints of both prudential reasoning and political practice.[21]

---

19   James Turner Johnson lists seven criteria: just cause, right authority, right intention, proportionality of ends, last resort, reasonable hope of success, and (idiosyncratically) "the aim of peace," in contrast to his earlier and more conventional seventh criterion of "just means" or "proportionality of means." See "The Just War Idea and the Ethics of Intervention," in *The Leader's Imperative*, ed. J. Carl Ficcarotta (West Lafayette, IN: Purdue University Press, 2001), pp. 115-16. Martin L. Cook lists eight just war criteria in *The Moral Warrior* (Albany, New York: State University of New York Press, 2004), p. 28, adding to Johnson's list a criterion he labels "Public Declaration" (which I will suggest below is a meaning of "legitimate authority" rather than a distinct criterion). In contrast to his earlier work (in which this criterion was omitted) Cook now includes Johnson's final criterion, "the aim of peace," which Johnson argues is greatly stressed in international law, bringing Cook's list of criteria to eight. The U.S. Catholic Bishops publish a slightly different list in "The Challenge of Peace" (1983), omitting mention either of Johnson's "ends of peace" or Cook's "public declaration," and inserting a criterion of "comparative justice" that includes consideration of whether "sufficient right exists to override the presumptions against war." Interestingly, both the order and description of these seven criteria are different a decade later in the Bishops' revised stance, "The Harvest of Justice is Sown in Peace" (1993), specifically substituting a "presumption against *the use of force*" for the earlier description of "comparative justice" as a "presumption against war," presumably to take account of the need for humanitarian military intervention. Finally, former U.S. President Jimmy Carter invoked a list of six (rather than seven) criteria in March, 2003 to frame the terms of his opposition to military intervention in Iraq, citing, in this order, "last resort," non-combatant immunity, overall proportionality, right authority, and Johnson's "the ends of peace." These are only scattered examples.

20   Jeff McMahan, for example, has repeatedly called attention to the manner in which various members of the set of just war criteria, such as proportionality, are extremely difficult to define with precision in specific instances to which they are thought to apply. His analysis of these problems of conceptual clarity and applicability are summarized in his new book, *Killing in War* (Oxford: Oxford University Press, 2009).

21   Johnson, once again, describes this as a tradition rather than a theory, the intention of which is to guide statecraft, the behavior of military leaders, and the consciences of individuals. *Morality and Contemporary Warfare*, p. 26.

The underlying inconsistencies between the normative dimensions of the legal and the theological modes of discourse were seldom explored in the context of superpower rivalry and possible nuclear war. The dramatic increase in appeals to military force for the purposes of humanitarian intervention in the wake of the collapse of that superpower rivalry and nuclear threat have forced moral discourse (as I have argued elsewhere) increasingly away from reliance upon the specific provisions of international law, and toward increasing reliance on the underlying moral debate characterized by the classical or "theological" tradition. Pre-emptive wars of "anticipatory self-defense" that otherwise strain the credulity of our concept of "self-defense" are, in fact, wars of this very different, constabulary sort that Vitoria first clearly described, for which international law makes no allowance, and Catholic just war doctrine admits only with the gravest reluctance.[22]

One reason that the classical or theological approach might be more adept than its rivals at handling these new kinds of problems is that, unlike international law, there is no close connection between the doctrine and any particular form of political organization. International law presupposes the nation-state as the fundamental unit of analysis and also, by convention, as the basic bearer of rights. This is the Westphalian convention cited above, what Walzer, in his work (as we have also noted), terms the "legalist paradigm." *There is, however, no corresponding political or conceptual structure to which to tie (or, in this case, to bind) the provisions of classical just war theory.* There is no explicit mention of, or underlying need to presuppose conceptually, entities like nation-states, let alone anything like the modern conception of an "international community" in order to interpret and apply the list of necessary conditions that comprises the classical tradition.

Instead, in the medieval era in which this classical doctrine was formulated, sovereignty was *distributed* over a number of competing entities: national rulers (kings, emperors), regional authorities to whom these would appeal in order to raise funds and military manpower, national and international church authorities, and "supranational" religious organizations like the Jesuits or Dominicans, or the Papacy itself. Likewise, in what we might term the post-modern, post nation-state era, we find sovereignty increasingly distributed over national leaders, regional security organizations (like NATO), non-governmental organizations (still including religious organizations), and supranational entities like NAFTA, the World Trade Organization, the European Union, and of course, the United Nations itself. Thus, we now find ourselves driven back from the legalist paradigm to a conceptual scheme for evaluating the morality of the use of force that is independent of any particular arrangements regarding sovereignty.[23]

---

22   See my essay, "The Reluctant Interventionist," in *Perspectives on Humanitarian Military Intervention* (Berkeley, CA: University of California Press/Institute for Intergovernmental Studies, 2001), pp. 1-13.

23   See Maryann Cusimano Love, "Global Problems: Global Solutions," in Beyond Sovereignty, 2nd edition (Belmont, CA: Wadsworth, 2003), pp. 1-42.

In the past, one was likely to count it among the many weaknesses of the classical, philosophical tradition, not only that its provisions were individually somewhat vague and imprecise, but also that the doctrine itself seemed to justify too much, and to place insufficient limitations on the authority of individual rulers to violate the geographical spheres of influence of others. In the wake of destructive religious wars of the Reformation and Counter-reformation, the Westphalian or "legalist paradigm" was proposed as a solution, by legitimating and bounding those spheres of influence and granting them, for the sake of peace, the rights of sovereignty and self-determination within borders secured by a semblance of law.

That compromise was a steep price to pay for peace, even if it seemed a reasonable price to pay at the time. As Henry Shue notes, this convention appears to grant the state unlimited right to do wrong (at least within its own domain) which surely cannot be the intent, and which makes the notion of "right" itself incoherent.[24] The intent of the Westphalian paradigm was to grant the state the right to "do wrong," as judged from the perspective of neighboring states, who were nonetheless prohibited from interfering. The "wrong" in question was religious in nature: worshipping the "wrong" god, or worshipping God in the "wrong manner." These "moral errors" were nonetheless to be tolerated by other states. The notion of sovereignty and territorial integrity was never intended to permit the state or its agents to abdicate or violate their inherent duties to secure the basic human rights and liberties, and security of person and property, of their own citizens, as routinely occurs today—let alone was it meant to prevent other nations from coming to the aid of the victims of such oppression.

Despite the extraordinary confusion evident during the recent international debate concerning the moral and legal status of preventive war in Iraq, it turns out that it is only international law, grounded in this Westphalian paradigm, that explicitly and unconditionally prohibits the use of military force preventively. Despite numerous well-intentioned resolutions to the contrary, conventional just war doctrine simply does not. Rather, such questions are posed as *moral dilemmas*, underscoring a tension between competing moral obligations, which it is the responsibility of reasonable moral agents, through the use of practical reason, to adjudicate. John Stuart Mill eloquently captured the nature of this dilemma over a century ago in his analysis of humanitarian military intervention (1859), and in so doing refuted in advance the one-sided claims of those opposed in principle to any use of force preventively (to thwart the international analogue of criminal conspiracies, for example) or for any other purpose beyond self-defense.[25]

---

24   See Henry Shue, "Limiting Sovereignty," in *Humanitarian Intervention and International Relations*, ed. Jennifer Welsh (Oxford: Oxford University Press, 2003), pp. 13-16.

25   See "A Few Words on Non-Intervention" [1859]. Reprinted in *Dissertations and Discussions*, Vol. III (London: Longmans, Green, Reader and Dyer, 1867), pp. 166-67. There Mill writes: *"[T]here assuredly are cases in which it is allowable to go to war,*

Evidently there are, or could arise, occasions in which the use of force for purposes other than self defense would not only be permissible, but even obligatory, if the threat of harm from refusing to act were sufficiently grave. Indeed, it might turn out to be the case that self-defense, especially in the case of nations that do not respect the most basic rights of their own citizens, is not a right that it would be at all appropriate for them to exercise.[26] Michael Walzer's variation on this tradition proscribes preventive war, but only by arguing for a distinction between preemption and prevention derived from an historical analysis that may, in the end, beg the very question of "imminence" and intent that it purports to solve.

Suffice it to observe at this point that paradigms have histories, and enjoy only finite lifetimes. It is the fate of theoretical models in all disciplines eventually to show their age, and, under the stress of anomalous circumstance, to reveal the fractures and inconsistencies long obscured by compromise and familiarity. It has often been remarked of late that the Westphalian paradigm in international relations is showing its age, and increasingly labors under the stress of irresolvable anomalies. Political and legal discourse has, as a result, been driven back toward reliance on the older, philosophical tradition of just war discourse in terms of which there is no fundamental and incoherent equivocation between the *conditional or conferred* rights of collectivities like nation-states, and the *unconditional* or inherent rights of the biological individuals that compose them.

Law, Morality, and "Vigilante Justice"

Against this decidedly anomalous historical background, the instinctive reaction of many critics of U.S. President George W. Bush's original proposal in 2002 to wage a "preemptive war" against terrorism, unilaterally if necessary, was that such a proposal clearly constituted a direct violation of international law. One needn't have been an experienced scholar of international law to recognize that

---

without having been ourselves attacked, or threatened with attack; and it is very important that nations should make up their minds in time, as to what these cases are. There are few questions which more require to be taken in hand by ethical and political philosophers, with a view to establish some rule or criterion whereby the justifiableness of intervening in the internal affairs of other countries, *and (what is sometimes fully as questionable) the justifiableness of refraining from intervention*, may be brought to a definite and rational test" (my emphases). Endre Begby analyzes this essay in detail, including Walzer's misreading of Mill's position on intervention, in "Liberty, Statehood, and Sovereignty: Walzer on Mill on Non-Intervention," *Journal of Military Ethics* 2(1), 2003: 46-62.

26   In a brilliant and provocative study, *War and Self Defense* (Oxford: Clarendon Press, 2002), for example, philosopher David Rodin criticizes both the Westphalian paradigm and the reliability of Walzer's "domestic analogy" on which it is based. His argument, however, is that even wars of national self-defense are seldom justifiable. Wars should only be fought, if at all, for the purposes of very limited international law enforcement and protection of human rights (pp. 163-88).

this judgment seemed correct.[27] The conception of an international community of nation-states operating under a common rule of international law contains nothing to suggest that any individual member of that community may make itself an exception, solely on its own authority, to the laws governing the remaining members of that community. It tested the ingenuity of even the most perverse legal minds to cloak this doctrine in the legally-sanctioned guise of self-defense or collective security, as envisioned under the enforcement measures of Article VII of the United Nations charter.[28]

What I myself argued instead at the time was that such actions as the U.S. proposed, and subsequently proceeded to carry out, constituted the kind of vigilante justice that the terms of the United Nations charter was envisioned to supplant. This was awkward in the extreme since, according to the U.S. Constitution, this nation and its leaders were bound *by domestic law* to adhere to the terms and provisions of treaties, such as the U.N. Charter, and other international agreements to which any U.S. President has been signatory and which Congress has proceeded to ratify, assuming that these international agreements are fully embodied in appropriate enabling domestic legislation. Provided that these conditions are met, the restraints on the use of military force as well as on the behavior of individual combatants that result from international law are legally binding on this government *from the perspective of domestic law as well*. Thus, as was often asserted, the Bush administration's actions were "illegal" in a very strong and disturbing sense, unless the treaties and enabling domestic legislation were either revoked or else re-written.

In defiance of this legalist perspective, however, then-president George W. Bush declared, in his State of the Union Address in January, 2004 to the United States

---

27   Thus, despite claims of some international relations scholars that international law governing the resort to force had either broken down or been re-written in the wake of Rwanda, Bosnia, and Kosovo (e.g., Michael J. Glennon, *Limits of Law, Prerogatives of Power: Interventionism After Kosovo* [London and NY: Palgrave Macmillan, 2001]), the preponderance of scholarly opinion seemed to favor the view that states still supported the limitations on the use of force contained in Article 2: 4 of the United Nations Charter, and that "preemptive self defense" is a concept "without legal justification." See Gray, *International Law and the Use of Force* (NY: Oxford University Press, 2000), and Mary Ellen O'Connell, "The Myth of Preemptive Self-Defense," *American Society of International Law Task Force on Terrorism* (August, 2002).

28   Article 2(4) of the U.N. Charter prohibits the use or threat of force against the territorial integrity or political independence of any state. Article 2(7) extends this prohibition to the collective action of the U.N. itself, granting full domestic jurisdiction to member states and prohibiting the supranational body from intervening in matters "which are essentially within the domestic jurisdiction of any state," save in the case of collective self defense as determined through an appropriate deliberative body of the U.N. (such as the Security Council), as described in Article 51, and Chapter VII. It is as straightforward as such matters can be that none of these conditions pertain to, or were satisfied by, the international deliberations leading up to the most recent war in Iraq.

Congress and the American people, that the United States would never seek what he termed "a permission slip" in order to defend the security of its people. This declaration constituted a stated intent to ignore, or defy, or revoke earlier consent to existing international law whenever such laws were perceived to conflict with the interests or security of this nation, as judged by its elected leadership. This declaration *could* have been taken, in turn, as a statement of principled disagreement with specific provisions or statutes of the United Nations. It appeared instead to constitute an expression of outright contempt for the institutions of international law themselves, at least as presently constituted.

Yet even if the Bush administration were charged with "outright contempt" for international law, the charge would not, in and of itself, address the question of whether the ensuing war in Iraq was *morally* justified. Instead, such a charge would establish a strong burden of proof on the American leadership to provide a convincing case that relevant moral considerations *validly trumped* the provisions of international law in this instance. Arguments of this sort have, in the past, been offered in justification of otherwise "illegal" humanitarian interventions, as by NATO in Kosovo, for example. There the case could be summarized as a quasi-legal action by proxy: inasmuch as the legally sanctioned entity (the United Nations) is unable or unwilling to act, a proxy may be delegated (or, as happened, may delegate itself) to carry out the otherwise-justified intervention in the international community's behalf.

There was not at the time, nor has there been since, any similar, *univocal* defense of the U.S. military intervention in Iraq, though (as Walzer avers, in the conclusion of *Arguing about War*) a defensible case could have been made following the expulsion of U.N. weapons inspectors in 1998. Timing, it seems, is extremely significant in the justification of war, and the fact that a case for punitive or retaliatory military intervention could and should, in Walzer's view, have been made in 1998 did not license an "open-ended arrest warrant" for alleged criminal conspiracies that might arise indefinitely into the future.

There was, in fact, a deep divide within the Bush administration itself between those (like then-Secretary of State Colin Powell, and senior members of the Department of State) who adhered to an underlying respect for the institutions of international law, and others (such as former Vice President Cheney and former Secretary of Defense Donald Rumsfeld) who appeared to hold those institutions themselves in contempt. "Violating international law" from the first of these two perspectives could be seen as an act of protest or civil disobedience aimed at challenging the effectiveness (but, importantly, *not* the underlying legitimacy) of the law itself: in effect, shaming the international community into a greater awareness of its moral and legal responsibilities. This is the sort of complaint that scholars like Walzer and Ignatieff have lodged against the United Nations more generally, and which led some (like Ignatieff) to support armed intervention in Iraq, even absent United Nations authorization. Shame, however, does not accurately characterize the international community's response to this particular demonstration of force. In any case, this position of "principled" or "robust internationalism," does not seem accurately to capture the Bush administration's reasoning at the time in deciding to deploy military force.

A more accurate legal description of America's actions, as I argued at the time, was not civil disobedience, but *vigilantism*. The vigilante is one who acts to establish some form of law-like order, either in the outright absence of laws, or when the established structures and institutions of law enforcement appear to be corrupt, ineffectual, or otherwise lacking in the will or the power to enforce the law. Individuals and nations may decide upon this course of action for a number of reasons. Sometimes, of course, they do so simply because (as with a lynch mob, for example) they resent the restraints that law and due process place upon their exercise of passion, hatred, or desire for vengeance. Just as often in the domestic case, and quite frequently in the international case, however, the vigilante takes the law into his own hands when he or she judges that the normal institutions and procedures of the law are inadequate, weak, morally corrupt, or otherwise ineffectual in enforcing justice, providing security, and maintaining the rule of law. This appeared to be the crux of the position of the U.S. President and many of his advisers at the time: namely, that the specific provisions, and more importantly, the various institutions of international law themselves, were simply too weak, too morally corrupted by the prevailing selfish interests of individual member states, and otherwise too ineffectual to ensure an authentic and just rule of law in the international arena.[29] Hence, they seem to believe, the United States is perfectly justified in ignoring them.

Whenever such a judgment of moral decay and collapse is alleged regarding the normal institutions of the law, it falls to the vigilante (at least, in his own estimation) to provide, through powerful and often unilateral action—and solely on his or her own authority—the kind of security and enforcement of the ends of justice that the law itself is intended, but unable or unwilling, to provide. This is both a dismal and a highly undesirable state of affairs. Our experience in domestic law with vigilante justice—with citizens "taking the law into their own hands"—is not very encouraging. Even granting the most well-intentioned and socially-responsible of motives, the vigilante threatens to become as much or more a danger to public order and security than the criminal elements he or she

---

29   While he does not use the term "vigilantism" specifically, Michael Ignatieff does denounce the weakness, corruption, and anachronism of current statutes and institutions of international law, and calls for their radical reform in the defense and promotion of democracy and human rights in the struggle against the threat of terrorism in his Gifford Lectures, *The Lesser Evil: Political Ethics in an Age of Terror* (London: Penguin Books, 2004). His frustration and contempt for the repeated moral failings of the United Nations and for the moral and intellectual bankruptcy of the concept of "an international community" were forcefully expressed at the NEH institute on "War and Morality" cited earlier. My own concerns for the welfare of these institutions and their need for radical reform reflects more the attitude of "principled internationalism": see G.R. Lucas, "The Role of the International Community in the Just War Tradition: Confronting the Challenges of Humanitarian Intervention and Pre-emptive War," *Journal of Military Ethics* 2, (no.2), (2003): 141-8.

proposes to resist, especially when freed from the restraints, checks, and balances (particularly the kind of adversarial review) that legal institutions impose upon an individual agent's judgment or license to act.[30]

Recognizing this dilemma, however, in no way answers, excuses, or removes the underlying criticism by the vigilante of the moral bankruptcy of the prevailing institutions of law and order. The Bush doctrine has evoked numerous comparisons with images or cases drawn from the "lawless frontier" and the "wild west," not the least because his critics derived a certain satisfaction from caricaturing this U.S. President as a trigger-happy cowboy from Texas.[31] The more serious side of these comparisons is that there is something apt about drawing parallels between the early American frontier and the present state of international relations in terms of the rule of law (or its relative absence or ineffectiveness). Like the developing frontier, there has been in the international arena a gradual development from a primordial state of nature toward at least the outward trappings of cosmopolitan civilization and culture, with an increased need to restrict the liberty of individuals as the price of good order, discipline and security for all. In times of crisis, we note how exceedingly fragile are those veneers of law and order, absent genuinely

---

30   See Martin L. Cook's telling caution in this regard in "On Constituting the World's Sole Remaining Superpower," the opening chapter of *The Moral Warrior: Ethics and Service in the U.S. Military* (Albany, NY: State University of New York Press, 2004).

31   In January, 2004, I had the privilege of being the first invited guest on the inaugural edition of a new public radio broadcast, "Philosophy Talks," hosted by the distinguished Stanford philosophers John Perry and Kenneth Taylor (KALW-San Francisco: January 13, 2004, at "high noon" PST). Along with callers to the broadcast, we conversed on "The Bush doctrine of Preemptive War," during which numerous such references and interesting variations of "wild west" cases were discussed. Knowing, one might ask, that your adversary has publicly stated his intention to ride into town tomorrow and gun you down, might you plausibly ride out to his ranch the night before and carry out a pre-emptive strike? How imminent does such a threat have to be to justify the preemptive use of force? Can you draw your gun and shoot your adversary on Main Street at high noon before he has a chance to fire, or must you wait for him to attack first? Surely you couldn't justifiably kill either adversary preventively, say, a year in advance, merely on the speculation that they might later constitute a lethal threat. Wouldn't it be better, one exasperated caller inquired, to ride out to the ranch and first attempt to dissuade or deter the adversary, rather than simply killing him? And so forth. The western metaphors have evidently captured the public imagination, although other domestic analogies might ultimately prove more helpful, such as the plight of the dysfunctional family (failed states), spouse abuse (humanitarian intervention) and the raving lunatic neighbor amassing weapons and building fertilizer bombs in his basement (rogue states and counter-terrorist intervention). In the case of preemptive war in Iraq, it might be helpful to draw analogies with actual domestic cases like the FBI preemptive attack on the compound of the Branch Davidians in Waco, TX: carried out with good, solid justification, the best of intentions to prevent harm to the larger community and even to some of the more vulnerable and likely involuntary inhabitants of the compound itself, based upon what seemed to be reasonably reliable intelligence, but with extremely unpredictable and unfortunate results.

authoritative and efficacious institutions for establishing *and enforcing* the law. Nations, like individuals in a provisional state of nature, are armed of necessity in order to protect themselves, and are (like hearty, self-reliant denizens of the frontier) all too prone to "take back" the delegated authority of self defense and enforcement of justice from established legal institutions when they find these inadequate to that task.

In the "international community," according to this analogy, we find that there are recognizable if rudimentary forms of law and order, encompassing the international analogues of a town marshal, or a county sheriff, and a town council —the U.N. Security Council—and the district court, far away (the international criminal court in The Hague, perhaps). But there are no guarantees that when things deteriorate in a given neighborhood (in, say, Rwanda or Bosnia) that the reluctant or largely powerless "marshal" (the U.N. Secretary-General) will succeed in raising and bringing a posse of utterly disinterested and risk-averse fellow "citizens" to aid the victims of violence, or that the reach of the court will be sufficiently broad to apprehend and punish those who imperil the lives and violate the rights of the inhabitants of that neighborhood.

The public fascination for western frontier metaphors at least attempts to capture, in an imaginative and fanciful manner, some of the genuine frustrations and limitations encountered in attempting to understand, let alone enforce, international law. The disturbing image of the frustrated vigilante, acting at best in a quasi-legal fashion, both portrays the intentions of the U.S. and its coalition partners after September 11, 2001, and also helps to underscore the growing fear and resentment with which our "fellow citizens" in that international community, (especially the nations of Europe and the Middle East) regarded America's unilateral and unrestrained posture of defiant enforcement of justice in total disregard of the established procedures and due processes of international law. Vigilantes quickly come to be feared as much or even more than the criminals they seek to restrain.

The recourse to vigilantism underscores *the inherent fragility of international law itself.* International law rest broadly upon three sources: international consensus (as codified in specific treaties and conventions), the "unwritten" or "common" law captured in settled custom (*jus gentium*), and (somewhat more contentiously) "tolerated practice," the sorts of behaviors that nations are disinclined to condemn or attempt to punish.[32] Unlike domestic law in the U.S. (in which the Constitution is viewed as the ultimate authority for legal interpretation) there is no established hierarchy or priority of authority among these distinct sources of international law. Thus, the time-honored concept of diplomatic immunity, for example, while nowhere codified in treaty or convention, enjoys roughly the same status in international law as do the "bright-line" statutes of specific treaties and conventions. This rough parity of competing sources or traditions of law functions reasonably well, except when the settled customs or the tolerated practices diverge sharply,

---

32   See Anthony C. Arend, *Legal Rules and International Society* (Oxford: Oxford University Press, 1999). I basically follow the argument of this work in the account above.

say, from the alleged "consensus" enshrined in black-letter legal statutes. In such instances, it is difficult to know what to make of the claim that such conventions embody some kind of international consensus, if nations can be shown routinely to ignore or bypass them while other nations look away or do little more than complain ceremoniously. This is the anomaly we face in evaluating the morality (if not legality) of recent wars of intervention, whether for humanitarian objectives, or in the putative cause of "preventive" or preemptive self defense.

The U.S.-led military intervention with the goal of regime change in Iraq was a clear violation of existing international law in the first sense of that term: namely, a violation of international consensus as codified in the United Nations Charter and supporting treaties and conventions. *What, if anything, follows from this observation?* We are simultaneously confronted with a number of disturbing precedents that undermine the normative force this observation might otherwise have. The military intervention by the U.S. in the sovereign nation of Panama with the goal of "regime change" in December of 1989 was likewise a clear violation of international law. No permission slips were sought or received by the elder Bush administration for removing Gen. Manuel Noriega from power and placing him in custody (where he remains even after completion of his original jail sentence). Moreover, that mission proceeded no more or less effectively than did a similar intervention carried out unilaterally, but *this time with full international approval*, a scant five years later in Haiti. Both actions—one condemned the other approved —were effective in achieving their stated goal of regime change in the short run, extremely ambiguous in attaining their long-term objectives, and involved decidedly mixed motives and *results that seemed to depend little upon the legality or illegality of the operations under international law.*

In a very different example, the use of military force by the U.S. against targets alleged to be al Qaeda terrorist strongholds in the sovereign nations of the Sudan and Afghanistan in 1998 were classified as "preemptive military strikes," and were at the time roundly condemned as violations of international law. The 75 cruise missiles launched against Iraq following its initial expulsion of U.N. weapons inspectors the same year were not authorized by the U.N. Security Council, and were likewise condemned both by the U.N. membership and by many American citizens, who (mistakenly, as it happens) suspected all of these preemptive strikes suffered from ulterior, entirely domestic political motives. The marked differences in specifics in all these instances is beside the point in recognizing all to be examples of internationally tolerated practices that departed substantially from international law in the first sense: namely, international consensus enshrined in treaty or convention.

Perhaps all that these examples illustrate, however, is that the previously-limited arrogance with which a powerful nation has treated its less powerful neighbors in this hemisphere since the inception of the Monroe Doctrine in the 19th century, has now expanded into the broader international arena in defiance of international will. Yet this explanation likewise does not fully suffice, inasmuch as many nations other than the U.S. have likewise pursued their own independent paths to conflict resolution outside the bounds of black-letter law. The use of military force by President Jules Nyerere of Tanzania for the purposes of "regime change" in forcing dictator Idi Amin from power in neighboring Uganda was not sanctioned by the international community or the U.N. Security Council. It was and remains a clear violation of international law even though it seems very much the sort of constabulary action that Vitoria envisioned in defense of basic human rights. The preemptive military strike carried out by the Israeli Air Force against Iraq's French-built nuclear reactor in Osirisk in 1981 was likewise an unauthorized and illegal violation of sovereignty. The actions of NATO members in Bosnia and Kosovo, the latter partly aimed at "regime change" in sovereign Yugoslavia after the collapse and failure of the U.N. mission there, were determined by the member states of NATO themselves to constitute a violation of international law—one that they judged "illegal, but nonetheless necessary."[33]

The past quarter century is littered with examples of appeals to military force that can only be described as "vigilante justice:" wars of intervention, of preemption, of prevention, and of regime change, some fought for the sake of securing peace and maintaining the existing rule of law, others for purposes of providing humanitarian assistance, still others in order to combat terrorism. Most, if not all of these actions were carried out without international approval; most, if not all, were deemed by their perpetrators at the time "illegal, but necessary." What are we to make of the numerous examples of such evident disregard for international law? It seems as if the contempt for international law that critics ascribe to the previous U.S. president, or to this nation itself as a new and disturbing development in our foreign policy, in fact represents a prevailing fashion among nations, a preference for vigilantism in lieu of the investment of resources and hard work necessary to build workable international institutions.

These actions, of course, may represent something else entirely: *a conceptual crisis in international law itself.* On the one hand, as noted, international law supposedly captures and codifies, as well as guides, the practices tolerated by civilized nations and peoples (*jus gentium*). Yet some of the vigilante actions cited above have at least been tolerated, and even been deemed to be necessary, despite their violation of "bright-line" statutes of international law. If on the one hand, we persist in labeling such acts "illegal" (on account of their being explicitly proscribed by legal statute) then surely we would conclude that respect for the law at least needs to be strengthened by mechanisms for stricter enforcement of these laws. If this cannot be done, then it serves as an explicit indictment of the fundamental institutions of international law itself, and of the moral resolve of the community governed by that law. If, on the other hand, at least some and perhaps many of these instances of non-defensive use of military force can be justified on grounds other than the law, then our own historical experience with civil rights and

---

33   This interesting phrase gained currency through use in a committee report for the British Parliament: Patrick Witnour, "MPs say Kosovo Bombing was Illegal but Necessary," *The Guardian* (June 7, 2000).

civil disobedience in this country might lead us to conclude that *when otherwise justifiable practices consistently run afoul of the law, the law itself is in need of reform.*

Vigilantes are self-deputized constables, performing (as in all of the above examples) police-like functions, in some cases wholly divorced from any clear reference to explicit national interests. Their behavior constitutes "methodological anarchy" in the very worst legal and moral sense. What is lacking, and clearly needed, are notions of legitimate authority (sovereignty or jurisdiction) and proper adversarial review necessary to authorize such actions. We require an effective means of licensing this unilateralism, and restraining it to deputize nations to carry out law enforcement activities legally, in order to represent the authentic needs and wishes of the international community, properly formulated, rather than merely some individual nation-state's own best perceptions of these.[34]

From this vantage point, it is hardly surprising that the classical just war concept of "legitimate authority" turns out to be the most vexed question in all of these cases. Even when one's cause appears just, it is clear that the moral agent (whether individual or nation-state) is not simply entitled or licensed to rely solely on his or her own authority in arriving at that judgment. There is always a demand for what philosophers like John Rawls, Jürgen Habermas, Onora O'Neill, and many others (following Kant) term a "principle of publicity:" the moral agent bears a burden of proof for presenting his case in the form of just cause, right intention, last resort, proportionality, and reasonable means to an impartial jury of peers. Michael Ignatieff, in *The Lesser Evil*, labels this the "principle of adversarial review," and argues that this constraint, essential to democracy, must form the cornerstone of any political procedure designed otherwise to protect nations or their citizens from harm by overriding the rights (including the right of sovereignty) they ordinarily enjoy.[35]

I have thus argued that the toleration of numerous exceptions to existing legal statutes (whatever the specific reasons for tolerance might have been in each individual case) may also point to an internal incoherence in the basic institutional

---

34　I have proposed some guidelines, termed *jus ad pacem*, to guide the formation of relevant international law in this respect. They differ substantially from guidelines subsequently proposed by the International Crisis Group's "Responsibility to Protect" [R2P; see above, n. 14] in that they pertain to preventive self-defense and law enforcement in the international community, as well as to humanitarian interventions. See "From *jus ad bellum* to *jus ad pacem*: re-thinking just war criteria for the use of military force for humanitarian ends," in *Ethics and Foreign Intervention*, eds Deen Chatterjee and Don E. Scheid (Cambridge: Cambridge University Press, 2004), esp. pp. 85-93.

35　*The Lesser Evil*, p. 11. I discuss this principle of publicity in greater detail, with particular reference to Habermas's theory of communicative discourse, in my analysis of the morality of military anthropology (see *Anthropologists in Arms: the Ethics of Military Anthropology* [Lanham, MD: AltaMira Press, 2009]) and of the issue of autonomy and individual dissent in the military itself (see "Advice and Dissent: the Uniform Perspective," *Journal of Military Ethics*, 8, (no. 2), (2009): 141-61).

structures of international law itself.[36] The increasing occurrence of vigilantism often signals a pressing need for major institutional reform. The United Nations, created over a half-century ago, is not a "federal" agency. It lacks the power to act autonomously, or to provide effective and impartial adversarial review. Its various provisions reflect a long-suppressed tension between cosmopolitan aspirations and universal concerns on the one hand, and the more narrowly construed needs and desires of its self-interested member-states on the other. The U.N.'s difficulties at present are of a piece with the difficulties in governance encountered by the former English colonies in America under the Articles of Confederation. This last comparison suggests the urgent need for revision and reform.

If we seek to avoid vigilantism and prevent preventive wars, perhaps it is time, as Allen Buchanan has proposed, to convene an international "constitutional convention" in order to write a more effective U.N. Charter.[37] The goal of this exercise would be to realign this organization so as to reflect its cosmopolitan evolution away from unlimited, and towards merely conditional sovereignty on the part of its member states, as well as to establish effective courts and a constabulary force. In this manner, the revitalized organization would be positioned more fully to represent and defend the authentic needs and rights of the only true bearers of rights, namely, the biological individuals of which any and all nation-states are ultimately comprised.[38] Such efforts to reform the law invariably proceed from a moral or philosophical foundation that lies beneath or beyond existing law, and aim—as vigilantism ultimately does not—to establish, rather than to undermine, the rule of law itself.

---

36   This is the conclusion of a lengthy study, several years ago, by Anthony C. Arend and Robert J. Beck, *International Law and the Use of Force: Beyond the United Nations Paradigm* (London: Routledge, 1993). I have merely amplified some of these authors' proposals in the current essay.

37   See, for example: Allen Buchanan and Robert O Keohane, "The Preventive Use of Force: A Cosmopolitan Institutional Proposal," *Ethics and International Affairs*, 18, (no. 1), (2004): 1-22. Also Shue, "Limiting Sovereignty," 11-28.

38   The proposal for an international criminal court with broad jurisdiction is one such reform, opposed by the U.S. It cannot prevail, or be effective, absent more basic reforms and the creation of complementary institutions of law enforcement as described here. Many voices are echoing this urgent call for the reform of international institutions, none more eloquently than Michael Ignatieff in *The Lesser Evil*, and the distinguished human rights scholar, Henry Shue in "Limiting Sovereignty," both cited earlier in this essay.

Chapter 3

Crossing Borders to Fight Injustice: The Ethics of Humanitarian Intervention

Richard W. Miller

[This chapter was the basis for a talk at a seminar on ethics and military affairs at the U.S. Naval Academy on October 6, 2001, when the mass murders of September 11 were a fresh, stunning memory. The participants' intense engagement with the ethics of restraint in war and their respect for fundamental criticisms of U.S. foreign policy were deeply impressive. A postscript applies the account of humanitarian intervention to the 2003 overthrow of Saddam Hussein.]

Suppose that within each country in the world, everyone had the reasonable, informed view that important laws and policies equitably responded to everyone's legitimate interests and deeply-held convictions. Suppose that this shared insightful approval of the institutions of each country combined with everyone's willing participation in a project of handing a common culture down to future generations, and that these two sympathies led everyone, loyally and intelligently, to commit herself to do her part in continuing the independent political life of her country. In such a world, the equal respect that individual people owe to one another (as well as the respect that peoples owe to one another) would be expressed in a stringent constraint on military action across borders. The only justification of military intrusion would be its use in defense against another country's attack.

Of course, our actual world is very far from this idyll of internal justice. Still, some countries come this close: the constitutional arrangements are basically just and are recognized as such by the vast majority; nearly everyone would be strongly opposed to the resolution of their disagreements with compatriots through pressure from outside; those with just grievances have a reasonable hope of making significant progress through continued political discussion; and these injustices are not grave, widespread violations of human dignity, systematically imposed. In these countries (mighty ones, such as the United States, and weak ones, such as Costa Rica) current injustices do not sustain reasons to ask for military rescue from outside that are more morally serious than the complaints against intrusion that would express the nearly universal goal of collective self-determination. These countries are close enough to the ideal to merit, on the same grounds of mutual respect, the same right to political independence and territorial integrity and the same right to defend this sovereignty that governments possess in the utopia I first imagined.

The deep difficulties concerning the morality of military intervention reflect further departures of global reality from my initial idyll. Many countries are much farther from the ideal than the countries that I have described: they depart through widespread violations of individual human rights or through unjust suppression of a fervent collective aspiration to autonomy of people dominating a subterritory who seek a government affirming their distinctive culture. When, if ever, do these departures from justice within a country's borders justify the intrusions that would be wrong in a better world? It might seem that a realistic view of the frequency and depth of these departures and of the imperviousness of tyrants to moral persuasion dictates a broad license for interventions to remove foreign injustices, so-called "humanitarian interventions." However, this view of tyranny ought to be accompanied by a similarly clear-eyed appreciation of the risks and prospects of intervention, the tendencies of interveners and the legitimate interests and aspirations of those who live amidst grave departures from justice yet have reason to oppose intervention. As the appreciation of these other troubling facts broadens, the moral license for humanitarian intervention shrinks.

In fact, I will argue, the formulas to which governments appeal in international criticism and justification should not include any explicit license for intervention above a horrific threshold of widespread massacre. In certain special circumstances, a responsible citizen should not oppose intervention to end injustices above this threshold, but these cases are extremely rare. Above the abysmal threshold, apart from these special circumstances, a U.S. citizen should have a strong, settled prejudice against humanitarian intervention by the United States.

Sovereign Injustice

When a government systematically wrongs many of its subjects in ways that violate their human dignity and rescue by actions of a foreign power is their only reasonable hope, it is sometimes obvious that military intervention to end the wrongs would unleash deadly violence that would make matters worse. Invading China to end the prolific violations of human rights there would be madness. But even when military intervention is not obviously inhumane, a deadly cure that no reasonable victim would invite, there can be serious moral reasons not to resort to this option. They fall under three headings: self-determination, imposed risks and systemic consequences.

Self-determination   In my initial idyll, three sources of valid patriotic pride reinforced one another, providing reasons why intervention would be wrong. The first is based on values of justice: someone in the target of intervention could protest, "Our basic arrangements do not include grave, widespread systematic violations of human dignity and provide a reasonable hope that serious injustices can be ended by just means." If the United States were to propose to invade Costa Rica to correct unjust measures too far to the left or if Sweden were to propose to invade to improve justice by movement farther to the left, then, even if the particular measures to be corrected were unjust, the intervention would constitute a failure adequately to value the virtues of justice embodied, over-all, in contemporary Costa Rica. The second form of patriotism expresses commitment to a widely shared political project, inherited from the past and handed down to the future, of interacting with others living in a territory to shape the political institutions dominating the territory: "It is for us to fight the battles for justice in our country, determining its moral future." Finally, most people in the pretty-good polities would affirm a political interest in cultural continuity, a desire for a shared independent government that represents, affirms and helps to cultivate a common culture: "For all our differences, we have a national way of life, which we and our government should protect, independent of outside interference."

In countries whose regimes are too unjust to sustain the first, justice-based form of patriotism, the vast majority are often patriotic in the other ways, political-historical and cultural. Shaping the terms of a shared political life in concert (and contest) with those who identify with a shared political history is an aspiration whose legitimacy does not entirely depend on its current moral success. This is, after all, a collective version of the project of individual self-reliance that is a central aspiration of any self-respecting adult. Circa 1960, Spaniards with utmost contempt for the Franco dictatorship were not morally confused if they thought it was inherently valuable to continue to work out the terms of Spanish governance with other Spaniards, even though the current institutional framework was profoundly unjust. Similarly, even in circumstances of injustice, developing and affirming a culture with those who share it is valuable so long as the defining projects of the culture are not fundamentally bad—and, so far as I know, no contemporary culture is so degraded. A citizen of Pakistan could coherently despair of interactions with fellow-citizens that advance the cause of justice, but still think it important that the evolution of culture and tradition in Pakistan should be the responsibility of Pakistanis, properly shaped through their own government rather than a foreign, better government.

The two non-justice-based patriotisms taken together are weighty reasons to object to foreign military intervention that would remove serious and widespread injustices. Even if through some miracle of military technology, the United States could bloodlessly invade and reshape China, transforming the current tyranny to a reasonably just polity on the model of Taiwan, the vast majority of people in China would have reason to complain of this coercive intrusion on their lives together. This would be reason enough not to invade China in order to end the sometimes brutal religious persecutions and widespread corruption of the current regime. Patriotic protests against humanitarian intervention gain moral force from the depth of the required intrusion. An invasion to remove serious, widespread, systematic injustice had better thoroughly reshape local attitudes and institutions through conquest and intimidation, so that injustice will not return, perhaps in even more brutal, vengeful abundance.[1]

Imposed risks   A military intervention in the name of justice has harmful side-effects in the invaded country, whose extent is unpredictable, just as its ultimate success in reducing injustice is unpredictable. So, quite apart from the interference with collective political and cultural aspirations, we need to ask whether the imposed risks are justifiable.

An important category of risks imposed by intervention are the lethal risks for invading troops. The use of conscripts to remove foreign burdens of injustice would give rise to especially serious concerns about risks that they are forced to endure. But even in volunteer armed forces, such as those of the United States at present, military missions ought to be rejected if they impose excessive risks on those who carry them out. And the level of acceptable risk ought to be relatively low when the mission that is contemplated is directed at ending injustice abroad. In exchange for the special terms of their employment, under which they cannot back out after lethal risks sharply increase, those who join the military are owed a commitment not to expose them to extreme risks, except in an extreme national emergency. This protective understanding is especially important in a society, such as the United States, in which men and women often enlist to escape grim employment prospects or a disorganized life emerging from a disorienting childhood.

To avoid imposing severe risks on the invaders, a project of humanitarian intervention will often make use of overwhelming advantages in military technology. But if the dominant regime in the target country is to be ended or turned from grave injustice, the resort to these advantages often causes widespread death outside the invading force. According to the then-editor of *Foreign Policy*, Central Intelligence Agency officials "concede that the U.S. military may have killed from 7,000 to 10,000 Somalis" while America lost 34 soldiers, in the unsuccessful effort in 1993 and 1994 to depose Mohammed Aidid.[2] So concern for risks to humanitarian invaders makes it all the more important to ask whether risks are justifiably imposed on those who live in the target country.

Some of these victims have no standing to complain. A person actively engaged in inflicting brutal injustice, Saddam Hussein, say, or a member of his secret police, has no good reason to complain of the effects of rescue needed to end his projects of unjust violence. Others have standing to complain, but voluntarily give up their right to protest: like someone who accepts the risks of a surgical intervention,

---

1   The independent value of self-determination was powerfully affirmed in work of Michael Walzer's which transformed the modern discussion of intervention. See his *Just and Unjust Wars* (New York: Basic Books, 1977), chapter 6. I will not give self-determination the unique moral authority it has in his account. But it will serve as one consideration among others in support of stringent limits to intervention that broadly resemble those that he defends.

2   Charles W. Maynes, "Relearning Intervention," *Foreign Policy* 98 (1995), p. 98.

they give reasonably well-informed consent to the risks of humanitarian military intervention, because of their hope for relief from injustice. Evidently, virtually all Albanian Kosovars wanted NATO military intervention, in spite of its foreseeable risks.

Still, putting to one side those who consent to the risks of intervention and those who have no standing, a great many people in any country exposed to humanitarian intervention have serious reason to complain of the imposed risks. Of course, serious risks imposed on civilians generate important reasons to complain. And these reasons do not just respond to immediate deadly side-effects which the U.S. military can reduce by smart targetting. Large scale dispossession and despoliation are also serious harms. In addition to concern for the Serbian civilian death toll of bombing at a height that protected NATO pilots' lives (a death toll of about 500 in the actual event), a just decision to press for the bombing campaign would have considered the prospect that Serbs living in Kosovo would be driven out by vengeful persecution if the intervention succeeded. (About 100,000 were.)[3]

The moral significance of harm to civilians is widely appreciated in arguments about whether to launch a humanitarian war and in assessments of its conduct. But this concern tends to crowd out attention to another group of people, who must be attacked in the course of the war yet must be objects of serious concern in judgments of its launching: armed defenders of the unjust regime who would not, in the absence of the invasion, engage in conduct that is rightly stopped through the use of deadly force. These victims may be unwilling cannon fodder, like the conscripts massed at the Iraqi border in 1991 when the U.S. invaded after Iraqi forces were expelled from Kuwait and Iraq had offered to give up its territorial claims; many were buried alive in trenches by bulldozers or suffocated and set ablaze by fuel diffusion bombs. Others who have reason to complain of deadly risks, even though they are armed fighters themselves, are patriots who rally to the defense of the homeland under the inspiration of the non-justice-based forms of patriotism. An invasion of Iran to end the tyrannical abuses of the theocrats would, presumably, kill thousands of patriots of this kind, many of whom would otherwise regard the dominant political arrangements with disinterest, condemnation or even disgust. Finally, some consideration is due to the usual rank and file of most well-established tyrants' professional armed forces, fleeing poverty for one of the few situations in which the lot of poor young men is improved at public expense, hoping that their job will not include anything more brutal than somewhat rough police work. Such a person's choice (for example, in a thug-state such as Zaire) was sufficiently constrained and his hope of avoiding grave injustice was sufficiently

---

3   Independent International Commission on Kosovo, *The Kosovo Report* (Oxford: Oxford University Press, 2000), p. 94, p. 108. The Commission had the official support of the United Nations but pursued its inquiry as an independent body. Richard Goldstone, former Chief Prosecutor of the International Criminal Tribunal for the former Yugoslavia, was co-chair.

reasonable that his death in an invasion should be counted (perhaps with some discount) as a reason on the side of not launching an invasion to liberate others.

Launching a war is wrong if its likely costs sustain reasons to object that are more serious, as a whole, than the reasons to object to the best feasible path of peace, in light of *its* likely costs. So a citizen asking whether her country's humanitarian intervention would be just needs to answer a hypothetical question: "Are the risks that my country would impose by invading justifiable by gains to be expected beyond what the best path of peace would yield?" In the real world, such questions are almost always very hard to answer. They are hard and relevant questions about any decision to launch large-scale political violence, not just a humanitarian intervention, but also a war defending against unjust invasion or a rebellion against grave injustice. *But the threshold of adequate assurance is much, much higher when the goal is the ending of injustice that others suffer in a foreign land.* The Tibetans who fought against the Chinese invasion and the Sandinistas who rose up against the Somozas' tyranny certainly imposed grave risks on their compatriots. But they could declare, "I refuse to tolerate these assaults on our dignity. Join me. These are your oppressors, too." Someone fighting against her own oppression may be well aware that many fighters on the other side did not perpetrate injustices against which she rebels. But she can say, "I should not be held hostage to the need to avoid harming deadly opponents to my pursuit of my own dignity." Those who can assert these prerogatives of self-defense against grave injustice are justified in launching a deadly struggle on the basis of a just cause and a fighting chance of achieving it through legitimate though deadly means. However, this mere fighting chance is not enough to justify outsiders in imposing death and dispossession on those with standing to complain in order to defend others from grave injustice. At a minimum, outsiders who responsibly launch an armed intervention ought to have warranted confidence that the vast majority of the intended beneficiaries of the intervention consent to the risks on the basis of adequate information and that the benefits of the intervention, as compared with realistic alternatives, probably outweigh the costs among those whose interests demand serious concern.

Uncertainty as to whether this two-pronged test is met is a powerful moral reason for preferring negotiation and compromise. For example, uncertainty as to whether NATO intervention would meet the second test, of probable benefit, is reason to believe that the Clinton administration was wrong to steer the Rambouillet conference to an ultimatum over Kosovo that needlessly intruded on Serbian sovereignty, in ways that guaranteed its rejection. (Under the Rambouillet ultimatum, NATO was to determine the composition of the Kosovo occupying force, which would have "unrestricted access throughout the FRY [Federal Republic of Yugoslavia] including associated airspace and territorial waters."[4]

---

4   *Le Monde Diplomatique* text of "Interim Agreement for Peace and Self-Government in Kosovo," www.monde-diplomatique.fr/dossiers/kosovo/rambouillet/html, chapter 7, appendix b, p. 8.

The Serbian Prime Minister accepted the Rambouillet accord apart from the prescriptions concerning NATO-led military implementation, which Secretary Albright took to be "largely responsible for the failure to reach agreement.")[5]

Systemic consequences   In addition to the risks that they impose and the aspirations to autonomy that they thwart within the target country, humanitarian interventions can impose important costs on third parties, through effects on international trust and international power relations. Cumulative costs of this kind can add up to an enormous worldwide burden if great powers frequently exercise a license to intervene in response to grave and systematic injustice.

There would be no such danger if intervening powers were guided solely by considerations of justice in deciding where to intervene, extracted no geopolitical advantages from their practice of intervention, and were appreciated for this probity by the world at large. But this utterly nonexploitive practice of intervention is as far from reality as the idyll of domestic justice with which I began. It is certainly very far from the practice of the United States.

In 1999, the United States led the bombing campaign against Serbia in response to brutal repression of aspirations to autonomy in Kosovo which had led to a death toll of around 2000 (including Kosovo Liberation Army combatants and sharply declining in the recent past), and had displaced hundreds of thousands of Albanian Kosovars, many intentionally driven from their homes.[6] The campaign was an attack on a defiant tyrant in a strategic part of the world and a demonstration of American willingness to use awesome military capabilities after the end of the Cold War. If United States efforts to end foreign injustice reflected the depth of injustice, independent of geopolitical advantage, one would also expect vigorous U.S. initiatives to moderate the repression of the Kurdish insurgency in Turkey where, in the fifteen years prior to the bombing of Serbia, the toll of conflict over Kurdish aspirations which responded to such longstanding cultural indignities as the banning of Kurdish names, cassettes with Kurdish songs and Kurdish-language schools was over 20,000.[7] At the height of the Turkish government's counter-insurgency, in 1994, the Turkish State Minister for Human Rights (who was soon replaced) described his government's conduct in one region in that year as "state terrorism": "In Tunceli it is the state that is evacuating and burning villages. In the southeast there are 2 million people left homeless."[8] The previous year, the

---

5   *Kosovo Report*, p. 156.

6   *Ibid.*, pp. 74, 83.

7   See Human Rights Watch, "Weapons Transfers and Violations of the Laws of War in Turkey" (www.hrw.org), 1995; Nicole Pope and Hugh Pope, *Turkey Unveiled* (London: John Murray, 1997), p. 256, p. 258; Stephen Kinzer, *Crescent and Star* (New York: Farrar, Straus and Giroux, 2001), p. 132. Nicole Pope and Kinzer had been Istanbul correspondents for *Le Monde* and *The New York Times*, respectively.

8   See Jonathon Randal, *After Such Knowledge, What Forgiveness?* (New York: Farrar, Straus and Giroux, 1997), p. 259.

U.N. Committee on Torture confirmed an Amnesty International allegation of widespread and systematic use of torture, including torture on mere suspicion of cooperation with the rebels.[9] In 1994, Turkey received $406 million in U.S. military aid in the form of subsidized loans, a $125 million cash grant under the Economic Support Fund program, largely used to offset military purchases, and surplus equipment with an original acquisition value of $109 million (preceded by a value in the previous year of $626 million.)[10] Eighty percent of the armament used by Turkish forces in its offensives against Kurdish villages was American.[11] According to the U.N. Registry of Conventional Arms, the United States was the only country in 1993 and 1994 to supply Turkey with the most deadly weapons of its offensive in the Kurdish countryside, military helicopters with integrated air-to-surface weapons.[12]

The Carter administration was notable for its public advocacy of a foreign policy based on the promotion of human rights. The need to defend Afghans against oppression was a prominent justification of its massive military aid to those fighting against the Soviet-backed regime and against the Soviet troops who brutally supported them. The administration had a different response to Indonesia's invasion and subjugation of East Timor. In that conquest, about 200,000 died, the vast majority civilians, mostly in 1977 and 1978. U.S.-supplied counterinsurgency aircraft used to destroy villages in the highlands were a crucial and very lethal means of conquest, by armed forces deriving 90 percent of their weapons from the United States. The value of the importation of U.S. arms to Indonesia in 1978 was three times that in 1976 (mostly through the government-to-government Foreign Military Sales program.) After 1975, the year of the invasion of East Timor, U.S. military aid increased, totaling $56 million in 1976-1978.[13] In his memoirs of his activities as U.S. Ambassador to the U.N., Daniel Patrick Moynihan reports how he was instructed to respond to massacres by Indonesian forces in their initial takeover of East Timor, which had been reported to have already claimed 60,000

---

9   Amnesty International, "Turkey: No Security without Human Rights," www. amnesty.org/ailib/intcam.turkey.turk5.htm [1996], p.3.

10   *United States Statistical Abstract 1995* (Washington. D.C.: U.S. Census Bureau, 1995), table 1305 and, on the basis of further government figures, Tamar Gabelnick, William Hartung and Jennifer Washburn, *Arming Repression: U.S. Arms Sales to Turkey during the Clinton Administration* (World Policy Institute and Federation of American Scientists, 1999), www.fas.org/asmp/library/reports/turkeyrep.htm, pp. 10-12.

11   See Randal, *After Such Knowledge*, p. 269; see also Gabelnick et al., *Arming Repression*, passim.

12   Amnesty International, "Turkey: No Security without Human Rights," p. 8. Thirty-one attack helicopters were supplied. In 1992 and 1993, the U.S. was the leading supplier of armored combat vehicles to Turkey, providing 250 (*ibid.*, p. 9.)

13   See William Hartung, "U.S. Arms Transfers to Indonesia 1975-1997" (New York: World Policy Institute, n.d.) worldpolicy.org/projects/arms/reports/indoarms.html, pp. 5f. Hartung's military aid total does not include such indirect help as grants of Economic Support Funds.

lives: "The Department of State desired that the United Nations prove utterly ineffective in whatever measures it undertook. This task was given to me, and I carried it forward with no inconsiderable success."[14]

In general, a stable tyranny that complies with the military, diplomatic and economic interests of a great power has little to fear from that quarter in the way of intervention. Rather, the targets of the power's humanitarian wars will be defiant tyrannies in parts of the world in which it is concerned to gain or regain influence. This independent force of geopolitical interests in shaping the interventions of military powers is universal, inevitable and even, to some extent, justifiable, since the evenhanded policing of grave injustice everywhere would constitute an intolerable burden. It makes humanitarian interventions a threat to other powers, in competition over access to raw materials, commercial opportunities, diplomatic coalitions and secure military shields. Such threats can give rise to distrust, militarization and an increased risk of violence worldwide. This was the fate of the many interventions in the Balkans, usually in response to genuine violations of human rights, in the death throes of the Ottoman Empire. It is the danger that usually restrained both sides from aiding in the overthrow of unjust regimes in the other's spheres of influence, in the Cold War. The same general worries about the use of American military might to advance American geopolitical power would take different forms today. But they are by no means obsolete. Someday, China will become a superpower. Very likely, Russia will become a superpower again. The level of violence accompanying such transitions is apt to be affected by the extent to which military invasion has been a means by which the old sole superpower has extended its dominance. China will remember.

Legal Norms and Moral Reasons

Understanding the many, diverse reasons why serious, systematic injustice is not enough to justify military intervention makes it easier to see on what terms sovereignty *could* justifiably be overridden, in order to end injustices of special kinds. The clearest candidates for humanitarian military intervention are governments currently engaged in widespread massacre, even though it has been exposed and condemned, with warnings to stop. Because the violations of human dignity are extreme and widespread, the reasons to rescue are especially strong. On the other hand, there are no overriding considerations of self-determination, so long as the ending of widespread massacre is the goal of intervention. A regime engaged in such projects is a regime whose continuance hijacks any cultural project or political history worth continuing. Considerations of imposed risk do not normally override the reasons to rescue. The potential victims can be assumed to accept the risks of rescue, for excellent reasons. Those who try forcibly to prevent rescue from such violence have gone beyond the limits of valuable patriotism, and

---

14   Patrick Moynihan, *A Dangerous Place* (Boston: Little, Brown, 1978), p. 247.

can be treated as mere perpetrators. The brutes engaged in widespread massacre are not apt to be stopped by milder interventions. Since the cause of intervention is rare and easy to discern using uncontroversial standards of good and evil, intervention on these grounds is not apt to excite a dangerous increase in distrust among great powers.

What about cases in which there is constant violence by groups seeking territorial dominance or loot, but no effective state, capable of imposing peaceful order, however unjust? It might seem that this absence of even an effective oppressor state eliminates moral barriers to intervention, since there is no sovereign government to be the object of patriotism and the status quo is full of risks. But this is to forget the varieties of patriotism and the sources of enduring order. As in Somalia, it is perfectly possible for those who are not united by an effective state to share a reasonable and powerful aspiration to determine their political fate among themselves, in a process in which they act as the cultivators and protectors of their shared traditions. Moreover, the very forces that have prevented the internal formation of an effective state are apt to make to make it profoundly difficult for a foreign power to create an enduring basis for stability. A long occupation, with its own costs in violent coercion, is apt to be required. Through such external domination, the process of mutual struggle that leads to eventual mutual accommodation and enduring peace with reasonable political justice may well be short circuited. Finally, because of the prospect of long-term dominance and the lack of internal political resources, intervention to end the disorders of a failed state is apt to extend geopolitical power in troubling ways. This was, after all, the standard excuse for U.S. interventions in Latin America before the Cold War, and the justification for the most extensive recent expansion of suzerainty in the Middle East, Syria's take-over of Lebanon. If the level of violence attendant on a failed state approaches widespread massacre within a significant region, the need for rescue may well combine with the absence of internal resources for rescue to justify intervention. But below this horrific threshold of carnage, the case for intervention will depend on further circumstances.

The other factor that plays an important role in justifying intervention is a fight for self-determination in a sub-territory. The horrific standard of widespread massacre was not met in Kosovo before the bombings, when atrocities against civilians were uncommon and diminishing, partly through the work of international observers. Certainly, it was not met by the Habsburg Empire in nineteenth-century Italy or the British Empire in eighteenth-century North America. But intervention in Kosovo was, at a minimum, worthy of serious consideration, and France's crucial interventions in support of both earlier independence movements were just.

These permissive judgments reflect the weakening of considerations that normally make armed intervention unjustifiable, when a secessionist rebellion achieves widespread support in spite of violent efforts to suppress it. Because a popular secessionist rebellion reflects fervent identification with a separate political history and the fervent aspiration for a politically independent culture, respect for self-determination no longer counts against intervention, at least if the territory in rebellion can secede without destroying the conditions for independent vitality of the rest. Because struggles for national independence often express widely held commitments to self-sacrifice, leading great numbers of people to risk their lives for the national cause, it is especially likely that people in a nationality struggling for independence would give their informed consent to risks imposed by intervention. Also, at least in the modern context, in which the dominating government itself professes to represent a nationality, the violent repression of a movement for independence is apt to mobilize, against the group seeking to secede, nationalist sentiments of contempt and vengeful victimization, which make future violations of human dignity more likely than future just reconciliation. Finally, the systemic worry about heightened world tension tends to be less pressing than usual, since a newly independent country, born of a fierce popular struggle, is not apt to be a mere extension of another country's sphere of influence.

However, this reduction of the force of the normal case against intervention does not create a general moral license to intervene. Indeed, characteristic features of popular secessionist rebellions generate their own anti-interventionist considerations. For example, a triumphant struggle against oppression can generate its own vengefulness and bigotry, as in Kosovo. Secession can inspire emulation elsewhere and dangerous recalculations of the regional balance of power, threatening the sort of destabilization that made Kurdish secession in Iraq a clouded prospect for the world community. So, while secession deserves special treatment, there is no general right to intervene in support of popular secessionist rebellions, even in the face of widespread injustice.

The considerations bearing on intervention have turned out to be diverse. So far, only rescue from widespread ongoing massacre has turned out to provide even a normally compelling reason why intervention is all right.[15] What further principles should guide deliberations over possible humanitarian interventions? The answer crucially depends on the kind of deliberation in question.

Often, the search for appropriate principles is a search for a shared repertoire of formulas to be used in justifications and criticisms that governments present in international forums. Currently, the repertoire consists of precepts that are nearly all extremely vague, collectively verging on inconsistency; a determinate interpretation of their dictates above the threshold of widespread massacre is bound to be forced. All governments agree that there must be no coercive interference with the domestic affairs of a legitimate government. That a government loses its legitimacy if it persists in engaging in widespread massacre is generally accepted.

---

15   "Normally" may seem callous. But the horrors of war that would have been unleashed would surely have made it wrong for a foreign power to rescue Tibetans from the carnage following the anti-Chinese rebellion. The first Bush administration's judgment that intervention to stop vicious suppression of the uprising in southern Iraq would have too dangerously increased regional instability was reasonable even if the administration was irresponsible to stimulate the rebellion in the first place.

Beyond this, there is probably general agreement that a government commits a kind of aggression that reduces the strength of its right to non-interference if, in the words of a cogent U.N. declaration on principles of international law, it uses "force to deprive a people of its national identity" or has no valid claim to represent "the whole people belonging to its territory without distinction as to race, creed, or colour."[16] But views of the extent to which the prerogative is lost and the terms on which these abstract precepts are to be spelled out differ widely from government to government and even from issue to issue. And the shared repertoire of formulas generally lends support both to the interventionist and anti-interventionist position, depending on interpretations that the repertoire permits. Thus, the same carefully drafted United Nations declaration at one point unqualifiedly asserts, "No State or group of States has the right to intervene, directly or indirectly, for any reasons whatever, in the internal or external affairs of any other State."[17] But the apparent blanket prohibition in this passage, which even seems to protect external conduct, no matter how unjust, is so extreme that it signals the need for a grain of salt. And elsewhere in the same document, the sprinkling of large grains of salt is facilitated, though not required—for example, in the statement, "The use of force to deprive peoples of their national identity constitutes a violation ... of the principle of non-intervention."[18]

Given the tendencies of potential interveners and of systematically unjust regimes, this repertoire of formulas ought to be maintained, because of, not despite, its vagueness and near-inconsistency. Because of the availability of anti-interventionist interpretations, military powers that intervene will face criticisms, which grow more pervasive and intense as their interventions become more violent, frequent and longlasting. These disincentives reduce the characteristic costs of intervention over the long run. On the other hand, because of the availability of interventionist interpretations, a tyranny above the threshold of widespread massacre has something to fear on account of its injustice. Such tyrannies usually will not be attacked and will be accepted as participants in international deliberative processes. But they will be subject to recurrent criticism in these forums and to costs other than invasion. There will, then, be incentives to move farther above the horrific threshold of widespread massacre, toward the pretty-good.

An unambiguous prohibition of intervention above the threshold would not be in the interests of humanity. It would remove incentives to improve justice. Proposals to move in the other direction, broadening the explicit license to intervene, are

---

16   Declaration on Principles of International Law concerning Friendly Relations and Cooperation among States in Accordance with the Charter of the United Nations in Hurst Hannum, ed., *Documents on Autonomy and Minority Rights* (Dordrecht: Martinus Nijhoff, 1993), p. 41, p. 43.

17   *Ibid.*, p. 41.

18   *Ibid.*

much more popular. (For example, Kofi Annan has been a prominent advocate.)[19] These revisions of the international formulary would explicitly deny the right of nonintervention to governments engaged in systematic, widespread violations of human rights, so that rescue from the tyrannical abuses of the Somozas, not just from massacre on the scale of the mass murders in Rwanda and East Pakistan, would be an appropriate goal of military intervention. Of course, those who propose this revision are aware that intervention in this cause might be wrong because of further costs or the improbability of sufficient gains to those who are to be helped. The whole revised system of precepts is supposed to include conditions on the just pursuit of the new goal. Humanitarian invasion is to be avoided if its further costs are too high, its prospects of improvement are too low, or the prospects of remedy by nondeadly means are sufficient.

But how are these constraints themselves to be interpreted and by whom? A requirement of a conclusive demonstration, compelling to any reasonable and informed deliberator, that the objections to humanitarian invasion are no more serious than the objections to the best path of peace is as good as a prohibition, above the threshold of massacre. Crucial comparisons of possibilities and prospects are always subject to reasonable dissent. But in the absence of a clear and determinate rule, the impact of the constraining precepts will be minimal. Given the greater ease of constructing a plausible justification on the basis of the new repertoire of formulas, military powers will be more apt to intervene in ways that serve their geopolitical interests, regardless of whether values of self-determination, imposed costs, and dangers of instability and hegemony are actually adequately honored. This implication of the American practice of intervention would, of course, be reinforced by reflection on practices of other governments, recently and throughout history, for example, the prolific interventions of France in francophone Africa.

The effect of the current intergovernmental repertoire of formulas concerning intervention is a mild discipline on countries that can intervene, leading to some rationing of interventions, rationing that favors the most flamboyant cases of injustice. Given military powers' insensitivity to relevant concerns, this is a healthy discipline. It no more expresses respect for tyrants than a rule excluding evidence improperly obtained expresses respect for the murderers, thieves and rapists who will, inevitably, gain freedom.

An alternative discipline, with considerable support, is institutional and procedural: a requirement of United Nations approval for humanitarian intervention, sometimes joined with a requirement of multinational military participation. Added to the explicit licensing of intervention against systematic, grave injustice if further conditions concerning imposed risks and peaceful remedies are met, this is initially attractive as a means of reducing worldwide injustice while keeping intervention within those limits: the divergent geopolitical interests of the participants will cancel each other out, reducing inclinations to violate morally relevant conditions;

---

19   See Kofi Annan, *The Question of Intervention* (New York: United Nations, 1999.)

especially if the intervening force is derived from military powers with divergent interests, assembled under the guidance of U.N. deliberations, the intervention will not increase distrust or produce objectionable hegemony.

The multinational procedure is certainly to be preferred, if I have accurately identified dangers of unilateral intervention. But the thought that it will sustain a more permissive license to intervene rests on the familiar combination of clear-eyed appreciation of the tendencies of individual governments and excessive optimism about the tendencies of the United Nations. Given the tendencies of governments, Security Council dominance of decisions to intervene and the great power veto are highly desirable. A military power that strongly dissents from a U.N. military project will resentfully detach from the United Nations, in fact if not formally, with results that are apt to threaten world peace. But with the veto, interventions will not occur if they threaten the vital interests of a great power. For example, Chechnya, the Kurdish provinces of Turkey and Gaza and the West Bank are beyond the pale. Given these realities, if international standards of intervention are not to fall into disrepute, they must be vague and subject to interpretation above the threshold of massacre. For similar reasons, multinational intervention forces are not a basis for expanding the current license to intervene. An effective multinational force requires a longstanding history of coordinated joint activity among the component forces. Such coordination does not occur among countries with sharply divergent interests. The alternative, a powerful genuinely independent standing U.N. army, would so threaten great powers that it will not be instituted and would threaten world peace if it were.

Moving beyond the official deliberations in which representatives of governments make their charges and offer their justifications, what more can be said to give structure to the moral deliberations of responsible individuals deciding whether to support humanitarian interventions? Except in the case of rescue from widespread massacre, there seems to be no reason to intervene that generally overrides reasons not to intervene. Because of the heavy burden of proof in the justification of large-scale organized killing for the sake of others' rights, we ought to be reluctant to approve of intervention above the horrific threshold. Still, such justifications may be available in special circumstances, even when it would be inappropriate to explicitly validate the justification in the repertoire of intergovernmental formulas.

While individuals' judgments of particular interventions must attend to facts of the case which would not be specified in the repertoire of intergovernmental formulas, they need not proceed case by case. Rather we can seek guidance in constellations of relevant characteristics which, at least in current global circumstances, tell strongly for or against intervention. The Tanzanian overthrow of Idi Amin suggests one such constellation. Tanzania was a neighboring country with a similar culture and history, lacking the capacity to dominate Uganda over the long run; Amin was an incurable and destructive tyrant, who had inspired widespread opposition including reasonably competent and tolerant people capable of leading a better regime; his power crucially depended on racist agitation and foreign arms bought through larcenous use of Ugandan resources. Even though they are not material for a U.N. convention, these characteristics furnish a compelling constellation of reasons to permit intervention. With some modification, this pattern can be fitted to other cases, for example, Vietnam's intervention in Cambodia.

Another constellation suitable for individuals' judgments takes special account of spheres of influence. The restoration of the Aristide government did not destabilize the hemisphere or reduce self-determination in Haiti, because Haiti was already a subordinate part of the American sphere of influence. But it would serve no purpose to convert these morally relevant characteristics into proclamations of superior and inferior status when official precepts of intervention are applied in the world public forum. The same pattern of reasoning applies to France's policing of tyranny in France's African sphere.

Thus, moral reasoning about humanitarian intervention acquires determinacy swathe by swathe, without producing comprehensive determinate principles. The pretty-good polities that I previously described are not subject to intervention. The situations of massacre are worthy of military rescue unless the side-effects of violence are especially extensive. In between the pretty-good and the abysmal, morally permissible intervention depends on diverse constellations of injustices and circumstances, which are not described by a determinate general rule, but can usefully be cataloged. Because of the imposed risks of intervention, its dangers to world stability and the non-justice-based patriotisms underlying even unjust polities, interventions outside these constellations will be wrong unless extremely rare special circumstances provide extremely powerful reasons to override a normal presupposition: foreign injustice is not to be ended by military means.

Postscript, 2009

This contribution was written when the NATO bombing campaign against Serbia in 1999 was the dominant recent fact in discussions of humanitarian intervention. Subsequently, a much more deadly war was launched that overthrew Saddam Hussein, with a humanitarian component in its justification that came to the fore as the appeal to possible weapons of mass destruction sank into disrepute. The cautionary precepts of the essay provided reasons to reject that justification. The sequel to the invasion has confirmed the force of those precepts.

A great power can be expected to protect its troops with overwhelming force. Contemplating the prospect of a U.S.-led ground invasion of Iraq, meant to quickly overthrow a long-entrenched tyranny, no one should have been surprised by a large Iraqi death toll. In the actual course of the military overthrow of Saddam Hussein, about 5,000 Iraqi civilians and about 5,000 Iraqi soldiers were killed.[20]

---

20   Iraq Body Count's tabulations from reports of civilian deaths in the invasion in at least two major news sources amounted to 6,616. See Iraq Body Count, "A Dossier of

Perhaps, in principle, the United States could have avoided an insurgency in the wake of his overthrow by holding quick elections, largely preserving the Iraqi army and bureaucracy, and withdrawing. But a citizen should judge the consequences of going to war in light of what her government is apt to do once its forces are engaged, without the selective realism that only attends to tendencies of the regime to be deposed. The United States could not be expected willingly to risk another defiantly independent regime in control of Iraqi oil or to destroy the opportunity the invasion had created to establish a secure position on the Persian Gulf and mold a leading Middle Eastern economy in U.S. interests. Once an occupation in pursuit of American power had inflamed nationalist resentment and insurgency, the United States would not soon withdraw or concede authority to those who regarded the United States as an oppressive occupier: great powers do not willingly sacrifice the credibility of their future threats of armed intrusion. In sum, a vast toll of violence in the attempt to reshape the polity of a fractious country, using troops with no local cultural connection but vast firepower, was to be expected. There was no evidence of informed consent to this risk by the majority of the Iraqis with standing to complain of being put in mortal jeopardy. Outside those borders, more terrorist attacks, rather than fewer, were apt to be suffered on balance, while heightened fears in China and Russia were apt to threaten long-run stability.

These expectations were horribly fulfilled, confirming the humanity of a deep settled prejudice against humanitarian intervention by a great power outside its sphere of influence, in the absence of widespread massacre. According to two major epidemiological surveys, excess deaths due to the invasion and its consequences in the next forty months were in the range of half a million.[21] These surveys only extended into the start of the fourth and most violent year after the invasion. Shortly after its end, a poll in which Iraqis were asked how many members of their household had died as a result of violence in the conflict since 2003 yielded

---

Civilian Casualties 2003-2005," www.iraqbodycount.net. The Associated Press's tally of deaths due to the invasion specifically characterized as civilian in 60 of Iraq's 124 hospitals was 3,240. See Niko Price, "AP Tallies 3,240 civilian deaths in Iraq," June 11, 2003. Reuters reported "unofficial think-tank estimates" of 4,895 to 6,370 Iraqi military deaths in the invasion. See "Table of military deaths in Iraq," April 7, 2004, www.reuters.com. The U.S. military estimated that at least 2,320 Iraqis were killed in the attack on troops near Baghdad prior to the taking of the city. See "Special analysis: Baghdad has fallen," *The Independent*, April 6, 2003, p. 7.

21   Gilbert Burnham, Riyadh Lafta, Shannon Doocy and Les Roberts, "Mortality after the 2003 invasion of Iraq," *The Lancet* 368 (2006): 1421-8 have a mid-point estimate of 654,965 deaths in excess of what would have been expected on the basis of death rates before the invasion, within a 95 percent confidence interval of between 392,979 and 942,636 excess deaths. Amir Alkhuzai et al., "Violence-related Mortality in Iraq from, 2002 to 2006," *New England Journal of Medicine* 2008 (358), 484-93 present estimates of death rates entailing about 400,000 excess deaths in the same period.

an estimate of about a million such deaths.[22] After the great surge of violence had receded, another poll asked whether the 2003 invasion would turn out to be in the best interests of Iraq in the long run. The "No"s outnumbered the "Yes"s by two to one.[23] Asked to judge the rightness or wrongness of the invasion in late February 2009, 56 percent of a large representative sample of Iraqis judged it to have been wrong, indicating condemnation by about two thirds of those living outside of the northern Kurdish protectorate that had been shielded from Saddam Hussein before the invasion.[24] The above account of humanitarian intervention supports this collective condemnation and is supported by it.

22   Opinion Research Business, "New analysis 'confirms' 1 million+ Iraq casualties," www.opinion.co.uk, January 28, 2008.

23   Opinion Research Business, "Iraqis Confident in Security but Concerned with Economy," Table 48, www.opinion.co.uk, March 14, 2008. 46 percent responded, "No," 23 percent "Yes," 19 percent "Impossible to tell," 11 percent "Don't know," and 2 percent did not answer.

24   ABC News, "Dramatic Advances Sweep Iraq, Boosting Support for Democracy," abcnews.go.com/PollingUnit, p. 20 and "Iraq Poll: Methodology", March 16, 2009, p. 2. Overwhelming majorities approving the invasion have, from the start, been an exceptional feature of the Kurdish north.

PART II
Jus in Bello

Chapter 4

The Proper Role of Intention in Military Decision Making

T.M. Scanlon

How does the moral assessment of an action, in particular the moral permissibility of performing it, depend on the agent's intentions?[1] This question arises in military contexts most famously regarding the targeting of noncombatants. The now standard understanding, deriving from the so-called Doctrine of Double Effect, is that it is impermissible to kill or harm noncombatants intentionally; it is permissible to kill or harm them only as the unintentional, even if fully foreseen, side effect of attacks on legitimate military targets, and only if the good thereby achieved outweighs the resulting evil. The Doctrine of Double Effect has appealed to many people because it seems to provide the best account of the distinction between permissible and impermissible conduct in these military cases and in other cases as well.

In what follows, however, I will argue that this doctrine should be rejected. Although it correctly identifies certain actions as impermissible, it provides the wrong explanation of why they are impermissible. I will argue that the permissibility of an action does not depend on the agent's intentions in performing it in the way that the Doctrine of Double Effect claims that it does, and I will offer an explanation of why this should have seemed to be the case even though it is not. I will begin by saying something about the idea of intention.

---

1   My first crack at this problem is described in "Permissibility and Intention I," *Proceedings of the Aristotelian Society* Suppl. Vol. 74 (2000), pp. 301-17. Pages 1-12 of the present chapter are largely drawn from that one and are used by courtesy of the Editor of the Aristotelian Society © 2000. I pursued these issues further in Chapter 1, pp. 8-36, of *Moral Dimensions: Permissibility, Meaning, Blame*, Cambridge, Mass.: The Belknap Press of Harvard University Press, Copyright 2008 by the President and Fellows of Harvard University Press. Portions of this contribution are reprinted and adapted from that book by the permission of the publisher. I am grateful to Roger Wertheimer for comments that have helped me to improve the present chapter.

Intent and Reasons

"Intention" is commonly used in wider and narrower senses.[2] When we say that a person did something intentionally, one thing we may mean is simply that it was something that he or she was aware of doing, or realized was a consequence of his or her action. This is the sense of "intentionally" which is opposed to "unintentionally". To say that you did something unintentionally is to claim that it was something you did not realize you were doing. But we also use "intention" in a narrower sense. To ask a person what her intention was in doing a certain thing is to ask her what her aim was in doing it, and what plan guided her action—how she saw the action as promoting her objective.[3] This is in part to ask what her reasons were for acting in this way—which of the various features of what she realized she was doing were features she took to count in favor of so acting. This narrower sense of intention is at least very close to the idea of intention involved in the distinction, central to the Doctrine of Double Effect, between the consequences of one's action that are intended (as ends or chosen means) and those that are merely foreseen.[4]

One thing that these two senses of intention have in common is that each tells us something about an agent's view of the reasons bearing on his or her action. This is most obvious in the case of the narrower notion. The broader notion of intention—the idea of what one does intentionally—is in the first instance a matter of what the agent understands herself to be doing. But it is also true that if an agent does something intentionally in this broader sense—if she is aware of this aspect of her situation—then even if she does not take this aspect of what she is doing to provide a reason for so acting she at least does not (insofar as she is not acting irrationally) take it to constitute a sufficient reason not to act in that way. In either case, then, to say what an agent does intentionally, or intends, is at least in part to say something about her assessment of the reasons that bear on acting in that way.

---

2   These may correspond, respectively, to what Elizabeth Anscombe calls an agent's "intention *of* doing what he does" and "his intention *in* doing it." See G.E.M. Anscombe, *Intention* (Oxford: Basil Blackwell, 1958), p. 9.

3   This aspect of intention is emphasized by Michael Bratman. See his *Intention, Plans, and Practical Reasoning* (Cambridge, MA: Harvard University Press, 1987).

4   The two may not, however, be identical. This is because there are many ways in which an agent can take some aspect of an action to "count in favor of it," and it may be that not all of these are cases in which that aspect is an agent's end or chosen means. For example, an aspect of a course of action can count in favor of it by offsetting what would otherwise be an objection to it. I may decide to go to an art exhibit only because I have been given a free ticket, but it would be odd to say that I went in order to get in free. Frances Kamm argues for the importance of distinctions of this kind in "The Doctrine of Triple Effect and Why an Agent Need Not Intend the Means to his End," *Aristotelian Society Supplementary Volume LXXIV* (2000), pp. 21-39.

Knowing an agent's intention in acting, and which things she is doing intentionally, can give thus us three kinds of information about her action. Knowing her intention, in the sense of her plan of action, tells us how she expects to move her body and to affect the world around her. Knowing what it is that she is doing intentionally, tells us what she believes about her situation and the likely effects of her action. It also tells us something about how she evaluates these factors—which things she sees as reasons for acting the way she plans, which things as costs to be avoided if possible, which as costs to be borne, which as inconsequential.

The Apparent Significance of Intent

With this as background, let me return to my main question, which is whether and how an agent's intention is relevant to the moral permissibility of what he or she does. It may seem that they are obviously relevant. An agent's intentions, it might be said, determine what the agent's action *is*—whether it is an instance of lying, for example, or murder—and what an action *is* in this sense must surely be relevant to its moral permissibility.

I want to identify at the outset, in order to set it aside, an important way in which this is quite true, but true in a way that makes it not directly relevant to the question I am pursuing. An agent's aim in acting, her plan in acting, her beliefs about the likely effects of her action, and her evaluation of various features of her situation— which of them she sees as providing reasons, positive or negative, and which as inconsequential—are, taken together, an important part of our basis for predicting the effects that her action will have. They are not a complete basis for predicting these effects. An agent's understanding of her situation is often incomplete or mistaken, and the effects of a planned movement may be quite different from what the agent expected. So, in order to assess an action we may need to draw on other information. But the agent's intention, and what she is doing intentionally, are a crucial starting point. Moreover, the agent's evaluation of various features of her situation tells us how her action is likely to be guided—which aspects of her situation she will attend to and how she is likely to respond if things do not go as she expects them to.

These factors are all clearly relevant to the permissibility of an agent's action, and I will return later on to consider their significance in more detail. But this way in which intent can be relevant to the permissibility of an action is in an important sense derivative. What is of fundamental relevance in these cases is the effects of the agent's action on the world around her (or what it is reasonable to expect those effects to be.) Her intention is relevant in the ways just described only because it tells us something about these effects. This is what I will call the *predictive* significance of intent. The question I am interested in, however, is whether an agent's intention is itself directly relevant to the permissibility of an action— whether, holding effects (or expected effects) constant, the permissibility of an action can depend on the agent's intention in performing it or, more generally, on what he or she saw as a reason for so acting. So I will set aside for the moment the predictive significance of intent and concentrate on the question of how intent might be more directly relevant to permissibility.

Various lines of thought support the conclusion that intent is directly relevant to the moral assessment of an action. There is obviously an important moral difference between intentionally harming someone, causing harm negligently, and doing so through a freak accident. The difference between causing harm intentionally and doing so negligently, however, is not a difference in *permissibility*. Both are generally impermissible. The difference between them lies rather in the kind of fault that is involved when an agent acts impermissibly in these ways. The difference between causing harm in either of these ways and causing harm through a freak accident does appear to be a difference in permissibility. But what makes the difference here is not intent. What differentiates negligence from a freak accident is not necessarily what the agent knew but what he or she *should have known*, under the circumstances, about the likely effects of his or her action.

It has, however, seemed to many people that there are cases in which not just the overall moral assessment of an action but also its permissibility depends on the agent's intention. Specifically, it has seemed to them that some actions are wrong because the agent intended another person's death either as an end or as his or her chosen means. This doctrine is controversial, but it is appealing to many because it seems to offer the best explanation of examples such as the following:

Drug Shortage   There are five people in Room B, and one person in Room A, all of whom have the same disease, and all of whom will die if not treated soon. There is enough medicine on hand to cure all five of the people in Room B, but since the person in Room A has a more advanced case, it would take all of the available supply just to save him.

In this case it is clearly at least permissible to use all of the medicine to save the people in Room B. Now consider:

Transplant   The five people in Room B are in need of organs—one needs a heart, two need a lung and two a kidney—and they will all die if they are not given transplants soon. Unfortunately, no organs are presently available. But there is a person in Room A, in for a check up, who could be given a lethal injection instead of the inoculation he is expecting, thereby making his organs available to save the five.

This is clearly impermissible. It might be tempting to explain the difference between these cases by saying that although it is permissible to let one die in order to save five, as in *Drug Shortage*, what is proposed in *Transplant* is to kill the one in order to save the five, and this is not permissible.

Drug/Transplant   The people in Room B are the same as in *Transplant*, and the person in Room A is the same as in *Drug Shortage*. If this person dies of his illness, his organs will not be damaged and thus can be used to save the five. Is it permissible to withhold the drug?

Everyone with whom I have discussed these cases agrees that it is not. Why not? One answer would be that, as in *Transplant*, this would be a case of killing one to save five. But this cannot be the basic explanation. What it is proposed to do to the one in this case is the same as in *Drug Shortage*—to refrain from giving him the available drug—and it was said in that case that this was not killing. If it is killing in this case, then this is because "killing" is being used as a moral notion—that is to say, it is killing because it is wrong (for some other reason) rather than being wrong because it is killing. What, then, is this other reason? One explanation that naturally comes to mind is that whereas in *Drug Shortage* the death of the one is merely a foreseeable consequence of giving the drug only to the five, in *Drug/ Transplant* the death of the one is intended: what is proposed is to withhold the drug from the one precisely in order to get him dead right away, so that his organs will be available for transplant in time to save the five. This is, on the face of it, extremely plausible as an explanation of the difference between the two cases, as a result of which what is proposed in *Drug Shortage* is permissible, but what is proposed in *Drug/Transplant* absolutely impermissible.

One might suspect that our reactions to these cases depend on ideas that are peculiar to the hospital setting—on ideas about the duties that hospital personnel owe to patients. I will return to this possibility below, but it is worth noting here that similar problems can arise in cases that do not involve hospitals or the obligations of doctors and nurses.

Rescue I   As I am driving home, I hear on my citizens band radio that a car is stalled along a seldom-traveled road that I could easily take. The car is delivering medicine to someone who will die unless he receives it within the next few hours. I could easily take that road and restart the stalled car.

Clearly I should do so.

Rescue II   This is the same as the previous case except I also hear that along another road I could take there is a stalled car that was taking medicine to five people in equally urgent need. There is not enough time for me to go to the aid of both cars.

Clearly in this case it is at least permissible for me to aid the latter car, so as to save five rather than only one.

Rescue/Transplant   This scenario is the same as *Rescue I* except that I know that there are five people in urgent need of transplants who will be saved if the patient awaiting the medicine dies very soon, as he will if I do not go to the aid of the stalled car. May I therefore refrain from aiding the car?

It seems that I cannot. Why not? As before, one plausible explanation is that in this case, but not *Rescue II*, I would be intending that the one should die, as a means to saving the five.

Like many others, I have found this explanation appealing. But there are well-known problems with it. First, no one has, to my knowledge, come up with a satisfying theoretical explanation of why the fact of intention in the sense that is involved here—the difference between consequences that are intended and those that are merely foreseen—should make a moral difference. Second, there are cases in which applying this distinction seems to give the wrong answer. For example, in the trolley problem case, famous among philosophers, it seems permissible to switch a runaway trolley onto a side track on which it will hit only one person rather than allow it to continue straight ahead and hit five. But it also seems permissible to turn the trolley in the Loop case, proposed by Judith Thomson, in which the side track loops around and rejoins the main line, so that if the trolley were not going to hit the one person, and thereby be stopped, it would continue around a loop and hit the five from the other side.[5] The answer in this case may be less clear than in the original one, but it is at least quite plausible to maintain that if it is permissible to turn the trolley onto the side track in the first case it is permissible in the second as well.

These cases seem to differ in just the way I have described: in the second, but not the first, one switches the trolley only because it will, by hitting the one person, be prevented from hitting the five. So it seems that this person's being hit by the trolley is intended as a means to the end of saving the others. Perhaps the distinction between intended and merely foreseen consequences, even though it makes a moral difference in the cases described above, does not make a difference in these cases. But this needs to be explained.[6]

Thomson also presents, as counter-examples to the kind of analysis we are considering, cases involving the use of lethal drugs for pain relief. Suppose that a patient is fatally ill and in great pain. The only course of medication that will relieve this pain will also cause the patient's death. Suppose that the patient wants to be given this drug. Does the permissibility of administering it depend on the doctor's intention in doing so—specifically on whether the doctor intends to relieve the pain by causing the patient to die or intends to relieve the pain by giving the drug which will, inevitably, also cause the patient's death? Thomson says, plausibly, that it does not.

This conclusion may draw support from the thought that it is not a bad thing, morally speaking, for a person in such circumstances to die sooner rather than later,

---

5   See Thomson, "The Trolley Problem," in her collection, *Rights, Restitution and Risk*, edited by William Parent (Cambridge, MA: Harvard University Press, 1986), pp. 101-2.

6   Frances Kamm has suggested one explanation. She questions whether it follows from the fact that one does X only because it will lead to Y that one intends Y. See "The Law of Triple Effect," *Proceedings of the Aristotelian Society* Supp. Vol. 74 (2000), pp. 21-39.

so the usual moral strictures against causing death may not apply. But Thomson's objection retains its intuitive force in other cases in which death is clearly a bad thing. It is plausible to claim, for example, that it can be permissible in wartime to bomb a munitions factory even though this is certain to kill some civilians living nearby, but that it would not be permissible to kill the same number of civilians just as a way of undermining public support for the war, even if doing this would do just as much to hasten the end of the conflict as destroying the munitions plant would. These two strategies clearly differ in moral permissibility. But is it equally clear that the moral difference between them is a matter of what is intended by the agents involved?

Thomson says that it is not, and she supports this claim with thought experiments such as the following. Suppose you were Prime Minister, and the commander of the air force were to describe to you a planned air raid that would be expected to destroy a munitions plant and also kill a certain number of civilians, thereby probably undermining public support for the war. If he were then to ask whether you thought this was morally permissible, you would not say, "Well, that depends on what your intentions would be in carrying it out. Would you be intending to kill the civilians, or would their deaths be merely an unintended but foreseeable (albeit beneficial) side effect of the destruction of the plant?"[7] Holding fixed the actual consequences of the raid and what the parties have reason to believe these consequences to be, might an action be permissible if performed by an agent with one intention but impermissible if performed by an agent with a different strategy in mind? I agree with Thomson in finding this implausible.

Explaining the Appeal of Double Effect

If this is implausible, why should the Doctrine of Double Effect have seemed so appealing as an explanation of the cases I considered earlier? Thomson suggests that the appeal of that doctrine depends on "a failure to take seriously enough the fact—I think it is plainly a fact—that the question whether it is morally permissible for a person to do a thing is just not the same as the question whether the person who does it is thereby shown to be a bad person."[8] As she says, a doctor who dislikes her patient and administers a lethal dose of pain killer, relishing the thought that this will be the last of him, is moved by morally objectionable reasons, even if an earlier death is in fact better for her patient. If she is moved by such reasons then she is a morally bad person. But it does not follow that it is impermissible for her to administer the drug (or that the patient should have to wait until a different doctor, with better intentions, comes on duty.)

There is something right in the suggestion that the appeal of the Doctrine of Double Effect arises from a confusion between assessing an agent and assessing the permissibility of her action, and I will later try to say what this is. But in

---

7   This example is derived from one suggested to me by Thomson.

8   "Physician-Assisted Suicide: Two Moral Arguments," *Ethics* 109 (1999), p. 517.

the form in which Thomson states it, this does not seem to explain the apparent significance of an agent's intention in cases of the kind we have been considering. Malicious thoughts of the kind just described, whether or not they operate as motives, certainly reflect badly on the character of the doctor. But no such thoughts have been involved in the cases we have been considering. The doctors in *Transplant* and *Drug/Transplant* are, we assume, moved purely by the desire to save as many lives as possible. The fact that they aim to do this by sacrificing an innocent person does not show them to be of bad character unless this is something that it is wrong to do. It therefore does not seem that we are tempted to think that it is wrong because it clearly indicates bad character and we fail to distinguish between the assessment of character and the question of permissibility.[9]

I believe that the truth in Thomson's point can be captured by putting it in a different way. The illusory appeal of intent as a way of explaining cases like *Drug/ Transplant* flows, I suggest, from two facts about moral principles. The first is that although principles stating moral requirements specify that certain considerations normally count decisively for or against acting in a certain way, these principles almost always allow for exceptions. So, for example, according to the principle of fidelity to promises the fact that one promised to do a certain thing is a reason for doing it, and normally a conclusive one—a reason that determines what one ought to do even if it would be more convenient or more advantageous to do something else. But there are exceptions. For example, one need not, and indeed should not, fulfill a promise to one person to do something fairly trivial if doing so would cause great harm to someone else. Fully understanding the morality of promising involves being able to recognize the considerations that do, and those that do not, justify such exceptions.

The second feature of moral principles that I have in mind is that they can be employed in either of two ways: as standards of criticism or as guides to deliberation. As guides to deliberation, moral principles answer a question of permissibility: "May I do A?" They also explain this answer by identifying the considerations that make it permissible or impermissible to do A under the circumstances in question. These considerations may concern what the agent sees as reasons for acting, or other features of his state of mind, but they need not and often do not do so. In what I will call their critical employment, however, a principle is used as the basis for assessing the way in which an agent went about deciding what to do on some real or imagined occasion. Used in this way it provides the basis for answering a question of the form, "In deciding to do A under those circumstances, did Jones take the proper considerations into account and give them the right weight?" An answer to this question depends on an answer to the prior question, of which considerations are relevant to the permissibility of such an action and how they should be taken into account. But it goes beyond this

---

9   Jonathan Bennett makes this point in "Morality and Consequences," *The Tanner Lectures on Human Values*, Vol. II, S. McMurrin, ed. (Salt Lake City: University of Utah Press, 1981), p. 99.

question in asking whether the agent in question in fact took these considerations into account in the proper way.

These two uses of moral principles are closely related, but there is a crucial difference between them. Criticism of the way an agent decided what to do is unavoidably predicated on assumptions (perhaps hypothetical) about the agent's state of mind—in particular about what he or she took into account in deciding what to do and took as a reasons for and against acting as he or she did. By contrast, when principles are used to guide deliberation they do this merely by specifying which considerations do, and which do not, count for or against various courses of action. I will refer to these applications of principles as their *critical* and their *deliberative* uses.[10]

It is easy to overlook this distinction. Since principles tell agents which considerations count for or against an action, it is natural to say that agents follow these principles when they take these considerations as reasons, and that when they do not, their failure to do so makes their actions wrong. But what makes an action wrong is the considerations that count decisively against it, not the agent's failure to give these considerations proper weight.

Suppose, for example, that I have promised to sell you my house, and that under the circumstances this counts as a decisive reason for doing so. In particular, the fact that I could benefit by breaking the promise and selling the house to someone else, who will pay me more money, is not a sufficient reason to do that. But suppose I break the promise anyway, in order to get this benefit. In describing what was defective about my action, you might say that I acted wrongly in taking my own advantage as sufficient reason to break my promise. At a more fundamental level, however, what made my action wrong was not the fact that I acted on a bad (selfish) reason, but rather the fact that I had promised to sell you the house. Given that there were no countervailing considerations that would justify an exception to the requirement that promises be kept, this fact counted decisively against selling the house to someone else.

This is even clearer when we view the case prospectively. Suppose I ask, while deciding what to do, "Must I do what I promised? Why shouldn't I sell to the other person, since it would be more profitable?" You would not reply, "That would be wrong, because you would be aiming at your own benefit (or acting for the sake of your benefit.)" It is true that I would be open to proper criticism for taking my own advantage as sufficient reason for breaking a promise. But this is criticism of the

---

10 In earlier versions of this paper I referred to these uses as "retrospective" and "prospective." But this was misleading because, as I have pointed out above, the question of permissibility that principles in their deliberative use are supposed to answer can be asked retrospectively and hypothetically as well as prospectively. Nor is the distinction one between first-person and third-person points of view. What I am calling the critical question—whether someone decided what to do in the proper way—is a question one can ask about oneself. And one can ask the deliberative question from a third-person perspective: one can ask, of a person in a certain situation, what that person should do.

way I went about deciding, not an explanation of why my action would be wrong. What makes it wrong for me to sell to the second potential buyer is that I promised to sell to the first one.

I believe that the two features of moral principles that I have just described provide the best explanation of our reactions to Transplant and to the other examples I have discussed above. First, although these examples differ in many ways, they all have the same structure: they concern general principles that sometimes admit of exceptions, and they raise questions about when these exceptions apply. For example, it is normally impermissible to act in ways that can be foreseen to cause serious harm. The runaway trolley case shows that this principle has exceptions: it is sometimes permissible to act in ways that can be foreseen to cause serious harm to some people if this is the only way to prevent similar harm to a greater number. *Transplant* shows that although the possibility of saving others sometimes justifies an exception to the prohibition against causing foreseeable harm, it does not always do so. Similarly, *Drug Shortage* and *Rescue II* show that there are exceptions to the principle requiring us to aid others when we can: in these cases it is permissible to fail to save some because this is the only way to save others. But *Drug/Transplant* and *Rescue/Transplant* reflect our judgment that the possibility of saving others does not always justify an exception to this principle.

The underlying problem raised by these cases is why the principles in question should have this particular form: why a consideration that justifies an exception to a principle in some cases should not do so in others. I will return to this question below. What I want to point out here is that if these cases have the structure I have just described, then the second feature of moral principles that I discussed above—the distinction between the critical and deliberative uses of a principle, and the ease of overlooking this distinction—can explain why it is tempting, but nonetheless mistaken, to think that the intentions of the agent play a crucial role in these cases.

It is tempting to say that what would make it wrong for an agent to fail to save the person in *Drug/Transplant* or in *Rescue/Transplant* is the fact that she would be intending that person's death, that is to say, she would be *taking* the advantages of his dying sooner as sufficient reason not to save him. It would be quite correct to say something similar to this if we were taking the relevant principle in its *critical* employment as a standard for assessing the way in which this agent decided what to do. That is, it would be quite correct to say that her way of making this decision was defective because she *took* a certain consideration (the possibility of saving five others) as justifying an exception to the principle requiring one to aid others, when in fact this consideration does not justify an exception to that principle in this case.

But the question of permissibility is answered by taking the relevant principles in their *deliberative* employment. What makes a proposed action wrong is thus the consideration that the relevant principle identifies as counting decisively against it (given the absence of relevant countervailing considerations.) In the promise-keeping example discussed above, this was the fact that I had promised to sell you my house. In *Drug/Transplant* and *Rescue/Transplant* it is the fact that there is a person who is in need of aid that the agent can easily provide. A person who takes the possibility of saving others via transplant as justifying an exception to the duty to aid in these cases, or takes the possibility of selling his house for a higher price as justifying an exception to the obligation to keep a promise, makes a mistake in so doing. But what makes this a mistake, and what makes the corresponding actions impermissible, are the considerations that support the relevant obligations.

The distinction in question here—between the deliberative use of a principle to decide whether a certain action is permissible and its critical use to assess an agent's process of decision-making—might be described, as Thomson suggested, as a distinction between assessing an action and assessing an agent. But the distinction I am calling attention to is narrower and, for that reason, easier to overlook. It is the distinction between the permissibility of an action and a special kind of agent assessment, in which what is being assessed, is not the agent's overall character but rather the quality of the particular piece of decision-making that led to the action in question.

The two features of principles that I have cited can also explain why it is mistaken, albeit tempting, to appeal to intent in assessing the permissibility of bombing the munitions plant, in the example Thomson discusses. Here the relevant principles are those applicable to the conduct of war. The example presupposes that these principles have something like the following form: In a war, one is permitted to use against one's opponents destructive and potentially deadly force of a kind that would normally be prohibited. But this is permitted only when its use is justified by a military objective, and only with the provisions that one takes sufficient care to minimize harm to non-combatants and that the harm that can be expected to occur despite this care is "proportional" to the importance of the military objective.[11]

---

11 My concern is with how this principle should be understood, specifically with whether it is best understood in a way that makes the permissibility of using deadly force depend on the agent's intent. I will therefore not enter into the difficult questions about how such a principle is to be defended, such as questions about why war should entail the suspension of ordinary moral requirements, about the permissibility of entering into war in the first place, and about what constitutes "war" in the relevant sense. It might of course be maintained that the permissibility of entering into war already depends on intent: that it is permissible to go to war with the aim of self-defense, for example, but not with the aim of conquest. My response is just the one given above: the permissibility of going to war depends not on what one sees as reason for doing so but on whether there actually are good reasons for doing so (given what it is reasonable to believe one's factual situation to be.) Of course there is such a thing as going to war for bad reasons in a situation in which good reasons are also present. But this is an assessment of the way the agent decided what to do (using the principles of jus ad bellum in what I called above their critical employment.) It should not be confused with the claim (based on the same principles in their deliberative employment) that going to war under those circumstances was impermissible.

In the example Thomson discussed it is assumed that the destruction of the munitions plant is a military objective in the relevant sense. The raid on it is therefore permissible if (and only if) the conditions just listed are fulfilled: if due care is taken to minimize harm to non-combatants and the expected harm to non-combatants is "proportional."

If there is no munitions plant, and a raid that killed many non-combatants would hasten the end of war only by undermining morale, then the raid (a pure case of "terror bombing") is not permissible. What makes it impermissible is not the intentions of the pilots who carry it out or of the commanders who order it. Rather, it is impermissible because it will kill people and the circumstances are not such as to provide a justification for doing this—that is to say, not such as to bring the case under any exception to the prohibition against doing what can be reasonably foreseen to cause loss of life. (Recall here what I said above about what makes it wrong to break a promise.) The civilians who would be killed in such a raid are not "military targets" even if killing them would hasten the end of the war.

In the case where there is a military target (the munitions plant, in Thomson's example), and the raid that would destroy it would also kill enough people to demoralize the country, this raid is permissible just in case it is permissible considered as a raid on the plant alone.

We should distinguish two lines of thought that might lead to the conclusion that the permissibility of what is done in cases of these kinds depends on the intentions of the agents. The first of these is the one I have been arguing is mistaken; the second, which turns on the predictive significance of intent, is quite valid.

The first line of thought leading to the idea that the impermissibility of terror bombing depends on the intentions of those who plan it or carry it out moves from the true premise that what is morally faulty about their reasoning lies in the fact that they take demoralizing the public as a consideration that justifies the bombing to the false conclusion that this fact about their reasoning is also what makes their action wrong. But, as I have been arguing, it is a mistake to treat the fact that in acting a certain way we would be acting on certain inadequate reasons as the consideration that we should take as counting decisively against so acting.

To understand the second line of thought leading to the conclusion that intent can be relevant to permissibility, it is helpful to notice that there is something artificial about the way I have been discussing these examples. I have been assuming that the consequences of an action (in these cases, the consequences of a bombing raid) can be predicted on grounds that are independent of the intentions of the agents who carry it out. It is of course true that two actions done with different intent, such as a raid carried out by a pilot who wants to minimize civilian casualties and one carried out by a pilot who relishes them, can have exactly the same consequences. But this is not what we normally have reason to expect.

To see the importance of this difference, consider an even more artificial case, in which consequences are certain to be independent of intent. Suppose that the raid in question is to be carried out not by piloted planes, but by missiles, which are preprogrammed to seek out certain targets and avoid others. So we can assume that the consequences of firing the missiles—the effects on the military target and on civilians in the surrounding area—can be predicted with considerable accuracy, and in any event do not depend on the way anyone involved in carrying out the attack responds after the missiles are launched. Suppose that the question the commander asks you, as Prime Minister, is whether, given these consequences, it is permissible for him to launch the missile. In this case it seems clear that your answer should depend on whether, given the likely consequences of the strike, there is a justification for it that meets the relevant criteria. You should not say, "Well, it depends on your intentions in launching it. When you push the button to launch the missile, will you be doing this in order to destroy the factory or in order to undermine morale by killing the civilians?" Here Thomson's criticism seems to me entirely correct.

But in the world as we know it things are not like this. If the planes dropping bombs are guided by human beings, then the effects of the raid will depend on how the agents carrying it out will respond to the changing circumstances that they may be presented with. We could, of course, assume that the pilots, whatever their personal valuations of the alternatives may be, will strictly follow prescribed orders and procedures. If this is so, then the case will be like that of the automated missile, and the intentions of the agents will not be relevant to the permissibility of the raid. But if it is not so—if the way the agents react, and how hard they try to avoid harm to non-combatants, depends on whether they intend to avoid such harm if they possibly can—then their intention will matter to permissibility. It such a case it will be quite appropriate for the Prime Minister to ask about the intentions of those who will carry out the raid. Their intentions will not have the kind of significance attributed to them by the Doctrine of Double Effect, but they will have what I called above predictive significance, which is by no means unimportant.

I have so far not said anything about why the possibility of saving a larger number of people by transplant does not justify the courses of action proposed in cases like *Drug/Transplant* and *Rescue/Transplant*. The most obvious principles at work in these cases are the one (in *Transplant*) specifying a duty not to kill and the one (in *Drug/Transplant* and *Rescue/Transplant*) specifying a duty to aid when one can (in the case of *Drug/Transplant* perhaps also a special duty on the part of hospital workers to aid those in their care.) The question posed is what exceptions there are to these principles—in particular, when the possibility of saving others gives rise to an exception.

But the discussion of these cases also presupposes another principle. This principle holds that it is impermissible simply to take a living person's organs, even if this would benefit others, but that once a person is dead his or her organs are available for use to save others. Like the distinction between combatants and non-combatants, this principle might be questioned, but it is presupposed in the examples as I have presented them. It is this principle that explains why it is necessary to bring about the patient's death (by giving him or her the wrong injection, in *Transplant,* or by withholding medication, in *Drug/Transplant*) in order for the organs to become available. This is what forces on us the question of whether the possibility of saving others justifies an exception to the underlying principles prohibiting killing, or requiring saving.

Once the question is posed in this way, however, the idea that there are such exceptions becomes bizarre. The general form of the question is this: as long as this person is alive, we have an obligation to him to do X. If we were freed from this obligation we could do something good. Does this count as a justification to kill the person, or fail to save him? The answer is clearly that it does not. Perhaps a justifiable form of the obligation in question would incorporate an exception for cases in which the good of the relevant kind could be achieved by abrogating it. (In the case at hand this exception would allow us to take the organs of a living person when they could be used to save the lives of a greater number.) Assuming that the obligation does not incorporate such an exception, however, the idea that this should lead to justification for bringing about the person's death is absurd.

In this respect, the rationale for the proposed courses of action in *Drug/ Transplant* and *Rescue/Transplant* is quite different from that in *Drug Shortage,* and *Rescue II.* In the latter cases it is claimed that an agent is released from a duty to save one person by the possibility of saving a greater number. But there is no appeal to the idea that the death of the one person makes this possible by releasing the agent from a duty that he or she has to that person as long as he or she is alive.

What makes the proposed courses of action in *Drug/Transplant* and *Rescue/ Transplant* wrong (and differentiates these cases from *Drug Shortage* and *Rescue II*) is therefore not the agents' intent. It is true that an agent in *Drug/Transplant* or *Rescue/Transplant* who accepted the proposed rationale for a course of action would be mistakenly *taking* the fact that the death of the one patient would release us from an obligation as a reason to save him or her. But to say this is to make the shift I have been calling attention to, from the deliberative application of the relevant principles (which is relevant to the question of permissibility) to a critical application of these principles (an assessment of the way the agent went about deciding what to do).

The account I am proposing thus differs from one based on the Principle of Double Effect in a very general way, which should be noted. According to the Principle of Double Effect, there is a deep similarity between the courses of action involved in *Transplant, Drug/Transplant, Rescue/Transplant* and terror bombing. What is done in all of these cases is wrong because it involves intending to bring about the death of innocent people as a means to some greater good. On my account there is a more abstract similarity between these cases. In each one, an agent who follows a certain course of action would mistakenly take a certain factor as justifying an exception to a principle ruling out killing, or requiring one to give aid. But what makes the proposed actions wrong depends on the applicable principles and the explanation of why the proposed exceptions are not genuine. At this more substantive level the case are very different. To understand them we need to examine the different principles that are at work, and the case for possible exceptions to them rather than appeal to a general prohibition against aiming at the death of an innocent person.

In the case of terror bombing the relevant principles are those governing the conduct of war, principles involving the distinction between combatants and non-combatants, the idea of a military objective, and the idea of proportionality. There are difficult questions about how these ideas are to be understood, and about how principles governing the conduct of war, are to be justified. I have not undertaken to answer these difficult questions. My aim in this brief discussion has been the much more limited one of explaining how these principles, like other principles governing the taking and saving of lives, can draw the distinction between permissible and impermissible actions in what seems, intuitively, to be the correct place without making this distinction depend on an agent's intention in the way that the Doctrine of Double Effect suggests that it does. My argument thus leaves many problems unsolved. What it shows, if it is correct, is just that there is one set of questions about intent that we do not need to worry about.

Chapter 5

Ethics for Calamities: How Strict is the Moral Rule Against Targeting Non-combatants?[1]

Jeffrey Reiman

Introductory Considerations

Many people's moral intuitions seem sensitive to scale in the following way: If asked about small-scale interpersonal interactions, they believe firmly that no innocent person should be deprived of his rights for the purpose of preventing harm to another or even to several others. However, if the number of others to be saved from harm increases—to a thousand, a hundred thousand, a million, more—many people seem to reach a point at which they think that it will be morally acceptable—perhaps as a necessary evil—to deprive one or a few of their rights in order to save that many. A widely accepted example of such a deprivation of rights to avoid a great deal of harm is the forced quarantine of people carrying potentially deadly diseases.[2] And some philosophers have endorsed the principle at work here. For example, Ronald Dworkin suggests that it is compatible with taking rights seriously, to limit the recognition of a right "when the cost to society [of recognizing it] would not be simply incremental, but would be of a degree far beyond the cost paid to grant the original right, a degree great enough to justify

---

1   An earlier version of this contribution, entitled "Is the Combatant-Non-combatant Distinction Morally Defensible?," was delivered at the US Naval Academy in Annapolis, Maryland, on November 16, 2001. I thank the officers and teachers in my audience for many useful and challenging comments. That version of the chapter was published in George R. Lucas et al., eds, *Ethics for Military Leaders*, 5th ed. (Boston: Pearson, 2002), pp. 537-42. In revising that version for this publication, I have benefited from numerous useful suggestions offered by George Lucas and Roger Wertheimer, and stimulating (albeit hostile) comments from an anonymous reviewer.

2   "Quarantined persons do not deserve to lose their liberty, for it is not their fault that they are disease carriers. They are deprived of their freedom in order to protect against widespread deadly infection" (Andrew von Hirsch and Andrew Ashworth, *Proportionate Sentencing: Exploring the Principles* [Oxford, UK: Oxford University Press, 2005], p. 54).

whatever assault on dignity or equality might be involved."[3] This is not about restricting or overriding individuals' rights whenever doing so would produce a greater net sum of satisfaction than not doing so.[4] Rather it is a matter of restricting or overriding individuals' rights when not doing so would likely lead to harms on such a scale as to count as a disaster, a catastrophe, or, as I shall say, a calamity.

The result of this widespread sensitivity to scale is that Kantians (along with whom I include Kantian-style or deontological theorists generally) are able to embarrass utilitarians (along with whom I include utilitarian-style or consequentialist theorists generally) by showing that utilitarianism is counterintuitive because it can justify sacrificing one for even a few others; and utilitarians are able to embarrass Kantians by showing that Kantianism is counterintuitive because it is unable to justify sacrificing one for even millions. If, as seems plausible, the problem here is not with people's intuitions, but with the moral theories, then we need to build scale-sensitivity into our moral theories. What I call *ethics for calamities* is an attempt to do this, at least with respect to a common problem of military ethics, namely, the rule against intentionally targeting non-combatants.

War is a condition in which calamities are either occurring or always near at hand. We might even say that war is the paradigmatic calamity. And, indeed, there is evidence of sensitivity to scale in common moral judgments about war. Writing about the morality of killing innocents in war, Jeffrie Murphy says that there are many among war supporters who could sincerely say: "Of course it is terrible to kill babies but I believe, *to save more lives*, we must regretfully do it in this case."[5] Though he defends a virtually absolute prohibition on the intentional killing of non-combatants, Thomas Nagel writes: "The policy of attacking the civilian population in order to induce an enemy to surrender, or to damage his

---

3   Ronald Dworkin, *Taking Rights Seriously* (Cambridge, MA: Harvard University Press, 1979), p. 200.

4   Numerous philosophers sympathetic to utilitarianism—e.g., Jonathan Bennett, James Rachels, Peter Singer—have questioned the soundness of the moral distinction between killing and letting die upon which the moral prohibition against killing a few to save many rests.

5   Jeffrie Murphy, "The Killing of the Innocent," in Richard Wasserstrom, ed., *Today's Moral Problems*, 3rd ed. (New York: Macmillan Publishing, 1985), p. 341 (emphasis mine). In the course of a defense of an inalienable right to be treated as a person, Herbert Morris writes, in more general terms, that "there are ... situations in which it is accepted by all that a person possesses rights of a certain kind, and the difficulty we face is that of according the person the right he is claiming when this will promote more evil than good. The just act is to give the man ... what it is his right to have.... But it is a mistake to suppose that justice is the only dimension of morality. It may be justifiable not to accord to a man his rights." Herbert Morris, "Persons and Punishment," in Jeffrie Murphy, ed., *Punishment and Rehabilitation* (Belmont, CA: Wadsworth Publishing, 1973), p. 62.

morale, seems to have been widely accepted in the civilized world, and seems to be accepted still, at least *if the stakes are high enough.*"[6]

Numerous intellectuals have roundly condemned the US for dropping atom bombs on the Japanese cities of Hiroshima and Nagasaki[7]—but ordinary American citizens supported it wholeheartedly. In a Gallup poll taken in the days immediately after the atom bombs were dropped on August 6th and 9th, 1945, Americans were asked: "Do you approve or disapprove of using the new atomic bomb on Japanese cities?" 85 percent said they approved, with no significant differences based on sex, age or education.[8] In a Gallup poll taken 50 years later, approval was down to 59 percent. However, among those 65 years old and over—people who would have been at least 15 years old at the time of the bombing—80 percent approved.[9] In an essay entitled, "Thank God for the Atom Bomb," Paul Fussell recounts his response and that of other soldiers in the Pacific theater to the news of the bombing:

> When the atom bombs were dropped and the news began to circulate that [the invasion of the Japanese main islands] would not, after all, be necessary, when we learned to our astonishment that we would not be obliged in a few months to rush the beaches near Tokyo assault-firing while being machine-gunned, mortared and shelled, for all the practiced phlegm of our tough facades we broke down and cried with relief and joy.[10]

---

6   Thomas Nagel, "War and Massacre," *Philosophy and Public Affairs* 1, no. 2 (Winter 1972), p. 127 (emphasis mine).

7   Most notably G.E.M. Anscombe in *Mr. Truman's Degree* (a pamphlet published privately in 1958), which Nagel cites approvingly. Nagel, "War and Massacre," p. 127, see also p. 139. Michael Walzer has also criticized the bombing. See Michael Walzer, *Just and Unjust Wars* (New York: Basic Books, 1977), pp. 263-8; hereafter cited as *JUW*. And John Rawls has written: "[T]he fire-bombing of Tokyo and other Japanese cities in the spring of 1945 and the atomic bombing of Hiroshima and Nagasaki, all primarily attacks on civilian populations, were very grave wrongs, as they are now widely, though not generally, seen to have been." John Rawls, *The Law of Peoples* (Cambridge: Harvard University Press, 1999), p. 95; hereafter cited as *LP*.

8   George H. Gallup, *The Gallup Poll: Public Opinion 1935-1972* (New York: Random House, 1972), vol I: 1935-1948, pp. 521-2.

9   George Gallup, Jr., *The Gallup Poll: Public Opinion 1995* (Wilmington, DE: Scholarly Resources, 1996), p. 111. It might be thought that the decline in approval in later polls reflects a sounder judgment due to distance from the heat of war. But the decision to drop the bomb was made in the heat of war—with all the uncertainty about the outcome that later generations would not face. Thus I think that the views of contemporaries provide the relevant standard of common people's judgments about the decision to bomb Japanese cities.

10   Paul Fussell, *Thank God for the Atom Bomb and Other Essays* (New York: Simon & Schuster, 1988), p. 28.

Fussell reports as well that other writers who served in the Pacific—James Jones, Joseph Alsop, William Manchester—supported the bombing. "Having found the bomb," President Harry Truman said, "we have used it … to shorten the agony of young Americans."[11]

Accordingly, it may be that the belief in an absolute prohibition on the intentional killing of non-combatants is on less secure ground than its advocates normally assume. Moreover, recent developments, in particular the striking increase in the role played by non-traditional military forces, e.g., al Qaeda and kindred groups operating in Iraq and elsewhere in the Middle East, have changed the nature of warfare in ways that warrant reconsidering even very basic principles. I aim here to provoke such reconsideration of the rule against intentionally targeting non-combatants (hereafter: "the rule"). In challenging the rule, I shall not be concerned with the details of particular international codes or agreements. I treat the rule as a moral principle and consider the moral reasons for and against it. Moreover, I do not hope to reach a definitive assessment of the rule here. My aim is to raise questions and provoke thought about a principle that is often treated as beyond question in theory, and even more often ignored in practice.

The rule against targeting non-combatants is a matter of *jus in bello*, justice in the practice of war, not of *jus ad bellum*, the justice of going to war. It's about the *how* of war, not the *why*. This suggests that rightness or wrongness of the targeting of non-combatants should be independent of whether justice is or isn't on the side that targets them. Thus, writes Michael Walzer, we must ask: "without reference to the justice of their cause, how can soldiers fight justly?" (*JUW*, p. 128). This formulation is, as we shall see, oversimplified. The justice of harming anyone depends on the justice of the cause for which they are harmed, and then the amount of harm that one is prepared to impose in war depends on how morally imperative it is to fight that war at all. This means that, to judge policies, we will have to consider the justness and gravity of the cause for which they were undertaken; and to judge policy-makers, we will have to consider the reasonableness of their beliefs about the justness and gravity of their cause. However, to do this fairly, we must try to judge the reasonableness of such beliefs, both our own and those of our enemies, from a starting point of neutrality. (This is one of the many ways in which philosophizing about war is a lot different from fighting one.) I shall try to abide by these strictures in the following way. I shall start by talking about the morality of military practices independent of the justice or gravity of the cause for which they are undertaken and then, as appropriate, I will introduce some considerations which hinge on the reasonableness of people's beliefs about the justice and gravity of their cause.

---

11   Fussell, *Thank God for the Atom Bomb*, p. 37; see also pp. 15, 20, and 21.

Reasons in Favor of the Rule

1. As Walzer points out, and John Rawls agrees, innocent non-threatening individuals have rights not to be harmed (*JUW*, pp. 135-7; *LP*, p. 96).
2. Combatants are armed and trained for war. Therefore, they are threatening to the other side as well as physically and mentally prepared to be targeted (*JUW*, pp. 44-5).
3. Following the rule will tend to reduce the overall number of casualties and that is a good thing, whether the reduction comes among combatants or non-combatants.[12]
4. Following the rule may create more promising conditions for a lasting peace since attacks on non-combatants are more likely than attacks on combatants to provoke lasting resentments (see, for example, JUW, p. 132).[13]

I think that these ideas add up to a strong presumption in favor of the rule against targeting non-combatants. In what follows, I accept this presumption as such, and point to factors that may either weaken it or justify overriding it.

Reasons for Doubting the Moral Validity of the Rule

First, the rule seems clearly biased in favor of the large powers. Consider: America bombs Iraq during the 1991 Gulf War, aiming at military targets and, despite precautions, kills thousands of civilians. (The Jordan-based Red Crescent puts the Iraqi civilian casualties of American bombing at 113,000.)[14] According to the rule, this is morally acceptable since the deaths of these non-combatants were the unintended but unavoidable accompaniment of morally acceptable attacks on military targets;

---

12   "Experience provides independent evidence of the importance and efficacy of having laws of war. They have worked to save human life" (Richard Wasserstrom, "The Laws of War," *The Monist* 56 [1972], p. 15).

13   "Means of defense that are not permitted [to a state against which war is being waged] include ... such underhanded means as would destroy the trust requisite to establishing a lasting peace in the future" (Immanuel Kant, *The Metaphysics of Morals* [Cambridge, UK: Cambridge University Press, 1996], p. 117). "[W]ar itself is characterized as something which ought to pass away. It implies therefore the proviso of the *jus gentium* that the possibility of peace be retained (and so, for example, that envoys must be respected), and, in general, that war be not waged against domestic institutions, against the peace of family and private life, or against persons in their private capacity" (Georg W. F. Hegel, *The Philosophy of Right* [Oxford, UK: Oxford University Press, 1962], p. 215).

14   Cited in *Press for Conversion!* (the quarterly publication of the Coalition to Oppose the Arms Trade), issue no. 51 (May 2003), p. 37; available online at: http://coat. ncf.ca/our_magazine/links/issue51/articles/51_36-37.pdf.

these thousands of dead civilians were "collateral damage."[15] By contrast, terrorists, lacking a mighty air force, attack civilians directly, kill many fewer of them than the US does as collateral damage, and this is called murder, even barbarism. "Military deaths plus collateral civilian deaths" is civilized war, but "civilian deaths alone" is barbarity. This strikes me as fishy.

It will surely be countered that the moral difference between "military deaths plus collateral civilian deaths" that are acceptable and "civilian deaths alone" that are not depends on the fact that in the latter case the civilian deaths are sought intentionally, while in the former case the collateral civilian deaths are an unintended but unavoidable accompaniment to otherwise legitimate military measures. But I think that this rests moral responsibility far too heavily on what one intends for one's action, and not heavily enough on what one knows will be the consequences of one's action. I think we are responsible for both. Of course, many moral theories—e.g., Kantianism as well as the traditional Roman Catholic doctrine of double effect (which is often appealed to on these matters)—put just this degree of emphasis on intention, and so it cannot be dismissed so easily. I do not dismiss it easily. I grant that evil done intentionally is worse than the equivalent evil done as the unwanted consequence of otherwise morally acceptable action, and both are worse than evil done inadvertently.

But how much worse? To my mind, the rule treats the difference as far greater than it is. I'd rather be harmed as an unwanted consequence than intentionally, but I'd much much rather not be harmed at all. Even if we grant that it is worse to be killed intentionally by a terrorist than as collateral damage, the thing that makes these things bad at all is that you end up dead—and that happens in both cases. Wouldn't you much rather narrowly escape a terrorist attack than be killed as collateral damage? Isn't it worse to be the victim of an unintentional harm than to be the unharmed object of an evil intention? Judging between the "evil intention without the evil consequence" versus "the evil consequence without the evil intention," the *evil intention without the evil consequence* is clearly the lesser evil. I think that this means that the presence or absence of the intention cannot carry the weight that is being placed on it by the rule. When civilians are being killed either way, the presence or absence of intention cannot be the difference between barbarity and civilized warfare. (I have elsewhere raised

---

15   Note that traditional just war theory as well as the Geneva Convention requires as well that "collateral civilian damage [not be] excessive relative to the military advantages" to be gained by a given military operation. Of such cost-benefit judgments, Kenneth Anderson, American University professor of law, writes, "By their nature, such judgments involve factual evaluations and guesses that cannot be legally challenged, unless something approximating willful, intentional gross negligence can be shown." Kenneth Anderson, "Who Owns the Rules of War?," *The New York Times Magazine*, April 13, 2003, pp. 41, 42. For our purposes, it suffices to say that, for large-scale military operations, collateral damage costing the lives of far more victims than the number targeted by terrorists will normally be found acceptable.

related questions about the focus of the criminal law on small-scale intentional killing and its looking away from large-scale unintended but foreseeable killing.)[16]

Walzer criticizes the doctrine of double effect for not including a positive duty to minimize harm to non-combatants (*JUW*, pp. 151-56). But, note that this is already a rejection of the idea that we are uniquely responsible for the harm we intentionally cause. It supports the idea of moral responsibility for the foreseeable, even if unintended, consequences of our actions, and that undermines the attempt to justify the rule by appeal to the distinction between intentionally targeted non-combatants and collaterally killed non-combatants. Indeed, I think that there is equally a positive duty to minimize harm to enemy soldiers as far as is compatible with pursuit of just war aims. But this principle cuts across the combatant-non-combatant distinction, and calls upon us to pursue our war aims with the least possible amount of harm overall.

Second, the combatant-non-combatant distinction does not line up with the distinction between those who are responsible for the war and those who are not. This can be seen from both sides. Non-combatants are often supportive of or instrumental to the war effort. Some may have voted for war or for candidates promising war. While those who produce weapons and other tools of war are clearly part of the war effort, even those who produce food and clothing, or those who just keep the domestic economy going, help their nation fight its war. Some may even be part of the very development that the enemy is opposing. For example, in the case of those who oppose the global expansion of American capitalism, financial workers on Wall Street are the enemy since they are helping spread the hated development. Civilian political leaders are often classified as non-combatants even though they are often more responsible than anyone else for military hostilities. And then there are civilian opinion-makers—e.g., newspaper editorialists, political activists, ideological lobbyists—who may be just as responsible for the war as the political leadership. On the other hand, combatants, say, uniformed soldiers, are not responsible for the war in which they fight. Rawls writes that, "leaving aside the upper ranks of an officer class..., [soldiers,] like civilians, are not responsible for their state's war. For soldiers are often conscripted and in other ways forced into war; they are coercively indoctrinated in martial virtues; and their patriotism is often cruelly exploited" (*LP*, p. 95).

---

16   See Jeffrey Reiman, *The Rich Get Richer and the Poor Get Prison: Ideology, Class and Criminal Justice*, 9th edition (Boston: Allyn & Bacon, 2010), especially chapter 2, "A Crime by Any Other Name."

Justifications for Overriding the Rule

First, most people are, I think, Kantian in their normal moral judgments. That is, they think it is wrong to harm non-threatening individuals even if necessary to avoid harm to one or more innocent others. (Most, for example, would think it gravely wrong to harvest the organs of a healthy person against his will in order to save the lives of several other people in need of healthy organs.) However, as I observed at the outset, many of the same people will allow as acceptable the harming of one innocent to save a very great number of other innocent persons. In sum, I think that people are effectively Kantians with respect to small-scale interpersonal relations, and effectively utilitarians when the numbers of people involved is much higher. One way to say this is that in normal situations, people are Kantians, but faced with what I have called a calamity, they are open to utilitarian-like considerations. (I say "utilitarian-like considerations" here, because I don't mean a strict obligation to act for the highest net sum of satisfactions. I mean, rather, a willingness to discount individuals' Kantian rights when necessary to prevent harm to very large numbers of others. In general, this is what I have in mind whenever I refer to utilitarian considerations.) If war is a calamity that justifies such considerations, then the rule against targeting non-combatants is an application of a Kantian-style morality to a situation whose large scale makes Kantianism inappropriate.

Second, we can reach the same conclusion by another route: In normal situations we confront the other as one individual to another. In war, we confront the enemy as one people to another people. War, writes Walzer, "isn't a relation between persons but between political entities" (*JUW*, p. 36). (I think this is why many people accepted the Allied bombing of Dresden, though it was militarily unnecessary and done to punish the German people—the logic, I suppose, was: they killed our innocent people so we may kill theirs, even though, obviously, the innocent individuals on their side are not the ones who killed the innocent individuals on ours.) In any event, when we confront individuals as individuals, the presumption of innocence as well as the prohibition against guilt by association are appropriate. When, in war, we confront an enemy people as a people, then the whole people is viewed as dangerous and individuals lose their presumption of innocence. Membership in the people is taken as evidence of guilt until proven otherwise—so, here, guilt by association is effectively accepted. Since both combatants and non-combatants are members of the enemy people, the distinction is eroded. Applying the rule, then, looks like treating a war as if it were a normal interpersonal confrontation.[17]

---

17   Nagel's argument for the near absoluteness of the prohibition of targeting non-combatants hinges crucially on the idea that war is a relation between persons and thus, by implication, that standard moral constraints on interpersonal relations obtain in war. He writes: "A positive account of the matter must begin with the observation that war, conflict, and aggression are relations between persons" (Nagel, "War and Massacre," p. 133).

I think that this is one reason that modern war has rendered the combatant-non-combatant distinction to some degree an irrelevant antique. The distinction harks back to a day when, in war, one army confronted another and they tried to keep their fight within something like gentlemanly rules of combat. In the era of modern warfare, where masses of people either directly fight as part of the military, or indirectly support the war effort by keeping the warring states' economies going, the situation that made the rule appropriate is no longer a reality, if it ever was.

Third, both of the preceding justifications are confirmed by consideration of the difference between domestic law enforcement and the sort of thing we accept at international borders. The police are supposed to treat people as innocent until proven guilty, not to interfere with them unless they show by their behavior (or it has been so testified by witnesses) that they have done or will do something illegal. At their borders, however, nations claim the right to interfere with people who have shown no sign of dangerous or illegal behavior. Customs officers have authority to search our belongings and bodies that would be regarded as outrageous if extended to domestic police.[18] Here again, it seems that we have something like a Kantian-utilitarian divide. Within the nation, we assume that people are friends unless they act like enemies, we give them the benefit of the doubt, we accept the risk of their harmfulness rather than invade their privacy or restrict they bodies. At the edges of the nation, by contrast, we try to minimize dangers, using statistical likelihoods, as well as hunches and suspicions, to justify invasion, restriction, and possibly injury.

It seems clear that a military operation is closer to a border situation than to a domestic one, and thus that the imperative to minimize danger gains prominence over respect for the privacy of individuals as well as over the presumption of innocence, and the rights of the innocent or seeming innocent are accordingly less weighty considerations in determining what to do. Likewise, it is at borders that peoples meet each other as peoples, and the morality of small-scale individual interaction is no longer applicable.

---

18   Of course, things have changed since the events of September 11, 2001, and searches of people about to board airplanes for domestic flights are now sometimes as intrusive as searches of people entering the country at borders. I do not think that this contradicts the point in the text because the searches are aimed at a very specific threat, that of either blowing up an airliner or commandeering it and using it to cause large-scale destruction; and thus these searches are not the same as those that come under the across-the-board powers granted to customs officials at borders. From another angle, however, the new intrusiveness of searches of passengers boarding domestic flights may be viewed as confirming the point made in the text: It reflects the fact that the events of "9/11"—a terrorist attack carried out by individuals already on American soil—have resulted in a blurring of the distinction between the domestic and international realms, with a predictable concomitant loss of the rights to noninterference that were based on the domestic presumption of innocence.

The First Principle of Calamity Ethics

I think these considerations support what I will call *the first principle of calamity ethics*: While Kantian-style ethics rightly govern small-scale interpersonal interactions, utilitarian-like calculations apply in large-scale intergroup or international interactions. Consequently, where intentional targeting of non-combatants can be expected to produce extremely large reductions in the number of people killed overall, such targeting is justified.

Simply viewing this as a two-theory sandwich—Kantianism here, utilitarianism there—is, however, not satisfactory. There needs to be some explanation of how the two approaches fit together as a coherent whole. I take that explanation to be implicit in a point already made, namely, that, while intentional harming is worse than unintentional harming, what makes them bad at all is the harming. To hold that it is so evil to kill an individual that we would refuse to do it even to save a large number of individuals from being killed is not a coherent moral position: It has drifted loose from its moral basis. It may be logically coherent to separate intentional from unintentional killing and direct especially severe condemnation to the former. However, in view of how little a difference the presence or absence of intention makes to those who get killed, it is not morally coherent to prohibit intentional killing when such killing might reduce dramatically the number of people killed overall.

Thus, we must steer a course between treating people as means to saving others, and refusing to prevent harm to large number of people. No formula or magic number will tell us when we confront a moral calamity and thus when utilitarian considerations begin to overtake Kantian ones. Indeed, sometimes the best indication we have that we do confront a calamity is that utilitarian considerations seem appropriate.

I think that there are enough clear examples of what I am calling a calamity that we can use the notion without a quantitative standard. I will leave it qualitative, then, and say that prevention of a calamity overrides the duty not to intentionally harm some innocent or non-threatening people. I think that Walzer's and Rawls's approval of the Allied bombing of German population centers, early in World War II, is an application of this principle; but that their refusal to approve similar practices under somewhat less urgent conditions—such as their condemnation of the US atomic bombing of Hiroshima and Nagasaki to shorten the war in the Pacific and substantially reduce the number of deaths of US troops—is due to failing to see that Kantian rights lose their force the farther they are extended beyond the small-scale interactions which is their native habitat (*JUW*, pp. 251-68; *LP*, pp. 98-101).[19]

---

19   Regarding the justice of the US atomic bombing of Hiroshima and Nagasaki, note that I am leaving aside the claim made by both Walzer and Rawls that the US should have offered negotiations to the Japanese before the bombing, a claim which I believe is true.

Note that Walzer's approval of the bombing of German cities shows the limits of his claim, cited earlier, that justice in the way we fight—*jus in bello*—must be considered in isolation from consideration of the justice of our cause—*jus ad bellum*. For this reason, when, later, I try to spell out the conditions that justify overriding the rule, I build consideration of the reasonableness of the belief in the justice of one's cause into those conditions.

The Second Principle of Calamity Ethics

So far I have given reasons for thinking that war justifies taking utilitarian-like considerations into account, and then I have given utilitarian-like reasons for overriding the rule, that is, for targeting non-combatants along with combatants to minimize the harm to both combatants and non-combatants on our side. However, I am enough of a Kantian to think that there must be Kantian reasons as well—and I believe that there are. I have already suggested that non-combatants are often responsible for a war and/or part of what makes it dangerous to the other side. Many share responsibility either for the onset of war or for its continued execution.

I want to develop this point further: In general, non-combatant civilians bear some responsibility for what their governments do. Governments require, at very least, the acquiescence of the great majority of civilians, and normally the positive cooperation of large numbers of them. At the limit, the citizens are responsible in the sense that, had enough of them risen in revolt, they could have stopped their government. Moreover, most citizens cooperate in keeping the economy going that enables their government to wage war. Walzer thinks that only citizens who manufacture weapons or other things directly necessary for warmaking are responsible, and those who simply provide, say, food and clothing, or other things that would be needed outside of war are not. But later he points out that depriving an army of supplies of all kinds is a standard and legitimate military goal (*JUW*, pp. 146, 170-72). This suggests that all aid to the government's warmaking capacities is military aid—and all who provide it are part of the war effort and thus legitimate targets.

Rawls argues that only leaders are really responsible for war and ordinary citizens are not. I think that this is not only empirically false, but that, on Rawls's own terms, it does not exempt civilians from being rightly targeted. Though Rawls holds that soldiers are no more responsible for the war than civilians, and though he (unlike Walzer) holds that soldiers do not lose their rights by taking up arms, he contends that they can rightly be targeted because those who are defending themselves against the soldiers "have no other choice. They cannot defend themselves in any other way, and defend themselves they must" (*LP*, p. 96). But, if this is true of soldiers, then it is also true of civilians, namely, that, even if they are not responsible for the war, they can be attacked if the other side "cannot defend themselves in any other way." This is a claim that can be made by terrorists who lack the means to attack a large nation's military forces head on.

In other cases, however, general citizen responsibility for war is evident. It is quite clear that a large number of Germans supported Hitler's anti-democratic policies and his aggressive military actions, much as many supported his anti-Semitism (even if they personally would not have gone so far as killing Jews). Hitler could neither have gotten and kept power, nor waged war on the scale that he did, without this support, and thus the citizens who favored or accepted Hitler were responsible for his wars (cf. *LP*, p. 100n22).

But I want to go further and say that even those who could have but did not wholeheartedly[20] oppose Hitler and his policies are responsible. Suppose it is objected that they are not responsible because (a) they didn't decide on Hitler's policies, they only didn't oppose them, and/or (b) opposing Hitler's policies was extremely dangerous. Here I reinvoke the idea that in the case of calamities like war, a different moral standard is appropriate, not now a utilitarian standard but a different way of applying a Kantian one. This argument has three steps.

First, though people are not normally held responsible for failing to prevent harm (as long as they have not caused it), there are exceptions to this. People with special relations to vulnerable individuals—say, their parents or their doctors—do have obligations to prevent harm when they can. And some European nations have Good Samaritan laws that hold people legally responsible for not preventing harm when they could have done so at a small enough risk to themselves.

Second, consider that we do not normally blame a person for doing something when he has been threatened with death if he doesn't do it. However, this refraining from blame does not continue no matter how high the costs of the action go. We might not blame a driver for running down an individual, when the only way to avoid it would have been drive into a bridge abutment and kill himself. But, what about running down a whole class of school children? What about driving into a dam support that holds back a flood that will wipe out a whole town or city? My suggestion here is that, as the harmfulness of an action increases, so the amount of risk we demand that individuals take on to avoid the harmful action increases.

Third, I now want to combine these two ideas and say that citizens are normally in a special relation to their state and therefore have some positive obligation to stop their states from causing unjustified harms and, since the potential harm that states can do is enormous, citizens who have any chance at all of stopping their government from doing that harm have the obligation to try

---

20   I add this to emphasize that it is not enough to oppose the policies in one's mind. To be relieved of responsibility for one's government's policies, one must actively use the means available to one to try to stop them. Talking about how a will to do good is still a good will even if it fails to do good, Kant points out that by such a good will he means not "a mere wish but … the summoning of all means insofar as they are in our control." Immanuel Kant, *Groundwork of the Metaphysics of Morals* (New York: Cambridge University Press, 1997), p. 8.

wholeheartedly to do so even if that subjects them to substantial risks, including the risk of death.[21]

This leads to what I call *the second principle of calamity ethics*: While the acts vs. omissions doctrine rightly governs most small-scale interpersonal interactions, where large-scale harm is at stake, people have positive obligations, not only to refrain from causing that harm, but also, as far as they can, to try to prevent it. And the greater the harm to be prevented, the greater the risk one is obligated to run in attempting to do so.

Then, all citizens who could try to stop their government from doing harm, but do not try wholeheartedly to do so, share responsibility for what their states do, and may be justly targeted in defense against those states. The only exceptions would be people who literally cannot act (invalids, prisoners) and those who actively—and where appropriate, violently—oppose their state's action. Children would not be exceptions. Though children are individually innocent, if their parents (or rightful guardians) are rightly subject to retaliation, and the parents do not get their children out of harm's way, then it is the parents, not the army that targets them, who are responsible for the harm the children undergo.

Concluding Remarks

I think that the reasons for the rule against targeting non-combatants, which I listed earlier, still have force against the reasons I have given for overriding the rule. I think the result, then, is a prima facie case for the rule plus an expanded range of conditions under which it can be overridden. This leads to two principles:

1. Where nations can achieve their legitimate military aims by targeting only combatants, they should do so even if there is some increased risk to their own combatants.
2. Insofar as nations or other groups are unable to target combatants (the case of Hamas in Israel, and perhaps of al Qaeda versus the US), or

---

21   The plausibility of this claim gets some support from the common judicial practice in the US and England of applying the standard of *strict liability*, rather than insisting on proof of negligence or other fault, in cases of extraordinary risk. The precedent-setting court case is the English case of *Rylands v. Fletcher*, 159 Eng. Rep. 737 (Ex. 1865), rev'd, 1 L.R.-Ex. 265 (Ex. Ch. 1866), aff'd, 3 L.R.-E & I. App. 330 (H.L. 1868). In a recent article, one legal scholar observes that: "a strong majority of states [in the US] has consistently recognized this precedent for strict liability from about 1890 to the present." Jed Handelman Shugerman, "The Floodgates of Strict Liability: Bursting Reservoirs and the Adoption of *Fletcher v. Rylands* in the Gilded Age," *Yale Law Journal* 110 (November 2000), 333-77.

insofar as targeting only enemy combatants significantly increases the risks to their own non-combatants (the case of Allied bombing of German cities), or where targeting only enemy combatants dramatically increases the risks to their own combatants (the case of US atomic bombing of Japanese cities), they may intentionally target non-combatants subject to these constraints:

a. Their belief in the justice and gravity of their cause must be reasonable;
b. They must try to produce the least amount of harm necessary to achieve their military aims.

Finally, one consequence of my argument is that the difference between so-called normal warfare and terrorism (assuming they are done for equally just causes) shrinks to a vanishing point. I think this is correct. War is hell. Pretending that it can be carried on in a gentlemanly manner—that those who comply with its etiquette are noble and just while those who violate its etiquette are barbarians—is propaganda. This doesn't mean that somehow terrorism is okay. It means rather that war is as bad as terrorism. All war is mass murder, or murderous retaliation against it. War can never be justified as anything but a necessary evil, and even when justified, it stays an evil. It must above all be carried out with an eye to minimizing harm.

Chapter 6

Invincible Ignorance, Moral Equality, and Professional Obligation[1]

Richard Schoonhoven

Traditionally, members of the armed forces have been expected to concern themselves with questions of *jus in bello*, but they are generally taken to be exempt from considerations of *jus ad bellum*. The standard justification for this exemption proceeds in terms of a notion of "Invincible Ignorance:"[2] combatants[3] simply do not have access to all of the information that goes into the decision to declare war, and (therefore?) they ought simply to assume that those who do make such decisions are indeed making the right ones; the powers that be know things the rest of us don't, things that justify the decision to go to war. From this is supposed to follow not just the exemption noted above, but, at least according to some authors, the moral equality of combatants—that soldiers are *ipso facto* guilty of no moral wrong if they fight in an unjust war, given a strict adherence to the rules of *jus in bello*—and perhaps even an absolute duty on the part of military professionals to go to war when ordered to so.[4] For if combatants can never know whether the

1   The views expressed herein are those of the author, and do not purport to reflect the position of the United States Military Academy, the Department of the Army, or the Department of Defense. An earlier version of this contribution was presented to a very helpful audience at the Joint Services Conference for Professional Ethics in January of 2003. I am grateful to Anthony Hartle, George Lucas, Raymond Piereson, Elizabeth Samet, Calvin Schoonhoven, Peter Tramel, Michael Tubach, Daniel Zupan, an anonymous referee, and especially Roger Wertheimer for comments on earlier drafts.

2   Actually, that justification often proceeds in terms of three types of considerations: (*i*) epistemological worries, (*ii*) worries about agency, and (*iii*) issues surrounding the notion of patriotism. I am here concerned primarily with worries of the first type, although issues of agency will surface at various points throughout the paper. Issues of patriotism, it seems to me, divide without remainder into issues of the first two types, although I do not argue for that claim here.

3   I follow emerging usage and use "combatant" as a generic term for all members of the armed forces: soldiers, sailors, airmen and women, marines, etc. Whether the combatant/noncombatant distinction so construed is the correct one for purposes of moral reasoning is an important question, but beyond the scope of this paper. See my "Noncombatant Immunity and Truman's Decision," unpublished manuscript.

4   Cf. for example Walzer (2000, pp. 38-40 and *passim*) on the moral equality of combatants; Christopher (1999, pp. 211-12) on the notion of professional obligation. The

wars their governments prosecute are just, they cannot be held responsible for those wars, and they have no business refusing to fight them. A great deal then apparently turns on this notion of Invincible Ignorance.

Yet, under scrutiny the notion appears deeply unsatisfactory, if not utterly specious. First, as an empirical claim, it seems plainly false. Surely it is *possible* for a combatant—even the lowliest foot-soldier – to know in a specific case that the war his government is prosecuting is unjust. Undoubtedly there will always be information that the combatant lacks—information that his government does possess – but what is required here is not that a combatant possess all of the relevant information, but only enough to form a justified true belief about the justice of the war.[5] And surely any individual might have that.

Some authors would apparently deny this. They push a very hard line, bordering on outright skepticism, about the possibility of knowledge concerning the justice for war. Thus Paul Christopher claims that "we often never know objectively and with any degree of certainty which side in a war is just, even in retrospect" (p. 211). Maxwell Taylor is even more forthright:

> As for fear of involvement in an unjust or aggressive war, I do not feel that [an ideal officer] would be greatly concerned. He knows full well that there is no authoritative definition of either kind of war.[6]

It does often seem that there is no single, universally agreed upon standard for determining the justice of a war, and the justice of many wars remains in dispute even to this day. Moreover, the undoubted existence of so-called "victors' justice" could well make one cynical about any claim of objectivity. Taylor suggests that:

> If [the ideal officer's] side wins, he knows that there will be few charges of injustice save from the vanquished; if he loses, the victors, following the precedent of Nuremburg, are quite likely to charge him with crime and aggression regardless of evidence to the contrary.[7]

It can easily look as if the sole determinant of the justice of a war is who wins, and if this is the case, then holding combatants responsible for the justice of the wars they fight would seem unfair in the extreme.

---

notion of Invincible Ignorance can be found, for example, in Vitoria, *passim*.

5   Notoriously, knowledge has often been held to require more/other than justified true belief. But that is not a debate I need to enter into here.

6   Taylor (1980, 13). By an "authoritative" definition, Taylor may just mean one universally agreed upon in international law, but one gets the sense that his cynicism runs deeper than this. In any case, this reading would not materially affect my argument, for a lack of clear legal definition does not in general excuse one from worrying about the morality of an action.

7   Taylor (1980, 13). A minor typographical error has been corrected.

It is true that if knowledge concerning the justice of a war is impossible, then the corresponding ignorance will indeed be invincible. But I see no reason to grant the antecedent. In the first place, the situation suggested above is certainly not unique to questions about the justice of war. Many ethical issues remain unclear, hotly-debated, contentious—think of the debates that rage even today about the morality of abortion or the dropping of the atomic bomb on Japan. There is no universal or even widespread agreement on these issues. But we do not in general think that this means that there is no objective moral truth in these areas. That conclusion may be true—*tout court*, or simply in regard to questions of *jus ad bellum*—but it does not follow simply from the persistence of disagreement or the difficulty of settling on an answer. And in general—a point to which I shall return—we do not hold that such difficulty excuses people from at least trying to determine the right thing to do. At a minimum, we admire more those people who grapple with such issues, and thereby display a moral awareness and sensitivity, than those who simply shrug their shoulders and fall in line.

Moreover, the views cited above threaten to distort the facts, for in many cases the truth does not seem that far to seek. It should have been apparent when Hitler's tanks rolled across the border into Poland in September of 1939 (or Saddam Hussein's forces into Kuwait) that what was in the offing was an unwarranted act of aggression and a massive and apparently unprovoked violation of sovereignty. This may seem glib. Governments have a tremendous ability to manipulate and control information, and individuals are subject to all manner of rhetoric and propaganda: Germans were told that they *needed* to annex Poland, and perhaps Iraqis believed that they had a legitimate claim to Kuwait. No doubt many officers and soldiers in these armies sincerely believed they were justified in acting as they did. But such beliefs, in and of themselves, prove nothing. Some people believe that such aggressive acts can be justified—by long-standing grievances or a need for more room, for example. But people also sometimes believe that the systematic mistreatment of other groups can be justified—by long-standing grievances or racial superiority, for example. While some people did and perhaps still do believe that Germany was justified in invading Poland, some people did and unfortunately still do believe that Germany was justified in attempting to exterminate the Jews. If we are to do Just War Theory at all, we need to presuppose some universal moral standards that apply regardless of differences in backgrounds or beliefs.

This last point bears emphasizing, for indeed the existence of an objective standard for such questions is presupposed in the Just War Tradition itself. At least, it is difficult to see how else to interpret the talk in that tradition about standard criteria for a just war.[8] Certainly the existence of an objective standard of morality is presupposed by the strictures of *jus in bello*, to which most of the skeptics about *jus ad bellum* seem to adhere. And there can be as much and as persistent disagreement here: as I mentioned above, the morality of Truman's decision to

---

8   Cf. for example; Christopher (Chapter 6); Coates (1997, Part II); Johnson (1999, Chapter 2); Orend (2000, Chapter 6).

bomb Japan is still a matter of some dispute. So there doesn't seem to be a great deal of difference in this regard between *jus ad bellum* and *jus in bello*. And surely, for all Taylor's cynicism expressed above, nobody—at least nobody worth listening to—really thinks that Nuremburg represents nothing more than victors' justice. I therefore see no reason to grant that knowledge is impossible in regard to questions of *jus ad bellum*.

Here the defender of Invincible Ignorance will claim that I have mischaracterized her position. It's not that it is impossible to know whether a given war is unjust or not, but given how difficult such determinations often are, and given the limited information and perspective available to any individual, it would be unfair to expect servicemen and women to settle these issues before going to war. How can we expect those in the service to determine the justice of a war in advance, when the rest of us can hardly agree even decades later? Thus, an officer ought to trust in his government to make the right—or at least a wiser—decision. Even given a certain amount of evidence to the contrary, it might be argued that *for all the combatant knows* his leaders may yet be in possession of certain facts that establish the justice of the war. So given that the war has been properly declared, he is entitled to believe, and ought to accept, that the war is in fact just; there is and ought to be a strong presumption in favor of obeying the commands he is given. This presumption is particularly weighty in regard to questions of *jus ad bellum*, because in general such commands come from the highest authority in a given state or society, and are made only after due deliberation.[9] In this vein, Taylor argues that:

> [i]n the absence of authoritative means to identify an unjust war in time to avoid participation, an officer has little choice but to assume the rightness of a governmental decision involving the country in war. Having made this assumption, he is honor-bound to carry out all legal orders and do his best to bring the war to a prompt and successful conclusion.

On the face of it, this presumption seems quite laudable: it seems simply to register a proper and healthy humility, for who is any individual to second-guess the decision of his government, which undoubtedly does have access to more information than he?[10] The question, however, is what undergirds this presumption and what follows from it.

First, it is important to note that, as the above examples show, such a presumption is defeasible. It *is* possible for a service member to be in possession of information that reveals the injustice of a war in a particular case. In the extreme, think of a

---

9   I owe this point to Roger Wertheimer.

10   Thus we can understand Christopher's talk of arrogance: "it is profoundly arrogant … to take the view …that after the national debate takes place, and the president and Congress decide to act, then the officers should have the latitude to follow their own conscience" (1999, p. 212).

soldier who accidentally opens the wrong envelope and stumbles across the entire battle plan, including the true motives for the war and the lies to be told to the press. Surely such a soldier *knows* that the war is unjust. This means that while such a presumption may be a reasonable starting point, that a particular war is in fact just can only be the conclusion of an investigation into the justice of the war, not a premise in an argument that precludes such an investigation. One cannot know in advance of such an investigation that a war is in fact just, or even that its justice is a matter beyond one's own abilities to determine. Even in a criminal trial, for all that a presumption of innocence guides our conduct, it does not relieve us of our duty to look at the evidence, nor does it prevent us from declaring the defendant guilty, if that is the way the evidence points. Of course, if the evidence is inconclusive, the presumption tells us to declare him innocent; similarly, it may be that if the evidence for a just war is genuinely inconclusive, a member of the armed services may have no choice but to fight.[11] But again, this verdict can only come *after* the investigation. And I take it to be obvious that there always must be such an investigation. War is a serious matter—people suffer and die on massive scales—and it ought not be entered into frivolously or unreflectively.

Here the objection will be that while this may all be true, it is not the *service member's* job to provide the requisite scrutiny. Rather, the presumption at issue is precisely that those who do make the decision have indeed done their job and are making a responsible and informed decision; therefore members of the services ought to fight.[12] Christopher's version of this presumption relies on a notion of "formal justice." He claims that "wars fought in accordance with [judgments made according to the accepted formal procedures of a nation] are formally just" (1999, p. 145), and that formal justice is "as close to objective justice as we know how to get" (p. 212). Therefore,

> [i]t is as though professional soldiers have taken the following oath: "Recognizing that I may never know in advance whether the use of force being contemplated is objectively just, I swear to respond as a soldier on behalf of my nation to all wars that are formally just"(1999, p. 145).

---

11   But cf. McMahan (2007a) for an argument to the opposite conclusion. McMahan (2007a, 58) points out that if one grants what seems incontrovertible—that more wars have been unjust on both sides than have been just on both sides (which the tradition in any case deems impossible)—then it follows that more wars have been fought unjustly than justly. Simple induction will then lead to the conclusion that any given war is probably unjust, and this, McMahan claims, ought to be enough to break the tie. The argument, however, strikes me as a little too clever; it seems to overlook what McMahan himself cites elsewhere (2007b, 99); *viz.*, the pervasiveness of in-group bias.

12   Perhaps unless the evidence to the contrary is extremely strong. This is apparently Vitoria's view; see below.

But if this is the presumption involved, then everything turns on the particular forms and procedures that constitute that formal justice. Here we need more than an abstract notion of formal justice. For a notion of formal justice to do this kind of work, it has to have some specific content; the mere fact that somebody somewhere has formally certified a war to be just is not enough to make it reasonable to believe that it really is just. Moreover, inasmuch as Invincible Ignorance is meant to apply to all members of the armed forces who fight at the behest of a legitimately constituted government, this content would have to be shared across all (possible) formal systems.[13] But this is simply not the case. Formal procedures vary widely, and while some formal systems may be well-constituted to arrive at the truth, not all are. So even if one has a great deal of faith in the formal procedures of one's own nation to guarantee just decisions, not everyone in every land is entitled to be so sanguine.

This discussion of formal justice points up another feature of the presumption at issue: this presumption goes far beyond a claim of mere factual ignorance —perhaps crossing into the realm of blind faith. There are two possibilities: (1) service members simply do not need to care whether the wars they fight are just or not, and (2) service members are entitled to believe that those wars, assuming the decision to fight has been made in accordance with the proper formal procedures, are in fact just. We shall return to the first of these possibilities below, but it is the second that is at least strongly suggested by the foregoing discussion. If this is the position at issue, however, then it is obviously not enough simply for the government to have access to more information than any given individual. Even if we grant that the government will always have access to information beyond that available to the rest of us, more would still be required before we were off the moral hook. Before we could rest secure in the morality of our nations' wars, we would have to believe that our governments would always interpret that information correctly, and would act on it from moral motives and for moral goals. That is, if the issue is trusting that one's government is doing the right thing based on the (additional) information available to it, one would have to trust not only that the government *had* such information, but that it was interested in and trying to do the right thing, and that it was not making any mistakes.[14] And that, sadly, is something that we all have occasionally had reason to doubt. So there does not seem to be any general immunity here from questions of *jus ad bellum*, at least none founded on an impossibility of knowledge or on a reasonable belief on the part of all members of all armed forces that their governments are acting justly.

---

13   As I understand Invincible Ignorance, and as classically conceived, it is meant to apply universally. Certainly a universal claim of the moral equality of combatants only makes sense if the Invincible Ignorance on which it relies is itself understood to be universal.

14   Even if you adopt the cynical view that justice just is fighting for the best interests of the state, it is simply naïve to think that all governments make just decisions about when to go to war; nations often act contrary to their own best interests.

This does call into question the moral equality of (all) combatants, which seems to me in any case a rather suspect notion. Nothing I say in this paper is meant to discount the fact that combatants are subject to coercion of many different forms: they are often forced to fight against their choosing, and given the power of governments in terms of propaganda and the control of information, even their choosing can sometimes hardly be considered free. Moreover, combatants sometimes fight for commendable reasons, even when they suspect their cause to be unjust—loyalty to one's comrades or unit, for example.[15] It would be morally insensitive to ignore these facts. But it is nevertheless unrealistic to think that all combatants always either fight for commendable reasons, or are forced into it.[16]

Nor do I mean to claim that we could often be in a position to make the relevant determinations—that we would ever be able to tell who was who—after the war is over; so we may have no choice but to treat all combatants as if they are morally equal. But notice that while there is certainly ignorance here, it is ignorance on our part, not on theirs. In any case, I am concerned in the first instance with making moral as opposed to, say, legal distinctions; and from a moral point of view, it is important to realize that combatants sometimes fight for the wrong reasons, and those reasons can properly affect our moral evaluations.[17]

The standard line, of course, is that so long as combatants fight according to the rules of *jus in bello*, they are morally equal, at least *qua* combatant. This suggests that the reasons for which a combatant fights are irrelevant to his moral status as a combatant. After all, the moral equality of combatants was never meant to cover all facets of a combatant's character. Some combatants may be adulterers and tax-dodgers—more to the point, some might fight out of hatred or bloodlust. The doctrine of moral equality does not excuse them from these crimes, but as long as their actions *qua* combatants are relevantly similar, we must judge them similarly. I see no reason to buy into such a rigid compartmentalization of moral judgment and moral responsibility, however: it seems neither to do justice to our moral intuitions nor to serve any useful purpose (although I shall return to this issue below). In general, when someone does something wrong—and intuitively fighting for an unjust cause at least *seems* wrong—it matters to us whether they reasonably believe they are doing the right thing.

Part of what I want to insist on in this paper is precisely that intentions and motives—the reasons for which one fights—*are* relevant to one's moral status as a combatant. Our moral evaluations, even in war, go beyond overt actions, and

---

15   Cf. Wertheimer (2007) for a sensitive discussion of how these various commitments may weigh against one another.

16   Walzer sometimes seems tempted in this direction; cf. for example Walzer (2000, p. 39).

17   In the Just War Tradition, there are a number of criteria beyond that of Just Cause – the reason(s) for which the war is fought—that are required in order for a war to be deemed just. Since I incline to the view that Just Cause is nevertheless the dominant criterion, I focus almost exclusively on it.

there does seem to be an important *moral* difference between the GI fighting on the battlefields of WWII because his country called him to or because he believes in such ideals as duty, honor, country—or even his German counterpart—and the soldier who scrubbed out of the *Waffen* S.S. (and so perhaps never actually commits a war crime), but who nonetheless fights in full support of Hitler's expansionist, imperialist, and genocidal ideals. Intuitively, (among combatants who fight willingly) there is a spectrum that ranges from those who fight nobly for a just cause, through those who fight nobly for an unjust cause, to those who fight ignobly for an unjust cause.[18] But the doctrine of the moral equality of combatants would require us to treat the first two cases as being on a par; it thus obscures distinctions we might reasonably and naturally want to make. Even combatants who fight knowingly, though perhaps not enthusiastically, in an unjust war are, I would argue, suspect.[19] Rommel, for example, is often cited as the example of a combatant who fought nobly for a bad cause, but my admiration for him is at least diminished by the fact that the cause for which he fought was evil, and he was well-positioned to know that it was evil. Again, it will be objected that Rommel did not fight *for* Nazism, but for some other cause—for German national sovereignty or out of a sense of duty, perhaps—but the two are not so neatly separable, and to the extent that the second furthered the first, it ought seriously to be questioned whether there was anything admirable about fighting for it.[20]

Also suspect, then, is the notion that officers have an absolute duty to prosecute the wars their government tells them to, unless we want to require that officers

---

18   I do not know where combatants who fight ignobly for a just cause fit in on this spectrum: are they better or worse than those who fight nobly for an unjust cause? But to the extent that the question is live, it displays the poverty of the doctrine of the moral equality of combatants. According to that doctrine, the question is a non-starter: the reasons for which a combatant fights being irrelevant, the individual who fights nobly is clearly superior, no matter what his cause.

19   Indeed, it might even be the case that combatants who in fact *are* ignorant are morally diminished by having fought for a bad cause. Apparently, some German combatants were plagued by guilt after the war for fighting in the service of Nazism, even though they had fought scrupulously according to the rules of *jus in bello*. Such feelings may not be universally misplaced. Cf. also Wertheimer (2007, 68) for the idea that while ignorance may be exculpatory, it is hardly justifying.

20   It is sometimes similarly claimed that Robert E. Lee, for example, fought not for slavery, but for Southern self-determination or states' rights. But Southern self-determination entailed slavery (at least for some continued time), and thus to fight for it was *de facto* to fight for slavery. I can do no better than to quote W.E.B Du Bois:

> Either [Lee] knew what slavery meant when he helped maim and murder thousands in its defense, or he did not. If he did not, he was a fool. If he did, Robert Lee was a traitor and a rebel – not indeed to his country, but to humanity and humanity's God.

The Lee case is particularly problematic, because it cannot even be claimed that he acted out of loyalty to his nation and his oath as an officer.

fight even when they know their government is wrong. We might distinguish three possible positions here:

1. Obedience is obligatory: officers are morally required to go to war, even when they (ought to) know that their government is wrong;
2. Obedience is optional: officers are morally permitted to obey, but also morally permitted to disobey when they (ought to) know that their government is wrong; and
3. Obedience is prohibited: officers are morally required to disobey when they (ought to) know that their government is wrong.

There are deep and interesting questions here, about which I will not have much to say, about how certain an officer would have to be before he refused to fight.[21] Given the sanctions usually attendant upon such a decision, the bar here is likely to be quite high—and considerably higher still before we would ever *require* such disobedience. Nevertheless, the first of these positions at least strikes me as too extreme, for it would require us to convict of a serious moral failing a German officer who refused to participate in the invasion of Poland, recognizing it for the aggressive act it was. I do not have to claim that all German officers ought to have refused to fight, but given the horrors of Nazism, I am inclined to admire those who did.

If the foregoing is correct, then the notion of Invincible Ignorance—understood either as an empirical claim or as a reasonable presumption that a formally declared war is in fact just—is highly suspect. The implausibility of this notion becomes even more apparent if we consider the case of a modern democratic state, for here the notion of Invincible Ignorance seems particularly inapt—and quite dangerous if insisted upon. That is, if members of the armed forces—who after all in this country at least are citizens—can never (be in a position to) know whether their country's wars are unjust, it is hard to see how or why ordinary citizens—the rest of us—should be better situated epistemologically. All of the arguments just considered seem to apply with equal force to ordinary citizens: most of us are no more, and often less, privy to the inner workings of the governmental decision-making process and its intelligence sources than the average combatant.[22] It is of

---

21 Vitoria exempts a combatant who *knows* a war to be immoral from fighting (173), but argues that in all lesser cases—i.e., cases of doubt—the combatant must fight. Notice how this, coupled with the doctrine of Invincible Ignorance, leads immediately to a requirement of absolute obedience. For if one can never have such knowledge, then one must always fight. McMahan (2006c; 2007a) argues that if anything—given what is at stake in war—the bar is actually higher on the side of having reason to believe that a war is just before one can morally fight. I am inclined to agree, though I don't directly address the issue here.

22 It is no help here to claim that ordinary citizens are part of the system of formal justice that makes the decision, whereas combatants are not, for the question at issue is in effect precisely what distinguishes combatants from citizens in this regard. See below.

course true that those in the service are busy people who do not have a great deal of time to worry about such things; but doctors and stock-brokers and plumbers are busy people too, yet arguably they have a responsibility to be aware of what their government is doing (and moreover, we think it's *possible* for them to do so).[23] And admittedly, given the speed with which decisions sometimes have to be made and the sensitivity of the information involved, we all sometimes simply have to trust that our government is doing the right thing. One doesn't want to be naïve about the fact that wars have been fought without the mandate of the people, but one of the cornerstones of democracy is that the government is accountable to the people, and a claim that we can never know whether the wars our country fights are just or not, even when our leaders can know, threatens seriously to undermine this central pillar of democracy. Moreover, if it is impossible for us ever to know, why would we even bother to inquire? And the suggestion that there is no point to ordinary citizens worrying about the justice of their country's wars seems a dangerous thing. To adopt a "hands off" position is simply to cede too much power to the government. None of this, of course, shows that ordinary citizens *can* have such knowledge, but it ought to make us less ready to embrace the suggestion.[24] So unless a line can be drawn between combatants and ordinary citizens in regard to a claim of Invincible Ignorance, that notion would seem to encourage a head-in-the-sand mentality that is inimical to the idea of democracy.

Of course, there are differences between service members and civilians regarding the sort of interest they are expected or required take in a war. Members of the armed forces, for example, are not allowed to criticize publicly political decisions about which wars ought and ought not be fought, and, famously, officers have gotten into trouble for doing so. So one reason we do not require combatants to stay informed about and do research on the decisions of their government is that it is in some sense irrelevant what they think or know, for they are not allowed to act on it anyway.

23　Vitoria contends that "Senators and petty rulers and in general all who are admitted on summons or voluntarily to the public council or the prince's council ought, and are bound, to examine into the cause of an unjust war. This is clear; for whoever can save his neighbor from danger and harm is bound to do so, especially when the danger is that of death and greater ills, as is the case in war. But the persons referred to can avert the war, supposing it to be unjust, if they lend their wisdom and weight to an examination into its causes. Therefore they are bound so to do" (p. 174). In a democratic society, this would presumably include all of the citizens, at least to some extent, and it does seem that, given the enormity of the suffering that war generally occasions, to the extent that one is capable of preventing an unjust war, one ought to do so.

24　It would be inconsistent given my argument here, simultaneously to insist that combatants bear (some) responsibility for the wars they fight and to exempt ordinary citizens from all responsibility for those wars. Indeed, I do think that citizens bear some such responsibility, but how much responsibility attaches to individual citizens of course depends on their particular governmental structure, and this and what follows from it is a matter for another paper.

This suggests a different way of understanding the claim of Invincible Ignorance. Rather than treating it as an empirical claim, perhaps we should treat it as normative; that is, we should treat combatants as if they are imbued with Invincible Ignorance; we should treat them as if it is impossible for them to know, and therefore they have no need to inquire. The claim of Invincible Ignorance then becomes a stance we adopt, underlying a commitment to treat all combatants as morally equal. This approach may seem patently obvious,[25] and is perhaps already in the literature, but the two senses of the term have not been as sharply distinguished as they need to be, and in fact have often been conflated.[26] And in any case, this reading of Invincible Ignorance only pushes the problem back. For now we should want to know what justifies this normative attribution. If the claim of combatant moral equality doesn't rest on a real notion of Invincible Ignorance, on what does it rest? Why should we exempt combatants from inquiring into the justice of the wars their countries fight, when we don't similarly exempt ordinary citizens? The answers to these questions will be what do the real moral work.

One obvious difference between members of the armed forces and civilians is that service members have sworn an oath to fight for their country when called upon. It might then be thought that they have no choice but to fight: they are morally bound by their oaths to do so. But this seems unlikely. A detailed examination of the obligations imposed by and the limits of oaths is beyond the scope of this paper, but while oaths certainly ought to be taken seriously, it is not clear that one can have a moral obligation, however arrived at, to do something immoral. Can one morally commit oneself to do whatever one is ordered to do, no matter how immoral it may turn out to be?[27] And if he does it, can he then claim that he was only fulfilling his oath (here it might be well to remember that Nazi officers presumably took and felt bound by oaths as well)? It does not seem that one can absolve oneself of moral responsibility so easily.

Vitoria gives three reasons why combatants do not need to concern themselves with the justice of war.[28] He argues that:

---

25   So much was probably already implicit in the name anyway. As much as those of us who spend a great deal of our time in the classroom are sometimes tempted to the opposite conclusion, no actual ignorance is truly invincible. Even the most benighted and recalcitrant student can occasionally stumble headlong into the truth, and thus, I shall suppose, into knowledge.

26   The normative reading is at least suggested by Christopher's discussion at (1999, p. 212), but cf. the passage from him quoted above. Does this represent an empirical reading, or a normative one? At best, the line is blurred.

27   Cf. Tramel (unpublished) on the moral acceptability of volunteering to fight whatever wars one might eventually be ordered to.

28   Vitoria is not actually interested in a distinction between combatants and citizens; he instead relies on an ungenerous distinction between those "who are admitted ... to the public council" and "other lesser folk" (p. 174). But this seems to parallel the distinction we are interested in, in that in a democratic society all citizens are in some sense "admitted

1.   It is impossible and inexpedient to give reasons for all acts of state to every
member of the commonalty ...

2.   Men of the lower orders, even if they perceived the injustice of war, could
not stop it, and their voice would not be heeded. Therefore any examination by
them of the causes of a war would be futile ...

3.   It is enough proof of the justice of war (unless the contrary be quite certain)[29]
that it is being waged after public counsel and by public authority. Therefore no
further examination on their part is needed (p. 174).

The second consideration here obviously fails to motivate a distinction between
combatants and ordinary citizens, for in any society in which ordinary citizens
could stop a war, presumably combatants would have at least as much power
—unless we especially prevent them from doing so, the propriety of which is
precisely what is at issue. And in a society in which both citizens and combatants
truly are powerless, then it seems neither ought to be held responsible.

Vitoria's first reason apparently has to do with the security of the state.
Elsewhere he writes that:

A prince is not able, and ought not, always to render reasons for the war to his
subjects, and if the subjects can not serve in the war unless they are first satisfied
of its justice, the state would fall into grave peril.[30]

Here, too, Vitoria is clearly thinking of the relationship between a monarch and his
subjects, as opposed to that between the executive of a democracy and its citizens;
we do expect our government to give us an accounting in such matters. But in any
case it is not obvious what the danger is supposed to be. One possibility is that
were service members to be held responsible for the justice of the wars they fight,
they might well refuse to fight at all, and so we let them off the moral hook, so to
speak, in order to secure their obedience. This seems a rather cynical view to take
of the matter, although in a less cynical vein it might be thought that we simply
agree not to hold our armed forces responsible for our moral decisions; that is, we
in effect indemnify them against liability for our moral mistakes.[31] Either way, this

---

to the public council, and the "lesser folk" presumably includes those who will do the
fighting.

29   Cf. note 21.

30   Vitoria (p. 176). Also quoted in Walzer (2000, p. 39). I am greatly indebted to
George Lucas for urging me to look at Vitoria directly.

31   I owe this way of looking at things to George Lucas. Zupan (2007) seems to worry
about the unfairness of holding combatants responsible for following the orders "we"
issue them, but it is worth noting that we do precisely this *re* questions of *jus in bello*. See
below.

in effect makes the attribution of moral equality into an agreement between a state and its combatants. However much there may be to be said for such an agreement, it leaves it somewhat obscure why we should let other militaries off the moral hook, or why they should so absolve ours (although I return to this issue below). In any case, it seems that if combatants are genuinely morally responsible for the unjust wars they (freely) fight, then a governmental policy of not holding them legally responsible does not alter this fundamental fact.

Vitoria suggests that "if subjects in a case of doubt do not follow their prince to the war, they expose themselves to the risk of betraying their State to the enemy" (p. 176), and Christopher writes that to "permit soldiers to leave military service whenever they do not agree with a political decision" would be to "make a mockery of the very notion of having a standing army" (p. 212).[32] But this is not obviously true. If the concern here is that our armed forces may refuse to fight when we want them too, and if we take seriously the idea of a citizen-soldier, then convincing one's soldiery ought to be no different from convincing one's citizenry, which is something most democracies at least are concerned to do. And in any case, it would seem that this would represent a substantial threat only if a great many combatants refused to fight; but if our government (or any government) were prosecuting a war such that mass defections (resignations) from the military were a real concern, it might be just as well to rethink that war.[33]

On the other hand, the worry might be that if we allow combatants this degree of autonomy, then obedience in general will be undermined, and in particular, combatants might be inclined to launch wars that are not sanctioned by the state. This does not seem likely, however. While no one doubts the importance of obedience to a properly functioning military, (almost) no one thinks that the obedience required is absolute. What is presupposed and required here is an asymmetry in (dis)obedience, such that those in the service in some sense have the option of not fighting when their government tells them to, but must obey when their government tells them not to fight.[34] Such an asymmetry does not seem

---

32   Christopher is thus firmly opposed to allowing officers to resign in protest of an unjust war. This sentiment may seem extreme, but I do not believe it to be idiosyncratic. A case in point: during the writing of this paper, an American diplomat, John Brady Kiesling, resigned his position over the then-impending war in Iraq. His decision was greeted by a great deal of disapproval on the part of a number of military officers, who made it clear that in their minds resignation was simply not an option.

33   The overall idea here is apparently that the military is the arm of the state, and one very much wants one's arms to do what one tells them. But I am not convinced that it would be an entirely bad thing if every time I got to feeling ornery and decided to go out and beat up on old ladies and small children, my arms refused to obey—as long as they did obey whenever I needed to defend myself.

34   In part, the answer here is to impose much higher sanctions for such transgressions (see below), but it may also be time to consider some sort of provision for selective conscientious objection. Much interesting work is currently being done on this topic; see for example many of the papers delivered at the 2008 International Symposium on Military

psychologically implausible, and is in any case presupposed by the tradition of *jus in bello*. Combatants are generally allowed, even expected, to disobey when obedience would violate the strictures of *jus in bello*, and nobody really worries that the disobedience of such orders will lead to a general breakdown of discipline. Of course, arguably, what is allowed in this regard is only the disobedience of *illegal* orders, and so it might still be thought that to allow for the disobedience of legal orders would be to invite a general breakdown in discipline.[35] But even here, "legal" can only be understood in some broader sense than "according to the laws of a given country"—I take it that shooting Jews was in fact legal in Nazi Germany—and if we are going to hold combatants accountable to an international standard *in bello*, there seems no good reason here not to hold them similarly accountable *ad bellum*. In general, obedience to superior orders—legal or not —is not considered a viable defense for violations of the rules of *jus in bello*; why then should the situation be so different when we move to the realm of *jus ad bellum*? Granted, the rules of *jus in bello* are much easier to follow, much more clear-cut, and thus it is easier to tell when they are about to be violated.[36] But in the weeks and months leading up to a war, one often does have the luxury of time for consideration and reflection (and rulers have the time to "render reasons" to their subjects). So again, there seems to be no good reason here to exempt combatants from such concerns.

It might be thought, however, that I have mislocated the worry. Daniel Zupan (2007) argues from what he terms the "logic of community:"

> Part of what I'll call the logic of communities is to be under communal laws, to consent to the rule of law, and reject individual acts of retribution and all the arbitrariness, fallibility, and injustice that are pervasive and dangerous features of the 'law of the jungle.' As such, there is an inconsistency if we ignore this moral feature of communal activity, which differentiates it from individual action in terms of moral responsibility. The individual gives over certain rights and responsibilities to some government, or representative, and it is considered legally and often morally impermissible for individuals to take into their hands matters that are the purview of the state. It is as if we demand of the individual that she refrain from certain activities (private wars) and cede that authority and responsibility to the state, but at the same time we reserve the right to condemn her for fulfilling the terms of the contract: she is to be in the state of nature and out of the state of nature at the same time (2007, 43).

Ethics, available at http://www.usafa.edu/isme/ISME08/isme08.html. Cf. also McMahan (2006c, 392) for the suggestion that the asymmetry may not be quite as strong as I here make out.

35 I owe the point to Anthony Hartle.

36 Maybe not. As McPherson (2005) points out, "The rules themselves may be straightforward. How the rules apply in specific circumstances is another matter." McPherson makes a point similar to mine here.

Here the worry goes beyond concerns about obedience, to concerns about justice and fairness, or even logical consistency. The state reserves unto itself a monopoly on the use of lethal force (outside of cases of self-defense, etc.). It is inconsistent, suggests Zupan, to grant that power to the state and then to turn around and hold individuals responsible for obeying that power. There is truth in the old adage that with awesome power comes awesome responsibility; but if that power is reserved to the state alone, does not the responsibility reside solely with the state as well? Here too, though, the situation is plausibly asymmetric; symmetry is often pleasing, but it ought not be mistaken for consistency. There is nothing inconsistent in saying—or in writing a social contract that says—I will use force only when the state authorizes it, but perhaps not even then.[37] From the fact that we allow people to use lethal force only when the state authorizes it, it does not follow that they have to use it whenever the state authorizes it. Admittedly, there would seem to be something inconsistent and unfair about the very same authority both issuing an order and then condemning those who follow it, but that is not really what is at issue here. What is at issue is the morality of the resort to force, and that, I am arguing, cannot be changed simply by the fact that it happens in obedience to an order.[38]

Thus we come to Vitoria's third reason. We have already discussed the presumption implicit in this consideration, and I have argued that such a presumption is in many cases unwarranted, and is in any case defeasible. This leaves us with the possibility, bruited above, that those in the service simply need not care whether the wars they fight are just (given that the proper authorities have "signed off" on them). Why might this be? There is at least one other area in society—one profession—where not only do we not expect the members of that profession to concern themselves with the justice of the particular causes they represent, we expect them *not* to so concern themselves. I am thinking, of course, of the legal profession.[39] When a criminal defense attorney, say, defends a client, there are certain rules she must follow—she may not knowingly suborn perjury, for example—but within those rules, she is expected—required—to defend her client zealously and to the best of her abilities, without regard for his actual guilt or innocence.[40] Indeed, we expect her to defend her client zealously, even if she

---

37   Obviously, there would be difficulties with any mechanism for selective conscientious objection; cf. note 34. I also take it to be clear that I am not talking about, e.g., instances of self-defense here.

38   Cf. McMahan (2007a, 53) where he comes to a similar conclusion; for a version of this asymmetry applied to the moral risks run by the agent, see McMahan (2007a, 56-7).

39   McMahan (2006c) closely parallels my reasoning in what follows, although in general I focus less on the specific harm that unjust combatants do to just combatants.

40   It might help to think here of a public defender. Public defenders effectively surrender a good deal of the discretion that many lawyers do enjoy, in that when one becomes a public defender, one in effect agrees to defend any client one is assigned, whether innocent or not.

knows him to be guilty. The analogy with combatants is immediate and obvious. Combatants too are expected to fight within and according to certain rules—the strictures of *jus in bello*—but according to the standard view of such things, so long as they remain within those bounds, they are not expected to concern themselves with the justice of their (nation's) cause. And indeed, by analogy, we might expect combatants to fight for their country, even when they know that country is wrong. So it might be thought that we can give a similar justification in both cases.

Yet as intriguing and suggestive as the analogy is—and it could obviously be deepened and extended in various ways—it ultimately breaks down. We have an adversarial system of law because we believe that it represents our best chance of seeing justice served. That is, we believe that by having a zealous advocate on each side, we stand the best chance of uncovering and arriving at the truth, or at least of punishing the guilty while protecting the innocent. We have a certain amount of faith in the system and consider its proper functioning to be of paramount importance, and the insistence that lawyers fight for their clients whether those clients are innocent or guilty is an integral part of that system. But it is not clear what the analogous hope would be in the case of war. What is the system in which exempting combatants from caring about *jus ad bellum* would play a necessary or even a useful role? How, precisely, does absolving combatants of personal moral responsibility for the wars they fight contribute to a just and lasting peace? Truth doesn't seem to be at issue here, and absent some fond belief that the good guys always win, or the cynical belief that might really does make right, there seems to be no good reason to believe that adopting such an attitude toward combatants will really conduce to justice, even in the long run.

It might be thought that the system of which the moral equality of combatants is an ineliminable part is the war convention itself, the body of rules and understandings that makes war a rule-governed activity. One might worry, for example, that by holding combatants accountable for *jus ad bellum* considerations, we undermine their incentive for adhering to the strictures of *jus in bello*.[41] That is, if combatants fighting in an unjust war are going to be treated as criminals in any case, why would they bother to obey the (other) rules of war? Why not, for example, begin torturing prisoners if it will help ensure a victory—and thereby allow one to

---

41   Brough (2007) suggests that by denying the moral equality of combatants, and thereby allowing combatants to see those on the other side as guilty, one opens up the door for the dehumanization of the enemy, which in turn leads to violations of *jus in bello* and inflicts psychological damage on those who do the dehumanizing. This claim strikes me as hostage to any number of empirical facts and as in any case implausible—police officers often pursue individuals they take to be guilty without dehumanizing them, for example —but if a sufficiently strong psychological connection were to be made out between the doctrine of the moral equality of combatants and the incidence of *jus in bello* violations and post-traumatic stress disorder, then I might have to qualify my views. It is worth noting in this regard, however, that Peter Kilner (2002) has recently argued that it might help combatants avoid PTSD to explain to them why the killing they do is justified. It might then help to see the other side as guilty. What empirical data there are strike me as equivocal.

escape prosecution? In a similar vein: one of the cornerstones of modern Just War Theory is the combatant/noncombatant distinction. Walzer ties this distinction to the moral equality of combatants: "Without the equal right to kill, war as a rule-governed activity would disappear and be replaced by crime and punishment, by evil conspiracies and military law enforcement."[42] But if we deny combatants the equal right to kill—if we are going to hold combatants criminally responsible even for killing other combatants in an unjust war—we threaten seriously to erode that distinction, and thereby encourage violations of noncombatant immunity. If killing even combatants is a criminal act, then what distinguishes it from killing noncombatants? And if nothing does, then what distinguishes war from wholesale slaughter?[43]

In part, the response here is to reiterate that I am writing philosophy, not policy; that is, I am interested in notions of genuine moral responsibility—what McMahan (2006a) calls the "deep morality of war"—as opposed to institutionalized, legal accountability. I admitted above that it might not be possible to make the distinctions necessary in order to hold individual combatants legally responsible for willingly fighting unjust wars; the foregoing considerations show that it might not be prudent, even if it proves possible. But even if we should choose not to punish such individuals legally, that is no in principle bar to our distributing moral admiration and condemnation differentially; moral distinctions, unlike legal penalties, can be indefinitely fine-grained.

Nor am I entirely ready, however, to concede that the argument against holding (some) combatants legally responsible for the justice of the wars they fight has been decisively made out, although we might want to restrict such actions to only the most egregious cases. Plausibly, all that would be required here would be a graduated system of punishments; we would simply have to assure that the sanctions for *jus in bello* violations remain discouragingly high, and therefore presumably a good bit higher than those for violations of *jus ad bellum*.[44] We make such distinctions in the law all the time. In his discussion of Rommel, Walzer claims that:

---

42   Walzer (2000, 41). Walzer is less confident that he draws the line in precisely the right place, but insists on the importance that some line be drawn: "I don't believe that this question must be answered in this or that specific way if war is to be a moral condition. It is necessary, however, that at any particular moment there be an answer. War is distinguishable from murder and massacre only when restrictions are established on the reach of battle" (pp. 41-2).

43   But cf. Wertheimer (2007, 63) for an argument that "the core *jus in bello* principles have no need of notions of combatant moral equality" even at the level of justification.

44   To impose a higher penalty for killing noncombatants than combatants, when both actions are criminal, might seem to make the combatant/noncombatant distinction arbitrary. But I would argue that the distinction is already arbitrary; "innocence," when applied to noncombatants, for example, is a technical term, not a recognition of moral desert; cf. also McPherson (2005) and my "Noncombatant Immunity and Truman's Decision."

> it would be very odd to praise Rommel for not killing prisoners unless we
> simultaneously refused to blame him for Hitler's aggressive wars. For otherwise
> he is simply a criminal, and all the fighting he does is murder or attempted
> murder, whether he aims at soldiers in battle or at prisoners or at civilians (38).

But the oddness here is not apparent to me at all. The simple fact is that we do
treat differently—morally and legally—the criminal who, say, kills only the
armed guard as opposed to killing his defenseless prisoners, and we do this even
though we think that such a criminal has no right to self-defense. Certainly we
might condemn the second killing more, and this condemnation might well be
represented in sentencing. Legal penalties, like moral evaluations, do not have to
be an all-or-nothing matter.

But perhaps I am too optimistic here, and in any case there might be further
worries. Beyond the above concerns, Wertheimer (2007) argues convincingly that
holding combatants legally responsible for the justice of the wars they fight is
an invitation to violations of *jus post bellum*. He argues that besides providing
a disincentive to surrender, and thus prolonging wars, punishing combatants for
the wars they fight is unlikely to eventuate in justice being done: "history," he
suggests, "offers scant hope of substantial good coming from punishing aggressor
combatants"(2007, 62). He therefore urges that we forego a good bit of retributive
justice, because the potential costs of doing otherwise are far greater injustices
and consequential evils.[45] If this is right, we might have no (moral) choice but to
absolve combatants of all *legal* responsibility for the wars they fight.[46] But it does
not follow that all combatants are genuinely *morally* equal.

This might be thought too fine a distinction. It might be argued that if there
are overriding moral reasons for equally absolving all combatants of legal
responsibility, then they are equally absolved of moral responsibility; there is no
point to any further moral distinction-mongering.[47] For if we nevertheless do insist
on making moral distinctions among combatants (*re jus ad bellum*), then we lapse
into hypocrisy in that we insist on treating them all equally, while at the same
time we insist that they are not equal. But it is hardly news that there is often a
mismatch between the law and morality; there are many actions that we might not
wish to criminalize but that are nevertheless immoral. So it does not follow that
all combatants are morally equal, even if legally we should treat them equally.
I very much doubt, for example, that all lawyers are morally equal, although it
might make perfect sense to treat them legally as if they were. Surely there's an
important difference between a lawyer who defends her guilty client—albeit with
some discomfort—out of a robust commitment to our system of justice, and a

---

45   Wertheimer, personal communication.

46   Cf. McMahan (2007b, 99), where he comes to much the same conclusion, although
McMahan grounds the "legal equality of combatants" primarily in epistemic considerations,
which I largely reject.

47   Walzer sometimes seems tempted in this direction. Cf. his (2006).

lawyer who simply doesn't care that his client is a murderer, but is just in it for the money. As a society, we might well want to encourage the former attitude in various ways, even if we refuse to recognize any legal distinction between the two. Something similar might be true for combatants; there might be strong consequentialist reasons for encouraging combatants to concern themselves with issues *jus ad bellum* even if we don't hold them legally responsible. As Robert Nozick points out, combatants "are certainly not encouraged to think for themselves by the practice of absolving them of all responsibility for their actions within the rules of war" (1974, 100). And it may not be hopelessly naïve to think that in the long run we have a better chance of seeing justice on earth if we expect combatants to care about the justice of the wars they fight.[48] At any rate, there does not seem to be anything inconsistent in holding that:

> ... most combatants who fight in unjust wars thereby act impermissibly, that most nevertheless have excuses that mitigate their culpability and are sometimes entirely exculpating, that many are not liable to punishment, and that even those who are morally liable to punishment because they have no excuse for participating nevertheless ought not, for pragmatic reasons, to be punished.[49]

And as Wertheimer himself points out, we can fully understand the war convention without relying on any notion of (genuine) combatant moral equality. "Combatant moral equality," he argues, "is not essential, let alone central, for rationalizing our collective, institutional responses to war conduct"(2007, 64).

But perhaps I have still focused too narrowly; perhaps what is ultimately at stake here is not the war convention, but the very system of international states whose conduct it regulates. That is, it will be said that a military willing to fight for and to take direction from its government is necessary even for the survival of a state, so if we are going to have an international society of states at all, we have to provide for the necessary preconditions, one of which is militaries willing —and morally permitted—to fight: states can only survive if their combatants have an equal moral right to kill. But if all combatants have an equal moral right to kill, then they do no wrong in killing (other combatants), and are therefore in this regard morally equal. States here are figured as the overriding good, which absolves their combatants of moral responsibility for war, and combatants are genuinely

---

48   See McMahan (2007b, 105) for some of the possible benefits of combatants caring about such issues.

49   McMahan (2007a, 50-51). As McMahan goes on to point out (51): "issues of culpability, punishment, and humane versus harsh treatment are all distinct from the moral equality of combatants, thought they tend to get run together in many discussions of the doctrine." Wertheimer (2007) comes to a conclusion similar to McMahan's – that "we have good reasons for not criminalizing aggressor combatant conduct" – though he rightly takes McMahan to task for characterizing such reasons as "merely" pragmatic (67). Cf. also McMahan (2006a, 25 and 38*ff*; 2006b).

morally equal, because of the role they play in the preservation of States. Much has been written about the importance of states, and of their role in preserving and safeguarding the rights of their members.[50] But of course not all states do an equally good job of safeguarding those rights, and in any case it is not clear that their existence requires letting their militaries off the moral hook.[51] In the first place, while the existence of States might require an equal right to fight defensive wars, it hardly requires a right to launch offensive, aggressive wars. Moreover, as history has shown, and as Taylor's cynicism cited above attests, combatants have often been willing to fight, even when they run the risk of being morally (and legally) condemned should they lose. The international system of states does not seem in imminent danger of collapse, even if we hold combatants responsible for the justice of their cause. So the same sort of consequentialist rationale does not seem to be available for the exemption of combatants from such considerations as operates in the case of lawyers. It is vitally important that someone defend even those who look—and perhaps are—guilty; it is far less clear that someone should fight even those wars that look—and so probably are—unjust. "Morally equal" combatants do not seem to play an essential role in a system that conduces to justice.

Structurally too, the two cases appear dissimilar. Lawyers are a part of the process that culminates in a (hopefully) just decision, whereas combatants stand at the end of the decision-making process (the decision to go to war—not, of course, the decision of who wins the war). In this way, they are perhaps more similar to executioners, who carry out the sentences handed down by the courts, or police officers, who enforce the laws.[52] Now at least as regards our own society, we do absolve executioners of those killings they commit, even if their victims turn out to have been innocent. And we do expect police officers to enforce the law, even if it is a law they happen not to agree with. Vitoria argues that "any doubt of mine about the justice of this war does not necessarily involve a doubt whether I ought to fight or serve in this war," but that I may nevertheless "lawfully serve in the field at my prince's command" (p. 177). For:

---

50   Thus cf. Vitoria: "The end and aim of war is the peace and security of the state" (p. 167). Also cf. Walzer (1970) for some more recent considerations.

51   And personally, I am worried about the hypostatization of states involved here and the attendant degradation of individuals. Indeed, I incline to a suspicion that this view of combatants as unable to adjudicate the rectitude of their nations' wars is a holdover from a bygone age in which combatants were considered to be little more than puppets, or perhaps extensions, of a monarch-as-state or state-as-monarch. But I lack the historical expertise fully to develop this claim. See McMahan (2007b, 96) for some of the dangers in this approach.

52   I owe the police analogy to Anthony Hartle; the example of the executioners (lictors) can be found in Vitoria.

[i]t is precisely the same as with a lictor who has his doubts whether the judge's decree is just, it does not follow therefrom that he doubts whether or no he ought to carry it into execution; he knows that he is bound to carry it into execution (p. 177).

But notice that even here a great deal turns on the particular case, and on how the case is described. If we think in terms of a police officer who happens not to agree with some particular law—a law banning prostitution, say—then we are perhaps inclined to think that he ought to enforce the law regardless of his personal views. But if we think in terms of an unjust law that does serious harm, then we are often not so sure. In fact, some laws and sentences, we feel, ought not be enforced. We admire those officers who refused to enforce Jim Crow laws in the South, and we condemn those officers who carried out state-ordered executions of Jews under the Nazi regime. More important still, perhaps, is how those laws and sentences were arrived at. That is, it matters a great deal whether those laws and sentences are the product of a system that is designed to and can reasonably be expected to achieve justice. In those cases, if any there be, where we think the enforcement of an unjust law or sentence is nevertheless required, it is only because we think there is something much more important at stake: social order or the continued functioning of a just system or the preservation of a free and democratic society.[53]

What all this shows is that there is no blanket immunity from having to concern oneself with questions of *jus ad bellum*, not even one that extends to all and only combatants. By now it is a commonplace that ignorance itself can be culpable. Sometimes, when people claim that "they didn't know," the only possible response is that they should have known, and in general it is not unreasonable to expect some minimal degree of diligence or awareness, especially where the application of lethal force is involved. Even when people are allowed simply to acquiesce in a decision handed down to them, this can only be because they have a reasonable belief that the decision is in fact a just one, or that failure to abide by it would have disastrous consequences (to the extent that they have any choice in the matter

---

53   This is perhaps the position of David Estlund. Estlund (2007) argues that given certain background conditions about the procedure that eventuated in the decision to go to war, a combatant is morally *obligated* to fight even in a war he knows to be unjust. The extremity of Estlund's position is perhaps somewhat ameliorated by his claim that the mistake must also be reasonable—not too far out of line with what is actually moral. But here it seems that what is actually at issue is a certain epistemic humility: if you are not absolutely certain that a given war is unjust, and if the right sort of decision procedure differs from you on the sort of thing about which reasonable people can disagree, then perhaps you had better assume your own fallibility, and give the state the benefit of the doubt. In the case where you *know* the war to be unjust, however, it seems to me that to the extent you have a choice, you ought not fight. At bottom, I simply do not share Estlund's fundamental intuition: that a jailer or an executioner has a moral duty to carry out a sentence she knows to be unjust, given that it is the product of an "honest mistake"—at least not without a further story about what higher good is at stake.

at all). Vitoria suggests that combatants may be "excused from sin by reason of good faith" (p. 177), but good faith requires more than just burying one's head in the sand, and combatants who fight knowingly and willingly in an unjust war are simply not the moral equals of those who do not.

Bibliography

Brough, Michael W. "Dehumanization of the Enemy and the Moral Equality of Soldiers." In *Rethinking the Just War Tradition.* eds Micheal W. Brough, John W. Lango, and Harry Van der Linden. Albany: SUNY Press, 2007.

Christopher, Paul. *The Ethics of War and Peace: An Introduction to Legal and Moral Issues*. Upper Saddle River, NJ: Prentice Hall, 1999.

Coates, A. J. *The Ethics of War*. Manchester and New York: Manchester University Press, 1997.

Estlund, David. "On Following Orders in an Unjust War." *The Journal of Political Philosophy* 15, no. 2 (2007): 213-34.

Hartle, Anthony E. *Moral Issues in Military Decision Making*. Lawrence, Kansas: University Press of Kansas, 1989.

Johnson, James Turner. *Morality and Contemporary Warfare*. New Haven: Yale University Press, 1999.

Kilner, Peter. "Military Leaders' Obligation to Justify Killing in War." *Military Review* (2002).

McMahan, Jeff. "The Ethics of Killing in War." *Philosophia* 34 (2006a): 23-41.

McMahan, Jeff. "Killing in War: A Reply to Walzer." Philosophia 34 (2006b): 47-51.

McMahan, Jeff. "On the Moral Equality of Combatants." *The Journal of Political Philosophy* 14, no. 4 (2006c): 377-93.

McMahan, Jeff. "Collectivist Defenses of the Moral Equality of Combatants." *Journal of Military Ethics* 6, no. 1 (2007a): 50-59.

McMahan, Jeff. "The Sources and Status of Just War Principles." *Journal of Military Ethics* 6, no. 2 (2007b): 91-106.

McPherson, Lionel K. "Innocence and Responsibility in War." *The Canadian Journal of Philosophy* 34, no. 4 (2005): 485-506.

Nozick, Robert. *Anarchy, State, and Utopia*. New York: Basic Books, 1974.

Orend, Brian. *War and International Justice: A Kantian Perspective*. Waterloo, Ontario: Wilfred Laurier Press, 2000.

Taylor, Maxwell D. "A Do-It-Yourself Professional Code for the Military." *Parameters: Journal of the U.S. Army War College* 10, no. 4 (1980): 10-15.

Tramel, Peter. "Voluntary Military Service and Conscientious Objection." Unpublished manuscript.

Vitoria, Francisco de. "De Indis Et De Iure Bellis Relationes." *On the Law of War*, ed. Ernest Nys, trans. John Pawley Bate. Washington, DC: 1917.

Walzer, Michael. *Obligations: Essays on Disobedience and Citizenship*. Cambridge, MA: Harvard University Press, 1970.

Walzer, Michael. *Just and Unjust Wars*. New York: Basic Books, 2000.

Walzer, Michael. "Response to McMahan's Paper." *Philosophia* 34 (2006): 43-45.

Wertheimer, Roger. "Reconnoitering Combatant Moral Equality." *Journal of Military Ethics* 6, no. 1 (2007): 60-74.

Zupan, Daniel. "The Logic of Community, Ignorance, and the Presumption of Moral Equality: A Soldier's Story." *Journal of Military Ethics* 6, no. 1 (2007): 41-9.

PART III
Jus ante Bellum

The Moral Singularity of Military Professionalism

Roger Wertheimer

Introduction

For the last century and more, professionalism has been the dominant concept of our military's self-image and self-ideal. Central to the concept of professionalism is a distinctive concept of responsibility: the concept of professional responsibilities. That general concept has both individualist and collectivist elements, and since militaries have a distinctive inherent collectivist dynamic, unlike other professions and other organizations, our military's conception of professional responsibilities has distinctive collectivist components.

This is not well understood by military professionals, so military professionalism is not well understood by them. That's partly because this is not well understood by military ethicists whose work should illuminate such matters. The available philosophical frameworks for understanding the moral character of military professionalism are well represented by the work of Michael Walzer and Richard Schoonhoven, whose contributions book end the prior chapters of this volume. In Walzer's case, I refer more to the work his present chapter refers to, his seminal *Just and Unjust Wars*[1] which promotes a collectivist conception of military responsibility that aims to explain and justify a moral principle he dubbed 'the moral equality of soldiers'. The framework Schoonhoven's contribution represents is implicit there and explicit in the extensive writings it cites of Jeff McMahan. Like McMahan, Schoonhoven denies the moral equality of combatants by relying on an insistently individualist conception of responsibility.[2]

---

1   Basic Books, 1977.

2   McMahan's individualism is encapsulated in his claim: "A war is nothing more than the constituent acts of those who fight it" (from an unpublished presentation at the 2006 Joint Services Conference on Professional Ethics). The schemata *X's are nothing but (no more than) Y's* is the standard formula of metaphysical *reductionism*, here regarding institutions (and their relations and activities) and elsewhere regarding the objects (relations, activities) of other metaphysical categories such as numbers, minds matter, meanings, properties and causation. Reductionist theses say that any truth about X's (nations, wars) can be restated without remainder in truths about Y's (individual persons and their actions). Such grand theses may initially seem truistic, with an appealing sleekness imparted by Occam's razor.

Their topic takes them to the heart of military professionalism, yet Walzer's and Schoonhoven's arguments (and those of McMahan and many others) hardly mention military professionalism at all. Their competing analyses jointly present the profound dilemma military professionals confront regarding their professional conduct when they believe their nation has no right to be warring. That ethos doesn't resolve the dilemma; it provides no coherent specific principle on this matter; it is irredeemably ambivalent and conflicted here. As the more reflective among them sometimes sense, military professionals really don't know what to believe about this matter.[3]

Moral Precariousness

The dilemma is rooted in the peculiar inherent precariousness of the morality of warrior work that distinguishes the practice of warrior skills from that of civilian professions and other respectable occupations. The ethical codes of civilian professions derive primarily from the specific ends and means of their work, its defining goals and appropriate activities for achieving those goals. The defining goals are distinctive benefits for the client, specific interests served, like restoration of health, acquisition of knowledge, and so on. The work of a professional has inherently valuable ends; it is well worth doing, and not just for the money. Further, the practice (the exercise of the professional skills, the activity attaining the goals) is normally benign. While achieving a legitimate professional goal may occasionally require harming someone, the client or others, generally the harms are mostly minor, incidental, and not inherent in the activity or its goal. In brief, professional codes of ethics presume that the profession's distinctive aims are laudable and its means are (normally) morally unproblematic.

In contrast, the warrior's goal is victory in violence. Victory never itself legitimates the violence. Only the cause for violence can do that. The warrior's skill and success are neutral among causes. Professional proficiency is measured by efficacy in battle, contribution to victory, not by the validity of the cause. Further, the work of the warrior is the deliberate infliction of the greatest evils on other persons, subjugation or death. Death, disablement, destruction of other

---

Things start getting hairy when reductionists try specifying the substantive import of their thesis. What common beliefs about wars would be false if wars are nothing but those individual acts? Wars are fights between nations, states, corporate entities whose identity does not seem to change just by changing the sets of specific individuals in combat (or holding political office or having citizenship). Individualists have yet to explain adequately how we can think and talk about wars without referring to entities whose identity does not change with changes in some set of specific individuals.

3   This is finely expressed in Col. Daniel Zupan's "The Logic of Community, Ignorance, and the Presumption of Moral Equality: A Soldier's Story." *Journal of Military Ethics* 6, no. 1 (2007): 41-9.

people's goods, these are not inessential, incidental or peripheral consequences of military activity; these are the effects the warrior's tools and skills are specifically designed to cause. Absent some extrinsic legitimation, acts having such effects are monstrous, howling wrongs. In sum, the distinctive expertise of the profession of arms is a skill at causing intrinsic moral evils that cry for justification, while the profession's inherent goal is morally neutral.[4]

That sounds awful, and in the word's root sense it is, but it is not an indictment or criticism of the military. It's no ethical defect, no cause for shame or embarrassment that its work is inherently morally risky. Warring cannot but be a nasty, ghastly business, and it is very liable to be a great crime. There's no way around that.

This is a sensitive matter, frequently misunderstood and fiercely resisted, so though the point is plain and simple we need to dwell on this awhile to dispel some common distracting confusions. Throughout keep in mind that the problem presented is not whether warrior work is justifiable, but how, and the point thus far is only that the framework of functionalist reasoning applicable to civilian professions cannot work for military professionals.

Now, while some have denied it, we can take as a given that someone's got to fight our battles and do our killing for us. The military has the grand, grim duty of defending the nation, and to that end the killing and destruction may be necessary, justifiable, righteous work, worthy of great honor and glory. Military might has other uses no less noble, like the defense of allies and of the oppressed in humanitarian interventions. Certainly, the goods of protecting human health and life attained by medical work may also be attained by warrior work—and the work of plumbers and computer technicians—but those goods are *extrinsic* to these non-medical occupations. Those goods are internal to medical practice; the tools and skills of that practice are designed specifically to achieve those goals, and they are evaluated by their proficiency in that pursuit. Those goods do not guide the design of grenades and napalm bombs, or the development of skills in their effective employment. The warrior's tools and attendant skills are evaluated and evaluable by their proficiency, not in saving lives, but in causing death and destruction. And, note well, in the development and evaluation of the tools and skills, the identity of the victims is irrelevant.

Nothing here devalues national security as the paramount proper use of a nation's military, but no such extrinsic, distal goal identifies the military's distinctive nature or explains the distinctive character of its proper professional ethics. National security is an umbrella rubric, an "interest" threatened or affected

---

4   Contrast with the police, a paramilitary defense force against internal aggression. Police are agencies of *law enforcement*. That is a presumptively objective, impersonal good. The enemy within is a criminal whose behavior is presumptively wrongful and must be controlled. Our external enemies are not morally disadvantaged by any such impartial presumption. Further, while police may resort to violence to accomplish their mission, usually they need not and commonly do not use violence—let alone lethal force—or other presumptively condemnable means.

by a dysfunctional economic or educational system and other factors outside the military purview. The military is distinguished not by its serving that interest, but by its serving that interest—and others—*by violence* (destructive power, lethal force) or its threat. More precisely, *de facto* and *de jure*, our military's essential function is to further, by violence or its threat, what its government leaders deem to be the nation's interest. It cannot defend without a capacity to aggress. Both capabilities are available for service. The military's essential nature isn't revised or reduced by deploying it only for legitimate defensive purposes, no more than the nature of a gun shrinks by firing it only at paper targets.[5]

Predictably, these truisms are persistently obscured by double talk. Hard upon our WWII triumphs, it was a neat piece of Orwellian newspeak to rename the U.S. Department of War the "Department of Defense". The old name was too ominous for the department controlling the newly world dominant military of a self-professed non-imperialistic nation. The re-baptism signaled no shift or restriction of basic functions. The department's core purpose remained to use lethal force to conquer, subdue or otherwise enforce the cooperation of other peoples (Indians, Mexicans, Filipinos, Central Americans, Vietnamese, Afghanistanis, Iraqis and the rest) to serve politically influential American interests—annexing the conquered territory when convenient or otherwise effectively controlling it without occupying or colonizing it. Engagements to repel an invasion of the homeland are singular. Clear compliance with principles of justice has been occasional, and often almost coincidental.

The renaming was motivated by political realities; it didn't revise them. Legislation restricting military activities to "defense" is also subject to revision by political realities, as Japan's shipping soldiers to Iraq shows. Terms like "national security" and "defense" have virtually unlimited rhetorical elasticity, readily expanded from repelling a territorial incursion to protecting any of a people's interests, legitimate or not, and on to proactively promoting any such interest—till we get a government proclaiming that defense of our nation necessitates invasion of a distant, militarily crippled nation that is not attacking us, nor equipped to, nor preparing to (since any attempt would be a national-suicide bombing)—nor really seeming to. Overtly or covertly revising the definition of "national security"

---

5   Whether combat (actual or threatened) occurs in something properly called a "war" or something "other than war" matters little here. Shifts in the specific warrior skills most needed and honored may influence the flavor of a military's ethos, but not its core. However, for military and police agencies alike, the equipment and skills acquired for proficiency in their defining mission make them the natural go-to-guys for all kinds of situations remote from that mission, and this inevitable systemic mission creep has its costs, immediate and long term. Bearing arms may be prudent to discourage violence when resolving family disputes and delivering humanitarian aid, but it may also provoke violence or otherwise risk poisoning the atmosphere and making the mission more difficult. In any event, routinizing such missions may strain the personnel's preferred self-image as warriors or crime-fighters, and tax morale. The consequences for the occupational ethos may be substantial but cannot be explored here.

or "defense" may inspire or require revision of terms defining it or defined by it. When our political and media propagandists first allege that preventive war is justified as a necessary defensive strategy against terrorists, and then designate as "terrorist" all who combat our invasion and occupation of their homeland, our propagandists nicely preempt the use of "offensive" or "aggressive" to condemn any military act we indulge in.[6]

The all too prevalent current characterizations of warrior work in such terms as "defense" only mask the moral precariousness of that work. Such stipulations hope to remove the troubling precariousness by treating a possible extrinsic good of the activity as an essential intrinsic good that secures its justification. This hollow verbal victory turns a whole cluster of terms like "warrior", "military", "armed forces", etc., into honorifics whose application is as contestable as the determination of the goal some agent or agency is pursuing, and it kicks down the road what to call those exercising the same skills in the same kind of activity for other purposes. Such stipulations are unsustainable: they inevitably motivate an expansion of the definiens, "defense", to make the definiendum "warrior" apply much as before, and that makes the imputed intrinsic goal into something that justifies nothing.

The morally precarious position of the military has only dismal civilian counterparts.[7] That position is not the lot of lawyers with professional obligations to serve their client's interests in legal "battles", despite the unrighteousness of the client's cause and the losses for others. The adversarial character of the legal profession is unusual for civilian professions and unlike a military's adversarial nature in many morally significant respects. First off, much legal work is not adversarial or a threat to anyone's interest (e.g., writing wills, negotiating mutually agreeable arrangements), and it is often adversarial without damaging anyone (society benefits when it unsuccessfully prosecutes innocent persons), and even when the outcome damages one party, the legal proceedings themselves are not inherently condemnable: they needn't discomfit anyone, beyond, perhaps, embarrassing a witness. Beyond all that, the "battles" of legal adversaries are

---

6   Cf. David Rodin's *War and Self-Defense* (Oxford, 2002), which debunks the commonly assumed conjunction in its title.

7   The closest civilian counterpart is the work of executioners. The telling contrast is that government executioners in our tradition have commonly preferred anonymity, often wearing masks when they work in public. Our culture has rarely celebrated these workers even when riotously celebrating a hanging or beheading. Our warriors are not to be executioners. Nowadays they are prohibited from killing disabled prisoners. (Nuremburg war criminals had civilian executioners.) An executioner's proficiency may win admiration from her peers but not public adulation and glory. Killing someone bound and disabled needs minimal skill. Opportunities for displaying courage, heroism or much else beyond conscientiousness and self-mastery or callousness are exceptional, occasioned by some broken routine. Society pays executioners a fair wage, convinced that this work is worth it, that it must be done. Society cannot well call it dishonorable work. But it doesn't honor it either. Even when deemed needed, it seems ignoble.

regulated by rules and policies—including their professional code—designed (imperfectly) to promote the discovery of truth and the justice of the result. By contrast, the war rules within which warriors today work do not, in intent or effect, favor those with justice on their side or disadvantage aggressors. Instead, current war conventions prohibit the pursuit of natural justice and the punishment of captive combatants, however deserved it may be. Nations wisely sign on because generally every nation benefits, aggressors and defenders, victors and vanquished. In this respect our war rules are insistently amoral.

And so are our codes of military professionalism. Civilian professional skill put to an ignoble purpose (as when a physician masterminds undetected murders) is a perversion of the profession, a misuse of those skills. A warrior's dutiful service in wrongful aggression is rarely deemed dishonorable, let alone "unprofessional".

Again, the moral precariousness of warrior work is not that practitioners may find themselves ordered to do something god awful. That circumstance may equally befall the nonmilitary government personnel under a vicious regime. The profession of arms is morally problematic because, unlike civilian professions and other government work, there is a very clear and very strong moral presumption against its primary activity. That presumption is overcome when a warrior fights on the side of justice. That fact further locates the precariousness of the warrior's position and doesn't eliminate it. The problem confronting military professionals is not that of *jus ad bellum*, the problem of whether and when nations may rightly war. The warrior's question is not whether and when individual warriors, acting like mini-nations, may rightly duel or privately battle to death. Rather, the question is whether a society's warriors may justifiably do their work *when and because their government so commands*.

If military professionalism is modeled on civilian professionalism the answer must be: no. Civilian professionals are autonomous agents; the decision to ply their skills is not outside their control. No contract or oath can—legally or morally—bind a civilian professional to maim and kill innocent (non-aggressing) people; no such commitment eliminates or much reduces the agent's legal and moral accountability. The agent might have some justification or excuse for doing whatever she is bidden if she could reasonably believe that her client/employer would never direct her to participate in a heinous wrong. As things are, no one can reasonably believe that about any nation.

Certainly, it matters that a warrior is serving her nation rather than making a living as a mercenary. The question remains: how does that matter, given that elsewhere a governmental directive does not by itself suffice to justify compliance independent of any consideration of its righteousness? Military victory is not an impersonal good like health or knowledge. It is inherently a good for the victor, and inherently an evil for the vanquished, so it is inherently morally unlike health and knowledge. Other people don't have your reasons for improving your health or your knowledge, but no one need have any reason to oppose your attainment of those goods. The asymmetry here is crucial. The partiality civilian professionals can or must have regarding their clients' good is consonant with universalist principles of justice. A warrior's partiality for her people may be unproblematic within a tribal morality. How a warrior's lethal partiality is compatible with the universalist principles of justice of our culture is a profoundly troubling puzzle.

This last point is crucial. The moral precariousness of warrior work—the amorality of its distinctive goal and the presumptive immorality of its distinctive means—is inherent to the activity, universal for all mankind (and extraterrestrials), but it does not present the same problem for all societies, or anyway, what comes to the same, the available responses differ profoundly.[8]

Many a warrior of yore was proudly unmerciful to disabled and defeated enemies deemed to have served an unjust cause. World-wide, pre-professional warriors have often been enthusiastically ruthless, glorying in plundering, pillaging, raping, enslaving, massacring, torturing, untroubled by any doubt that the victor may despoil the vanquished at his pleasure. More often than not, much of such mischief has been blessed and motivated by communal moral codes. However horrendous, the suffering was often inflicted as punishment, judged fully deserved. Its justice was often the roughest, assigning collective guilt, unmindful of the unwillingness of anyone's participation and contribution in the alleged wrong. Its spirit might be hot vengeance or cold pragmatic calculation or self-righteous retribution or holy obligation. Clear-eyed warriors have deliberately drawn buckets of excessive blood, unnecessary for victory, seen the blood on their very own hands and did not distance themselves from it or feel dirtied by it.

Some warriors have respected the correlative thought and refused to practice their deadly craft for morally repugnant causes. This too has been urged and honored by some cultures. Whatever the statistical frequency of such sentiments, they are stirred by principles of moral responsibility whose nub has as much (and as little) natural, universal appeal as the Golden Rule. These natural moral sentiments may be repressed but not readily obliterated. Whatever a culture's warrior code may commend, a warrior with an open mind or a healthy human heart is vulnerable to the thought that his life might be befouled by his killing people for reasons he cannot respect. That thought is not antithetical to military professionalism. It is elemental to the ambivalence inherent in its ethos.

Moral Singularity

In our culture the moral precariousness of the military has motivated a great range of conceptions of *the moral singularity of warriors* expressed in some reluctance

---

8 Many dream of the day when the world is rightly ruled by some single legitimate authority whose military polices our Earth and brings to justice any who disturb its peace or threaten its order. Among its bounty of boons, in this fantasy the moral precariousness of warriors disappears since this military has become a law enforcement agency whose personnel are police. (Cf. note 3 *supra*.) However realistic this possibility, it suggests no solution of the moral worries of current military professionals.

or resistance to regard someone's moral responsibility for service in condemnable warfare in the very same way we regard a person's moral responsibility for complicity in other horrendous injustices.[9] People, in and out of the military, commonly feel that such service is, at minimum, not dishonorable. Attitudes on this vary widely, and while they are generally vague and inchoate, their differences may be gross or finely nuanced. At one extreme, some people feel that (almost) any refusal to serve is dishonorable. At another extreme, others think themselves morally obliged to refuse service in an unjustified war and to publicly condemn the war and the political leaders and to laud those who eventually condemn themselves for their service—yet even such conscientious objectors are commonly reluctant to condemn those who never condemn themselves for their service.

Such conceptions may be expressed in various ways. As noted earlier, while civilian professionals are said to act unprofessionally when they put their skills to evil ends, this is not said of warriors. Further, such conceptions have varied along many dimensions. Among the most salient (historically, conceptually, and morally) is their degree and kind of universalism. Nothing truly comparable to Walzer's idea of combatant "moral equality" is available without a background acceptance of (some version of) the universalist egalitarianism that took hold in the Enlightenment.

Walzer's conception of warrior moral singularity is extreme in many respects: its egalitarianism, its simplicity, its incoherence. In essence, it says, for example, that while the nation and political leaders of Japan had no right to kill Americans at Pearl Harbor, and no right to command Japanese pilots to kill those Americans, nonetheless those pilots had the right to kill those Americans just because they were so commanded. That claims defies comprehension.[10] Happily, we have no

---

9   Throughout I let fly grand historical hypothesis with the unscholarly abandon of other philosophers who presume the propriety of arm chair social science that offers illuminating connections among familiar, apparently scattered facts. In the present instance, I rest with a challenge to those friends of the military skeptical of its moral precariousness to explain the popularity of conceptions of its moral singularity.

10   There's no end to the conceptual and moral dilemmas here. Walzer claims to believe that the American soldiers' and sailors' right to life was not violated by the Japanese pilots. He supposes they were *wronged* (if at all) only *by* the leaders, not by the pilots, because those pilots were executing the commands of their nation's legitimate authorities. That makes no sense unless those pilots are regarded as nothing more than weapons guidance mechanisms by which their leaders achieved their aims—but that makes it nonsensical to say that those pilots had a right to kill their targets, or to attribute any rights at all to them. Apparently, Walzer (and McMahan too, but not Schoonhoven) thinks we must think and talk this way to make sense of our war conventions and traditional principles of jus in bello presuppose this conception. Actually, our established laws and dominant moral doctrines make perfect sense—historically, politically, legally, morally and conceptually—apart from any close variant of Walzer's conception. The whole notion of combatants having a *legal right* to kill (assault, maim, imprison, etc) misconceives international law, for the alleged "right" is devoid of any legal content or consequence. The sole suggestion of such a legal right is the

need to try to make some sense of it, since nothing remotely like it is needed to make good sense of the war conventions and principles of *jus ad bellum* and *jus in bello* Walzer accepts along with most reasonable people today. Walzer cannot himself really believe what he says. His blanket absolution of moral responsibility for a combatant's contributions to horrendous evils directly entails the denial of *any possibility of* justified conscientious objection to military service. That implication is utterly unpalatable to Walzer (and most reasonable people), but it is the sole significant import of his principle. The whole subject of warrior moral singularity has near nothing to do with war conventions, crimes and institutional sanctions and everything to do with sin, conscience, and our extra-institutional interpersonal and intrapersonal attitudes and relations. That is how Augustine conceived this matter, and why this matter goes to the heart of professional military ethics.

Schoonhoven's criticisms of Walzeresque conceptions of warrior moral singularity are persuasive partly because they are commonsensical. As such they make it understandable why many a modern officer may be leery of Walzeresque conceptions of their moral singularity which salvage their honor by sacrificing their self respect, threatening their proud conception of themselves as professionals, morally responsible for their professional conduct. The flip side of this is that Schoonhoven leaves us wondering how it could be that (as he observes) many (perhaps most) military professionals, including relatively thoughtful ones teaching at the academies, profess some conception of their moral singularity, perhaps less elegant and extreme than Walzer's, but still quite robust.

While Schoonhoven does not offer some alternative, minimalist conception of warrior moral singularity, he may represent the outer limit of positions within that range for he does not rule out the possibility of some such singularity. He is more cautious than ethicists like McMahan who suppose that any moral attitude that appears to regard a warrior's moral responsibility as special in some way must be either indefensible or defensible by the same principles, concepts, and kinds of reasoning we properly employ regarding all other matters of moral

---

prohibition of the punishment or any abuse of captive combatants. Yet, what has actually motivated and fully justified governments around the world to establish and maintain that prohibition are considerations of national self-interest entirely independent of any idea of combatant moral equality or a right of all combatants to kill one another. Further, all this must also be said regarding those pilots killing 68 American civilians at Pearl Harbor. Some if not all of those civilians are paradigm cases of noncombatant casualties of aggression decriminalized by our war conventions. We prohibit punishing the pilots for those killings just as we prohibit punishing them for killing uniformed personnel, and for much the same reasons of national self-interest. On Walzer's reading (which McMahan accepts) our war rules and *jus in bello* orthodoxy must suppose that the pilots had a legal and moral right to kill those noncombatants (albeit unintentionally) and did not wrong them. Worse yet, those victims cannot even be the "moral equals" of their assailants, for they can have no right to assail their assailants except by forfeiting their "protected" status as noncombatants. These and most all of my criticisms of Walzer are explained more fully in my "Reconnoitering Combatant Moral Equality," *Journal of Military Ethics* 6, no. 1 (2007).

responsibility, so the apparent singularity is sheer illusion. Anyway, in practical terms, Schoonhoven's main disagreement with McMahan is not insignificant but not significant enough. For both, the moral responsibility of military professionals differs from that of civilian professionals not at all or only in degree. McMahan might allow some minimal presumption favoring a warrior's compliance with a governmental directive to serve. Schoonhoven seems sympathetic to a somewhat stronger but still anemic presumption unacceptable by his military professional colleagues.

The dilemma for military professionals is that neither Walzer nor Schoonhoven/McMahan offers an acceptable option, yet those are the only available philosophical frameworks. Western philosophy provides no alternative that makes sense of some compromise. It is principally our philosophical heritage—particularly the universalist, egalitarian, cosmopolitan, humanitarian, liberal, individualism emerging in the Enlightenment -- that has made the military's moral precariousness a peculiarly acute and apparently irresolvable problem.

Enlightenment Influences

Considered geopolitically, the Enlightenment begins with the mid-17th century Westphalian renunciation of religious warfare and the recognition of states as sovereign national communities. It culminates in the early 19th century rise of military professionalism and the civilian control of the military that professionalism promotes. That development may be well conceived as the Enlightenment's dialectical response to its intensification of a cultural and political problem made specially pressing by the Peace of Westphalia: the problem of military fealty. When a military and its personnel are alienated from religious motivations, and the nation they serve is a political fiction, an artifact of state sovereignty lacking the unifying communal bonds of kinship and common culture, then the problem of securing military loyalty to political leaders (a problem for [almost?] any human society) faces unprecedented challenges. The instability of that political condition is aggravated as a culture becomes increasingly individualist, liberal, skeptical of authority, resistant to it and resentful of it, and increasingly responsive to the callings of a transnational, trans-political common humanity.

America's military is a creature of a novel culture whose self-conception is documented by a resounding expression of Jeffersonian liberal egalitarianism. The unmistakable Enlightenment spirit shining through its founding documents has kept a steady pressure on the nation's laws and every dimension of culture. That pressure will always meet push-back from religions with imperialistic inclinations or ritual practices condemned by a conception of people as free and equal responsible lives. But most religions feel unthreatened by Enlightenment principles most of the time, for those principles protect religions from one another and enable them to flourish. Our humanist, egalitarian liberalism is inherently at odds, not with religion, but with the military and the ethos demanded by its organizational imperatives. The organizational totalitarianism needed for military proficiency is a massive, systematic violation of Jeffersonian democracy, its civil laws and social codes. Enlightenment principles do tolerate and sponsor the military's radical subordination of citizens in its ranks, because—and only insofar as—it is necessary to protect and benefit the civilian world. Our heritage had largely left its military leaders *carte blanche* to create and run a proficient military modeled originally on European militaries with centuries of aristocratic heritage. Over the last half century the civil government (executive, legislative, and judicial), often responding to civilian movements, has taken closer and closer control of the military, and called for justification of military practices and traditions in every corner of its culture. That trend is likely to accelerate.

Members of our military enter it with the consciences born of their national civilian culture and personal subcultures. Military training must reform that mindset to function effectively in an authoritarian agency. That is an imperative inherent in the nature of a military organization. Another imperative comes from military professionalism's commitment to the military's subordination to the civil government it serves: military culture must evolve within the evolving civilian culture, respect it and stay subordinate to it.

The conscience Professional Military Ethics Education (PMEE) must shape must continuously struggle with the civilian conscience from which it springs, respecting it while resisting it, sometimes envying or admiring it, sometimes straining to tolerate it, sometimes enhancing itself by taking civilian ideas and practices on board and redesigning them to accommodate the military's organizational imperatives. One consequence of this complexity is that the military conscience commonly sees its moral challenges and frames its inner conflicts in ways that may be opaque for civilians. Another consequence is that that conscience is susceptible to self-delusion due to the illusion of transparency natural to self-consciousness. Among its inner imperatives is a demand for unity, in thought and deed, throughout the organization. That demand is energized by its needs for decisiveness, confidence, certainty, simplicity—a cluster of concerns predisposing the military mind to suppose that it has some single, unified, coherent ethos and the primary purpose of PMEE is to transmit it. A pervasive assumption controlling its response to the moral conflicts it confronts is that its ethos is under attack from some hostile, alien ideology, so it must marshal its forces to crush this opponent. That is dangerously wrongheaded. The "enemy" is within.

Military professionalism is the Enlightenment's Trojan horse within the fortress of the military's ethos. The military wheeled that "enemy" in, transformed it and transformed itself by professionalizing itself. The military is constrained from without by the Enlightenment strains of the civilian culture it serves; it is pulled from within by its commitment to an occupational ethos born of that culture. It has encouraged professionalism for its Enlightenment spirit of scientific rationality to improve technical proficiency. Those habits of open critical inquiry—dissatisfied with dogma and skeptical of the epistemic authority of tradition and organizational authority—transfer to its ethical thought. Here the ethos of professionalism turns schizoid. A true professional internalizes the attitudes, values and principles appropriate for her occupation, so the military professional must somehow integrate a flexible, liberated intellectual spirit with the rigid, authoritarian mindset of militarism. Many aspects of this conflict are controversial, but its existence is widely recognized. Other implications of professionalism are not.

With the end of aristocracy came the end of officership as the aristocratic occupation, and with the rise of liberal egalitarianism came a pervasive meritocracy and conceptions of dignified labor that award prestige and social status to occupations called *professions*. The term and its cognates are generally honorific, so their precise connotations are variable and controversial. Nowadays virtually every occupational grouping aspires to this aristocracy of employment.

Professionalization of the military has been a target and a mission, with skirmishes, battles, and marketing campaigns, in America and abroad since the 19th century. Military academies have, perforce, been prime targets and theatres of these campaigns, because professionalization means nothing without systemized education and training. Professional Military Education (PME) must satisfy the demands inherent in professionalism within the constraints of the military's organizational imperatives. That complex demand must control every policy and program of PME, especially every aspect and detail of PMEE.

Professionalism is an Enlightenment spirit of occupational self-improvement, with two primary concerns, the cultivation of competence and the promotion of an ethos of its proper employment. Professionalizing the military resembles professionalizing other occupations in its raising the standards of skill and the competence of practitioners. As elsewhere, the big money for professionalizing goes to improving expertise, the technical skills that increase proficiency. Professionalization of the military ethos is not funded or manned on the scale of training programs for fighter pilots. It does not command that attention or invite the same cold, questioning eyes.

Still, as elsewhere, the ethos of professionalism motivates its own transmission. It presses for developing practitioners who exercise their expertise with professional integrity. Professionalizing the military's ethos resembles other professionalizations in this and other important respects. All professional codes are alike at some level of abstraction and generality. Professionalism always opposes an amoral spirit of unconstrained technical proficiency and bottom-line cost-benefit effectiveness. Military professionalism is no less morally serious; it is deadly serious about its codes. Civilian professional codes rarely have incompatible principles or values. They differ in their focus and emphasis. Each professional code is contoured to accommodate the profession's distinctive goals, expertise and circumstances. Normally, the contouring comes from directly applying general ethical principles applicable to everyone to the distinctive general features of an occupation. Not so for the military. Its moral reasoning must take a different route.

If the morality of military professionalism is modeled on that of civilian professionalism, our military is in a morally untenable position. The ethos of professionalism has been, as it had to be, retrofitted for military operations. *Militaries are professionalized by militarizing professionalism.*

Civilian Control

American foreign policy promotes the professionalization of all militaries, not just those of our allies. It employs its military professionals to assist other nations to this end—despite the evident dangers of increasing the proficiency of all militaries in developing and applying massive lethal force. The intent is to foster intra-national—and thereby, inter-national—political stability by converting others to our own military's professional code, whose First Commandment is: Stay out of politics. Governments anxious about their military's fealty submit them to professionalization.[11]

Military professionalism is premised on the civilian control of the military. Professionalism in the military is in the service of the political *status quo*. Whether this be desirable or deplorable is debatable, but it means that military professionals are walled off from the political world civilian professionals inhabit. Our culture systematically circumscribes their practical reasoning about their professional conduct. Their moral reasoning about their political relations is censured when they presume to deliberate with the unfettered reasoning of civilians.

The term 'military professionalism' may mislead, since we do call a politically independent organization of numerous skilled practitioners of martial arts an *army*, a *military*. A private army may be well moved to promote its self-improvement and publicize it as "professionalization" for its instituting higher standards of practitioner performance, improving the training and testing of skills, and inculcating a warrior ethos fit for a Jeffersonian democracy, a civilian warrior ethos. Since militaries share some basic, broad organizational imperatives which put a premium on certain skills and character traits, our PMEE might profitably consider the proper ethos for such civilian warriors, and our military might reasonably reform its ethos upon learning how a private military markedly improved proficiency by adjusting its ethos and altering some practices. However, various factors limit our military's interest in such social experiments.[12] In particular, the institutionalized decoupling of the military from civil politics is no adventitious plank in the platform of the

---

11   Cf. http://www.caii.com/CAIIStaff/Dashboard_GIROAdminCAIIStaff/Dashboard_ CAIIAdminDatabase/resources/ghai/toolbox6.htm.

12   For example, a professional ethos is determined importantly by the profession's distinctive skills. Far more than with other crafts, the concept of *warrior skills* is an empty abstraction apart from some specified tool kit. Many medical skills of ancient practitioners are still relevant in high tech health care, but nuclear submarine commanders have little call for expertise at hand-to-hand combat. The means of killing many people is a markedly more odd lot assortment of tools and actions than the means of achieving the goals of other professions like restoring health or imparting knowledge. No private army could be allowed

military professionalization movement. It is the cornerstone of our military's professional ethics. Whatever the military advantages of a civilian warrior code (or anything else) its features are adoptable by our military only insofar as they are adaptable to the moral constraints imposed by our military's political condition.

As a modifier of 'professionalization' and its cognates, "military" applies solely to a governmental agency, specifically, the agency empowered to develop and deliver massive deadly force. Civilian professions are not agencies. In the U.S., the medical profession is not the AMA; elsewhere it is not the national health service employing all practitioners. At its core a profession is a skill set, a valuable expertise. Generally, would be clients (beneficiaries of the skill) might be almost any person or organization, civil or government, in this or any nation. As such, professions have an apolitical or trans-political character. On the other hand, professions have an inherent tendency to organize and engage in political activity. And whatever their affiliation with or participation in such organizations, our civilians professionals have the rights and responsibilities of citizens of a Jeffersonian democracy.

Since the military's subordination to the civil government was codified in America's Constitution before it professionalized its military, that subordination may seem much the same as that for all citizens, just a matter of obeying the law. That similarity is a bare abstraction. Our nation's military is a state sustained semi-autonomous world, with its own legal order, culture and ethos.

Statutory law assigns active-duty military personnel a distinct civic status. They are not civilians. They are denizens of a totalitarian dictatorship welcomed within a liberal democracy as long as the people believe that the totalistic subordination is needed for their own peace and security. Military professionals have markedly less participation in the civic order and processes separate from their professional lives. Around and within the statutory structure has grown a richly textured heritage, having pre-professional roots, of rules, customs and expectations—official and unofficial—defining the whole public "conduct becoming" military personnel in general, and particularly the officers. Their professional responsibilities pervasively constrain their public conduct, in uniform and out. Military professionals respect all that and wholeheartedly embrace it. They know that no civilian profession, individual or organization, has comparable capabilities for challenging or defying civil authority. Professional officers take pride in not being civilians and being subordinate to the civic order. (Some military professionals have made it a point of honor to not exercise their right to vote.) That pride honors their dreadful power. In return, society honors them and glorifies them as long as they faithfully serve their government.

This civilian control is a social contract.[13] With its unsurpassable potential for political mischief, the military must be denied all opportunity and any right

---

command of any more than a miniature of our military's armamentarium. That massive difference in power sustains markedly different tones of martial spirit.

13   Cf. Zupan, *Ibid.*

—and thus any obligation—to participate in the political process determining the deployment of their power, except as technical advisors regarding their capabilities, limitations, likelihood of success, risks and costs of failure, and the like. Military professionals subordinate their will to the government, the legal authority of the society. They subordinate their political will, surrendering the rights and responsibilities of citizens to influence their government to do what they believe is right. They subordinate their professional will, surrendering the rights and responsibilities of autonomous agents to influence their employers to employ them properly, in a manner they may be rightly proud of. They wear a uniform marking their release from civil society and their subordination within a state sustained totalitarian organization that commands absolute obedience to their superiors, even in the face of death. All this is thought legitimated by providing the personnel an (allegedly) reasonably fair deal. The state supplies their basic material needs (food, clothing, shelter, health care), a living wage, and a retirement pension (below the civilian pay scale.) It supplies their psychic needs by sustaining both a military culture that exalts their work, fosters pride in themselves and their occupation, and also a civic culture that respects, honors and glorifies them and their ethos, and holds them blameless for faithfully serving the nation. In sum, our society strips those in uniform of responsibility for their contributions to state sponsored deadly force, and compensates for this divestiture by sustaining a culture honoring that divestiture.

Understandably, many military professionals have presumed it absolute and axiomatic that they are not to be in the business of determining whether there is due cause for their killing people in their professional capacity. That extreme conception of their moral singularity is not a dogma of military professionalism. As with many other compatible or competing conceptions of that singularity, military professionalism neither commands it nor condemns it. Instead, it both encourages that belief and discourages it. That belief is encouraged by a culture commanding an absolute, unquestioning respect for subservience to the civilian order. However what exactly is required by such respect—whether it mandates some unquestioning acceptance of the wisdom and justice of civilian directives—is open to question. That idea is called into question by professionalism's Enlightenment ideals and principles of autonomy, open inquiry, and individual responsibility.

The conflict here exemplifies the basic structure of the inherent ambivalence within military professionalism. Still, the cognitive, motivational, and emotional character of that ambivalence remains an abstraction without some accounting of some other salient peculiarities of the military. The remainder of this essay is devoted to providing that account, but the subject is immense, so the account here is only a beginning, a sketch. Throughout my intent is to understand before presuming to criticize and reform. The occasional sharp comments that may sound censorial are meant to jolt some recognition of some questionable features of this ethos, but not to answer those questions.

Collectivization

Recall, the ethos of military professionals is structured by its subservience to the professionalization of the military, a corporate government agency. Membership in a civilian profession is awarded for acquiring a distinctive expertise. The professional code is designed to bind and guide those and only those exercising the profession's distinctive expertise. But membership in the military profession comes from membership in a professionalized military, a nation's warrior agency. That agency needs some personnel with advanced warrior skills, but it also needs many personnel with civilian skills who will not need any warrior skills. Military professional codes are designed to bind and guide all and only the uniformed members of a nation's military, whatever their skills and expertise or lack thereof.

Civilian professionals submit to their military's professional code as an additional code when plying their skills in military service. Being a military doctor (lawyer, etc.) is not comparable to practicing two civilian professions like medicine and law. The activity as a military professional is not an additional concurrent employment, and not an employment of martial skills but only the practice of a civilian profession as a uniformed member of an agency whose function is military. (Indeed, a military's medical and priestly professionals are debarred by law from deploying martial skills in combat operations.) Such civilian professionals may be licensed as military professionals by their commissioning as military officers. That status commits them to the professional code without assuming or implying their possession of any warrior skills or knowledge.

So too for their fellow professionals who have and employ expertise in warfare. Fleet admirals and infantry sergeants aren't military professionals by dint of warrior skills, not unless their warrior's will is subordinate to the state. They are held to their warrior code, not for having or employing warrior skills, but for their employment by a warrior agency. Military professionalism would be largely unfazed by out-sourcing to civilians all but the tasks employing martial expertise. There would remain the ambivalence in our military ethos between the ethos of civilian professionalism and the ethos of a warrior agency.[14]

---

14   The centrality of the organization in military professionalization gets expressed in the current idiom of our soldiers, who now find it natural to talk of their membership in, not (just) the *military profession*—aka *the profession of arms*—but (also or instead) the *Army Profession*. That term *sounds* weird to civilian ears; its meaning is not immediately grasped. Soldiers write essays wondering whether the Army is an organization or a profession. (The question is repeatedly discussed in essays of the USMA anthology, *The Future of the Army Profession*, ed. Lloyd J. Matthews, McGraw-Hill, 2002.) The answer is that the profession is the organization. No comparable question arises in civilian professions; no sense can be made of the question in that context.

Intrusion

But as things are, an additional strain is there to be felt by the many officers and enlisted personnel having no combat functions and no need or possession of a distinctively warrior expertise. PMEE policy has been to imbue everyone in uniform with a single shared ethos, not just a code of conduct, but a spirit, temperament, sense of self, valuations of activities and character traits, etc.—all of which are fitted for their contribution to the proficiency of people engaged in battles to the death. Few in uniform feel strained living by a shared ethic's behavioral do's and don'ts, but much of the military ethos relegates the non-warriors to a second-class status. The codes of those doing the same non-warrior work in civvies spotlight virtues other than those exalted in warriors. The PMEE we know trains personnel to live by and live up to the military's ethos, whatever its disconnections from the non-warriors' work and the kind of person they need to be to do it well and take pride in their own abilities, accomplishments, and their whole person.

Our military anxiously rubs this sore spot, roaring reaffirmations over and over that everyone in uniform is a warrior. Some non-warriors happily hear their cog-like lives so glorified and romanticized—and snap umbrageously at assaults on their self image. Others are not so able to fool themselves. They hear the authority's words and feel a disconnect with their own day-to-day lives. They may ignore the noise when they can, and wrestle with cynicism and resentment. Meanwhile, properly proud warriors are frequently, fiercely unempathetic. They are comfortable in their own skins, living a reality confirming their self confidence.

The military has its reasons for insistently instilling the self-identification of warriors uniformly, in everyone wearing the uniform. Armies and navies in battle live off a secure communal sense of totally invigorated togetherness. That disposition for the warriors' shared shout appears to improve military proficiency. Yet, all the repetitive emphasis on this shared self-conception seems indicative of anxiety about how well the teaching is taking—a disconcerting result when the teaching gets treated as self-evident, not open for doubt or debate. Such anxiety would be appropriate. We might reasonably expect that some stateside secretaries or mess hall supervisors would struggle to specify any aspect of their existence reminiscent of real warrior work, with its world of occasions for heroism, honor, glory, gratitude, awe, adulation, and utter erotic power. It shouldn't surprise anyone to learn that some feel sorely put down and put upon by harangues to deny their own eyes and judge themselves by standards suited for some other life.

The emphatic reaffirmations of shared warriorhood seem indicative of some ignorance or indifference about the intrusiveness of it all. Hitherto, militaries of other eras were not given to compunctions about personal intrusions. Political interest in such invasions of citizens' selves is a peculiarity of Enlightenment culture, with its valorization of individuality, authenticity, privacy, and personal autonomy. The increasing political interest is a trend that looks to loom ever larger for the military of a Jeffersonian democracy.[15]

Our military is now more willing to refrain from what it deems unnecessary intrusiveness, but its ruling assumption remains that it can—and must—be as controlling as it needs to be to instill the *esprit de corps* requisite for military proficiency and the salvation of the nation. Under this banner of controlling on-the-job conduct, the military continues to presume the right and duty to take control of a person's whole ethos, on and off the job. Predictably, the consequent habits of thought hardened in military leaders often hamper their capacity to recognize the impropriety of commanding their subordinates to submit to religious instruction and participate in religious practices. Those habits were long abetted by civil society; the illegality of such commands was judicially recognized only relatively recently. The incidence of such commands, even after repeated, clear, authoritative judicial condemnation, testifies not to random outbreaks of religious fanaticism or uncommon religious zeal, but to the predisposition of the military mind, its engrained presumption of a high duty to impose totalistic indoctrination to accomplish its mission. Currently, our Jeffersonian democracy limits that

---

15   Professionalization has many effects, affecting military personnel differently. The differential impacts just alluded to cut across national militaries and service branches. Other differences are due to a corps' history. Each military's ethos gets its specific content and flavor from its professionalization within a thick historical context. The fine discriminations and valuations needed for applying essential, essentially vague notions like "conduct unbecoming" and "good order and discipline" are not deducible from abstract principles of liberal egalitarianism or professionalization alone. The 18th and 19th century European militaries professionalizing themselves had centuries of traditions as paradigms of aristocratic culture. Their movements needed no devotion to the egalitarian liberalism nurturing civilian professionalization, but only an Enlightenment openness to questioning their traditions. Early American military leadership created a new military world by tweaking the best practices of Europe's aristocratic military heritages. That world has always harbored more traces of aristocracy than any other in America. Our Army officers today may (perhaps not unreasonably) think they've shed more of their aristocratic baggage than their Navy counterparts, but everywhere old habits of thought and feeling perpetuate themselves by their unnoticed influence on the interpretation and application of liberal egalitarian principles in specific cases.

Yet, while the processes and products of professionalization are conditioned by historical circumstances, the world-wide trend toward military professionalization tends to lessen the influence of military legacies and increase the homogeneity of militaries. At the same time, this tendency toward uniformity is countered by professionalism's intellectual predispositions that encourages experimentation, dissent and innovation and discourages rigidity and dogmatism, even in the conception of professionalism. By its own nature professionalism tends not to be a single or unchanging ethos. So, a highly abstract analysis of the logic of professionalism, such as the present one, risks oversimplification and falsification.

indoctrination only regarding matters deemed "religious." That aside, our civic laws and social norms legitimize a whole world structured to inculcate patterns of moral thought and feeling that prioritize the motivations prioritized by the military's organizational imperatives: obedience and loyalty.

Such intrusiveness and valorization of obedience and loyalty are not unique to the military. They are not uncommon in religions, particularly those organized like military authoritarian hierarchies. But religiosity needn't go that route. Unlike religions, states and other institutions and organizations, militaries, by their very nature, favor hierarchical, authoritarian organization. No other organization has an inner imperative, an inherent goal like victory in battle that makes a comparable demand for that organizational form. (Organizations of civilian professionals tend in the opposite direction.)

Unlike most all other endeavors, military success is a matter of might, and military might has been mainly a matter of the sheer size of the force—and the skills of the commanders in managing masses of personnel. Of course, technological superiority may offset numerical superiority, but technological advantages tend to be short-lived. In any case, no other professional's success has been so dependent on sheer numbers. The development of human communities from scattered small tribes into kingdoms, empires, and nation-states has fed and fed upon the development of massive militaries, now even in "peacetime".

Generally, civilian professional expertise can be well exercised by independent individuals and small groups. While those professionals have increasingly united in organizations which acquire a life of their own with their own (alleged or real) inherent imperatives, there's nothing like the same pressure toward organization, and still less for massive scale and authoritarianism. Civilian professionals may compete for clients, but their lives and nations aren't at risk from larger, competing practitioners. More importantly, the impetus toward organization is the opposite of that in the military. Doctors form medical groups and attorneys form laws firms so each practitioner can better serve his/her own clients, and, not coincidentally, have more clients to serve. Militaries grow larger to better serve their sole "client", the state, not to improve their members' abilities to serve their own clients or enlarge their base. In secular civilian professions, the individual practitioners are, metaphysically and morally, prior to their organizations. In the military, the individuals are professionals only by their membership in and complete subordination to the organization. So, the organizational imperatives are opposites in both their logic and content.

Obedience

The military profession, its ethos and educational programs are all in the service of and constrained by the inherent imperatives of an agency that must be huge yet tightly organized to operate effectively despite disruptions of every kind. Any rule-maker or commander intends her directives to be obeyed, but (rigorist religious orders excepted) no organization matches the military's valorization of sheer dutifulness, obedience, and unquestioning, cheerful compliance. To avoid the calamities attending military failure, a military must aspire to be a monolithic organization maintaining close coordination despite every force and trick of Mother Nature and hostile nations. Disorganization and noncompliance can be lethal, catastrophic. Unity and conformity must be rigorously imposed and maintained. Cooperation and compliance must be automatic and unhesitant despite powerful, natural competing impulses. Habits of discipline—a steady propensity to be motivated by the mere fact of being commanded—must be inculcated. Occasions and latitude for dissent are limited. Fateful decisions cannot commonly be submitted to negotiation, bargaining, compromise or any protracted discussion. Meanwhile, law firms, medical groups, universities, religions, and states may tolerate and thrive on dissension and internal disharmony.

All this can be and often has been overstated. Increased toleration and encouragement of debate and disagreement, loosening of command and control structures, and softening of the old blunt, emotionally blind ethos have resulted from professionalism's valuation of liberated thought, technological innovations, alterations in the nature of military threats, and so on. Military organizational imperatives limit toleration and valorization of dissension, but what the genuine imperatives really demand, specifically and in detail, is increasingly controversial.

Still, however adaptable, flexible and justified military professionalism may be, its spirit of subordination is foreign to the culture of civilian professions. While civilian codes seldom consider obedience a vice, neither is it found on any list of lead virtues. Obedience is a cardinal virtue of Boy Scouts, butlers, bellhops and bus boys, not responsible professionals. This stark contrast in the valuation of obedience is a cause and consequence of a stark contrast in the structure of moral reasoning. Traits of obedience are less prized by civilian professionals because obedience has such a restricted, peripheral role in their reasoning. Their decisions are not so controlled by a chain of command. Generally those decisions are evaluated by direct reference to the likely objective goods and evils they entail, and their compliance with universally applicable principles of liberal egalitarianism.

Meanwhile, beginning with the absolute civilian control of the fundamental military decisions, then down the whole chain of command, officers and subordinates are systematically discouraged from the independent reasoning of civilian professionals, since it threatens to distract them from their paramount duty of compliance with the decisions of their superiors. Our military's ethos can recognize that the duty of obedience is not completely absolute; some disobedience is justified. Still, it presumes that an order is to be obeyed, and that that presumption is not to be questioned without due cause. The first presumption is a defeasible premise in practical reasoning; the second is a constraint on the topics of reasoning. Questioning the presumption of obedience carries some risk. Doing so habitually is ill-advised for career advancement.

Predictably, it seems a tad unreasonable to the inhabitants of this moral universe when their professional obligations of obedience are regarded on a par with those of civilian professionals. After all, they have been trained to valorize obedience and respect its requirement as befits the morality befitting a military, a morality honored and sponsored by its legitimate civilian leaders, and the civic laws and social norms of a free, democratic society.

Still, absolutist talk of the sacredness and sanctity of oaths, vows and contracts smacks of fanaticism. Despite all the weight, strength and solemnity of military obligation, its power to withstand *all* claims of justice and cries of humanity will be questionable in a nation justly proud of its creation by political revolution, and committed to the principles of Nuremburg. Such questioning is within the limits of military professionalism, if not within the moral imagination of all military professionals.

Loyalty

A military professional's sense of the obligation of obedience—her metric of its strength—is unnatural to civilian ethicists; an adequate feel for it is hard to acquire by classroom contemplation of hypothetical cases. It likely defies comprehension when abstracted from the peculiarities of the military's emotional world.

Our military ethos is not distillable into a single slogan: Salute smartly and obey! Its spirit is animated with an emotionality civilian professionalism need not and could not inspire: the passions of intense loyalties, not one but a structure of loyalties to the nation, the government, the corps, and, most especially, to one's own comrades. The military's unmatched valuation of these loyalties is motivated by both the demands of military proficiency and the pressure to reduce the precariousness of its moral condition. These moral bonds and their attendant emotions may differentiate military professionalism from civilian professionalism more profoundly than all else. Experientially it is a whole other world.

In combat, conscientiousness alone won't cut it. With all its fog and fluidity, warriors cannot manage with nothing more than routines and compliance with explicit commands. Their lives depend on their reliance on one another. They've got to trust that each of them is moved by a genuine, profound concern for each other, ready to risk their lives for each other. To get the job done and/or survive, there's got to be an intense commitment to the corps and to one's unit and one's comrades: the team and each individual.

Loyalty is needed to supplement obedience and also to sustain it. Military proficiency markedly declines when the sole motivation for obedience is brute fear. Any warrior code prizes loyalty as well as obedience. Our military did less of that a century ago, but militaries have long done far more of it than any civilian profession, and now must do more than ever as leadership by stark fear becomes less acceptable and effective.

All the loyalties the military prizes are forms of partiality whose consonance with Enlightenment universalism and the reciprocalism of our golden-rule Judaeo-Christian heritage is problematic. These commitments contend with a civic culture that honors patriotism (and nationalism too), while also trumpeting the Brotherhood of Man and calling everyone to render the same basal care and regard for everyone regardless of such accidents of circumstance as gender, race, ethnicity, national origin—and national affiliation. Military professionals must reconcile the ideal of egalitarian universalism with their defining commitment to their own nation and their comrades. They declare themselves willing—indeed, honor bound—to obliterate people of other nations when so ordered and to die in the process if need be. There is no more profound expression of favoritism than the oath of military allegiance.[16]

The tensions between the partiality of loyalties and the universalism and cosmopolitanism of Enlightenment ethics present little conflict for civilian professionals, for (a) their favoritism benefits their clients generally without threatening grave harm to others, (b) their clients can be anyone, and (c) they generally need not have deep commitments to co-workers, a corporate agency, or government.

Civilian professionals commonly have special obligations to their clients, and their codes prescribe loyalties to the client beyond the contractual commitments. Normally, those obligations and loyalties are consequences of the professional-client relation, not a cause or precondition of it. The client is often a stranger with no prior claim on the professional. The professional's commitments are creatures of the relation, and generally terminate with its termination. The client is well and dutifully served without the professional being the client's servant, but instead an independent, autonomous agent bound by her code to act on her best professional judgment in the client's best interests, even, in some cases, against the client's wishes.

Civilian professionals may truly love to help people and love doing it with their hard-earned skills. This may be particularly admirable when they're not out to care for particular individuals they have personal reasons to care about: their favored clients may be whoever is neediest. Civilian professionals may have admirable motives but not an analogue of patriotism or other warrior loyalties. Admirable it may be for physicians to have heartfelt concerns for their patients, and teachers for their students, but we haven't the same need or expectation of their deep and lasting attachments as we do for an officer's love of her country. With civilian professionals, the temptations of betrayal aren't so frequent or formidable; their enticement by our enemies is unlikely. Significant emotional attachment comforts

---

16   For what may be the most illuminating, and must be the wittiest, elucidation of the implications of a universalized patriotism or nationalism, cf: Curtis Stalbank, "I'm Prepared To Give My Life For This Or Any Country", *The Onion*, 3/28/07, http://www. theonion.com/content/opinion/im_prepared_to_give_my_life_for.

a client, but generally a decent wage, or if need be a hefty one, is incentive enough to secure steady professional performance.

Some adults soldier like children at play, without caring whom or what they soldier for. That attitude, acceptable, even admirable in civilian professions, is not a virtue of noble warriors. Nowadays, few adults wish to be soldiers apart from a willingness to serve their country when it is threatened. The arms-length commercial allegiances of mercenary troops to their client-employer must be exceptional in the military. A state cannot rely entirely on a military with only monetary motivations for fear that the mercenaries might simply seize the nation's wealth. The government must be the commander of its military, not a mere client. Its military personnel are its servants, not free-lancing pros.[17] An egalitarian democracy cannot reliably command its military personnel unless they usually enter the service with an allegiance secured, not by oath or greed or fear alone, but by motivations like patriotism that are not creatures of contract or calculation of self-interest. Bereft of such motivations, bare oaths bear little credence.

Military professionals take pride in their selflessness, their subordination and submergence of self. They think it a submission with greater nobility than a vassal's servility. The submission is a surrender and liberation, a total identification with The Corps! The Corps! A military professional may think of himself, day to day, dawn to dusk, down to his core, as, say, a Marine.

Civilian professional counterparts are pallid shadows and not prescribed by their codes. A doctor may think of herself as a doctor. It's what she proudly does, what she proudly is, what she devotes and shapes her life to being. She may develop bonds with co-workers and co-professionals, but normally nothing more than the bonds nonprofessionals make in their work. (Consider what it would take to spread a fierce conviction: We dentists have got to stick together!) As for the AMA, her allegiance is likely negligible, and her identification with it null. To her hospital she may have more allegiance, but it's rarely deep and is generally readily transferable. And however substantial the allegiance, exceptional circumstances are needed for her to think of herself, on and off the job, primarily in terms of her affiliation to that organization. The spirit of such institutions is not a martial *esprit de corps*. The conscience of its personnel doesn't hark to *Hooah* or any remotely

---

17   I have heard it said that the government (or nation) is the military's client, and, by transitivity, the clientele of its members is the state or its citizenry. That sophistry is the joke in approaching a cop and saying: "You're a public servant and I want my shoes shined, so snap to." Military professionals do not have clients. Officers have subordinates but no clients. They are managers of a professionalized government agency. (There is nothing ignoble in this: football Quarterbacks have no clients either.) The government or nation is no more a client of the military than it is a client of the Department of State or Commerce.

comparable call. A properly professionalized military mind must do precisely that —or so it now supposes.

When the question is whether to serve at all, patriotism is the first loyalty to come in play. Fans of war may stand on a three-legged patriotism, shifting from stance to stance. Sometimes they speak to the unconverted with a vulnerable faith that premises their nation's righteousness unbroken or in the instance. Sometimes they speak to themselves, sharing a faith premising national exceptionalism. Sometimes they proclaim a loyalty that premises itself as sufficient justification.

Patriotism in itself has little content beyond its egocentrism. It motivates pursuit of the nation's self-interest, but patriotic fervor may move us whatever our conception of the nation's interests. Bare love of country never tells us when to war. It can only motivate acceptance and execution of a decision made on some other grounds. Patriotism powers us to support, fervently and mindlessly, whatever the nation and its military do, and not just going to war. It influences the rest of the military world by this conservatism, its proud acceptance and glorification of what its civilian and military leaders put before it.

Patriots may think their passion legitimates their military's plying its skills when their impersonal reasons for warring run out—as though their trust in their nation's righteousness were a reason for foreigners to presume the same rather than retain the foreigners' patriotic trust in their own nation's righteousness. Each patriot's love and trust can legitimate only his/her own acceptance of the authority of a decision, and support of its execution. The natural prejudice of a patriot's perspective is the presumption of the righteousness of furthering one's nation's interests. That partiality may acknowledge that, looked at impartially, that presumption may be epistemically groundless, and in any particular case it may be mistaken and indefensible. Still, patriots insist that patriotism is a virtue, most especially in a military leader, and that loyalty demands trust in and support of one's nation's pursuits despite evidence and argument to the contrary. Vaguely stated, some such favoritism may be universalizable and impartially approved. One risk of the military's culture of uniformity and instant submission to authority is a sclerosis of the patriots' cognitive stance: a tightly blinkered trust in their nation's commanders, a steady propensity to presume that, despite appearances to the contrary, they mean well and know what they are doing. The oaths of officers and voluntary enlistees may also oblige them to trust and maintain faith, and military professionals might understandably believe that any distrust is inconsistent with the sacredness of those vows. That stance seems respectable until it becomes absolutist, brooking no conceivable exceptions, and dismissive of any demand to explain why the sanctity of those vows transcends all their other bonds of justice, humanity and decency.

Love of country commonly overpowers love of mankind. Both affections pale before the famed bonding of comrades in arms. No other occupation induces coworker ties of comparable depth and intensity. That bonding is said to motivate more heroic sacrifice than all else. It may as frequently motivate less noble conduct.

Patriotism may make for a willingness to serve. The more personal loyalties may make for an unwillingness to refuse service.

There is a profound disgrace in departing from a communal ethos obsessively insistent on obedience, loyalty, team spirit. An officer can expect (mostly if not exclusively) condemnation from fellow professionals and the nation for refusing to serve when he/she sincerely judges a war wrongful. Of course (it is near tautological), such refusal may be deemed permissible, even obligatory, by those who deem the wrong sufficiently blatant and heinous. That possibility is academic. Governments aren't wont to wage wars they expect to be generally condemned by officers and citizenry. Military professionalism recognizes that, in theory, refusal to participate may be honorable. In practice, only officers of our enemies (Nazi Germany is the paradigm) get condemned. Resignation on grounds of conscience is lawful—in some circumstances. In others, especially in wartime, all exits are blocked. Even when lawful, it is hardly reputable. The toll down that road is stiff. However sincere and agonized, the choice is mostly condemned (loudly or quietly) and rarely admired by professional peers or the press and the folks back home. The catch-22 comes with the details of concrete cases. There the purity of moral judgment is inextricably entwined with political judgments. Thus, the callings of conscience can be silenced by labeling them "political."

The disrepute of resignation, refusal, civil disobedience, and any noisy or disruptive dissent in the military is rooted in the loyalties sustained by the military ethos. However conscientious, dissent is bound to look like betrayal. And that cannot but rattle the certainty of one's convictions. It all calls for pig-headed courage.

This last remark and others might be read as offering no more than an excuse for participating in shameful warring. Doctrinaire individualists, I take it, recognize loyalty as a justification, not a mere excuse, only insofar as the object of loyalty is deserving; loyalty itself is deemed to have little or no value apart from the value of its object. That is an uncommon, attenuated conception of loyalty. The common conception is that one test of true loyalty is a willingness to stand by its object despite its wrongdoing—not all wrongdoing, but some nontrivial wrongdoing. Individualists are properly puzzled by this: if neither B nor C has a right to harm D, how could B's loyalty to C give B a right to aid C's harming D? Doubtless it doesn't: rights are matters of justice, and when loyalty conflicts with justice it cannot claim any rights. Loyalty might still have some value, merit some respect, and justify some complicity in some injustice. How that could be has never been explained, but neither has it been shown to be impossible.

Conclusion

Despite the absurdity of combatant moral equality, Walzer might be sufficiently vindicated if military professionalism needs some conception of its moral singularity and some such conception is intelligible. I have suggested that Walzer is right to that extent, but military professionalism cannot well commit to any specific conception, because it is committed to competing imperatives. I close with two final suggestions.

Perhaps the moral circumstance of the uniformed among us, with its political isolation, oaths and loyalties and obligations of obedience, justifies only a moral presumption against condemning their participating in some condemnable wars. This presumption needs no unreasonable assumption that their government always acts rightly or is doing so here and now. The presumption might stand despite the government's decision being reasonably deemed very bad (yet not horrifically evil) if that decision does not exceed or jeopardize the legitimacy of that decision's authority. That modest presumption is not easily rebutted in a relatively well-ordered society like the USA.

Further, perhaps something of that presumption might be sustained for a military ruled by a regime with lesser moral legitimacy. I have supposed that if a well-ordered society properly sponsors and honors totalistic indoctrination of an authoritarian moral code to secure the proficiency of its means of survival, then those subject to that training may justifiably live by that code. So, while we may often properly condemn gross violations of Enlightenment principles in the civilian world of other societies, perhaps we cannot so freely condemn such societies or their governments for sponsoring and honoring the inculcation of the same military mindset. If so, perhaps we best recognize some moral singularity of their military.

Chapter 8

The Morality of Military Ethics Education

Roger Wertheimer

Introduction

Modern militarism institutionalizes an ethos of professionalism. The model is the American military, the wealthiest, history's most world-dominant. Its professionalism is an occupational spirit of self-improvement. A military is not truly professionalized without a program of Professional Military Education (PME) with two primary assignments: the acquisition and transmission of the knowledge and skills that maximize military proficiency, and the transmission and perpetuation of the ethos of professionalism—the mission of Professional Military Ethics Education (PMEE).

American professionalism is an Enlightenment ethos. The American military is subject to the basic Enlightenment moral imperatives governing the fundamental laws of the nation it serves. A military has an inherent imperative to maximize its proficiency in attaining its military objectives. The morality of the American military is an evolving negotiation of independent imperatives from independent legitimating sources.

This essay is about the interplay of distinct, often competing imperatives within the morality of modern militarism exemplified in America's best PMEE practices: its Department of Defense (DoD) academies training officers for its Air Force (USAFA), Army (USMA *aka* West Point) and Navy and Marine Corps (USNA *aka* Annapolis). These schools are the focus because they are the best we've got and I know them best—from two years of continuous personal observation advising USNA administrators about their PMEE programs, and from a consequent network of contacts at all the academies.[1] Since American PMEE derived from European

---

1   This whole volume and particularly my own writings owe much to many people. Few anthologists have been so blessed to have each contributor be a paragon of anthological virtue, prompt in response, cooperative in revision, punctual in manuscript delivery, and supererogatory in comment on my own contributions. I insert my acknowledgements here because I have been helped here most of all. This chapter is written from the peculiar perspective of a professional ethicist hired to advise an institution on its ethics education programs. It is designed to inform and engage a general public about matters that concern them of which they are ignorant, but it is addressed to my client (and other administrators

models and has since influenced PMEE worldwide, my observations should resonate with PMEE practitioners and participants elsewhere.[2]

Respect

Over the past half-century military culture has been revolutionizing itself, or trying to. The moral progress of military professionalism is best learned, not from its academy required courses on military ethics and military law, but from those on leadership. Oversimplifying, the ethics courses are more concerned with how to reason about exceptional situations; the leadership courses with how a leader is to act day-to-day. Future leaders are presently taught that true leaders live by some Kantianesque principle of respect.

Professionalism has taken the tyranny out of military authoritarianism. Insubordination is not met with brutality. Leadership texts teach the modern management practices predicated on current social science (organizational theory, personality theory, etc.). Officers are to be managers and leaders, not dictators. Respect is to run all down the line, as well as up.

In our current civil society, public denials of the principle of respect are beyond the pale. Military professionalism salutes the principle and declares a commitment

---

of PMEE programs) as a consultant's final report on his findings. So, it takes an occasional tangent off the central theme of conflicting imperatives to report some related matter of importance. So too, as an advisor's report, it takes liberties in its tone and trappings sure to scandalize scholars. Where possible and appropriate, scholarly canons are sometimes met, but mostly the essay is riddled with reports from unnamed sources, and controversial opinions unsupported by due documentation. Skeptical readers have only my assurance that my provocative claims have been properly vetted by very well positioned participants at all three academies, who would happily have my expressions of gratitude remain private. While some needling judgments have not met unanimous assent, not a word here is my opinion alone. Certainly, my confidantes often become so because of our shared sympathies, so my sources are skewed and some judgments represent minority opinions, but none are dismissibly tiny minorities. I am most indebted to my most severe critics, especially my erstwhile office-mate, Adm. Hank Chiles, USN (ret.), for his extraordinary patience and generosity with his time, effort, and informational resources trying to rectify what he deemed so defective. I am grateful for his saving me from numerous embarrassing errors, and regretful that so much remains so disagreeable. Likewise, I am nearly as indebted to George Lucas for all his many objections, patience, and generosity. The support, encouragement and counsel of Lara Denis and Bredo Johnsen have, as always, been essential.

2   This chapter is written to be understandable on its own but it is better understood with the background of "The Moral Singularity of Military Professionalism," the preceding chapter here. That chapter articulates my understanding of the historical context and motivational structure of military professionalism—an understanding here guiding what I think worth looking at, and how I look at it, and represent it. If my lens here looks off kilter, check the prior chapter.

to the Enlightenment ideals of equality, fraternity, and respect. Yet, civil society, in the USA and elsewhere, has spent two centuries in conflicts, institutional and interpersonal, over the interpretation and application of those ideals. Still today, a million times every day, people get astonished to learn that someone else regards this or that act or utterance as disrespectful. What respect calls for in a democratic civil society will always be controversial when you get down to cases.[3] What you learn about the demands of respect in that world is unreliable guidance for success in the military world.

The military is profoundly unlike a business corporation. Successful business leaders can be disastrous Defense Department managers when they really don't get it that the military is morally unlike any civilian organization. From the outside, it is one among many component organizations comprising our communal totality, our nation, our culture. From the inside the military is its own world, a societally sanctioned semi-autonomous legal order, politically isolated, detached from our democracy. This organization has an authoritarian structure condemned by our basic constitutional principles, and by Kant's conception of a respect due all persons—condemned everywhere except in the military. And prisons.

We all create, sustain, and certify this organization to secure our most essential goal, the survival of our nation, our lives, our homes and pussy cats. To that end, we presume ourselves entitled to empower this organization to do the most horrible, horrible, horrible things to millions of other human beings when we so direct it— and to demand that this organization evaluate and structure everything within it— all of its equipment, practices and human relationships—by their contribution to military proficiency. The dominant message we twitter to military managers seems to say that they are to live by the principle of maximizing military proficiency, and thus regard and treat everything under their command as a means to achieving our most elemental end. We empower these managers to enforce compliance coercively. They are not answerable to civilian courts. The leaders' word is the law of their world. Of course, getting what they want when and how they want it still takes skill. Compliance as intended is hardly automatic. Still, military directives don't risk meeting responses of "I quit; I'll work for a competitor." Open-palmed or fisted, their gloved hands are mailed. What respect down the line there demands is limited by what respect down the line is possible there.

Within this world, its new professionalism commands a new respect for the principle of respect. The venerable debasement of Privates and Plebes, once glorified, is now prohibited and sternly condemned with some consistency. That prohibition is dramatic, symbolic, and it ramifies throughout academy and armed forces culture. It nicely exemplifies much of the new leadership style. Constraining hazing and harsh training has been an evolutionary process going back to the late 19th century, taking hold in the 1950s, and accelerating in the morally anxious post-Vietnam military. The data points of the leisurely sloped learning curve are

---

3   See my review of Alan Donagan's *The Theory of Morality* in *Nous,* May 1983, pp. 303-8.

events of moral discovery, controversy and official redefinitions regarding the specific forms and degrees of humiliation and abuse deemed consistent with due respect for bottom dwellers.

Formal prohibitions from the highest authorities are impotent when stated in terms like "disrespect" or "hazing"—until some communal understanding develops regarding the relevant, specific, precise criteria determining the proper application of such terms in a particular case. What one's superiors will deem proper may still be uncertain. Time after time leaders get dismayed by the discovery (and embarrassed if it's published) that, despite their ever-so clear, prominently-posted directives, some of their most decorated boot camp DIs or student commanders keep dishing routinized cruelties, physical and/or psychological, with the purest devotion to sacred duty. Leaders get confounded by their trusted subordinates' conduct, and even more by their sense of betrayal for being punished for their contributions to military proficiency.

What the accused or convicted say when confronted may be dishonest or self-deluded rationalizations masking ignoble motives of sadism, or callousness, or inexcusable insensitivity. Never mind. The rationalizations would not (be thought to) serve the self if they weren't (thought to be) appealing to principles recognized by the opposing perspective. Before and after conviction the condemned's defense is the argument of the old guard professionals who lost the cultural battle: to wit, however humiliating or painful, the training regimen is permissible and required insofar as it is permitted and required to maximize military proficiency.

The once honored old guard and the new culprits have lost out to new professionals who say or suppose that the military can't be entitled to deny or disregard the principle of respect. Our social contract assumes that we all have reason enough to accept our subordination to military superiors, but our consent would be crazy and incapable of legitimating anything if we allowed the military absolute and unlimited power over us as mere means to its end. Our own self-respect demands that we not authorize an organization that disregards our demand for respect. We'd lose our self-respect enlisting in a military that permits disrespect unnecessary for maximizing military proficiency.

Few old guard professionals have been so impolitic as to deny this, publicly. Most see no need to since they are certain that while of course there are limits to the harms trainers can inflict, the humiliation and suffering they've always allowed are well within those bounds, and they are indispensable for achieving the needed discipline so essential for successful combat. Even limp-wristed new professionals must admit that they cannot absolutely prohibit all acts causing pain or humiliation. That's infeasible even in the civilian world.[4] The new guard must realize that they still permit and require trainers to inflict far greater humiliation and physical discomfort to achieve their goals than our society allows elsewhere.

---

4   Feeling humbled by a course grade F is not unusual or pathological; for some of us, a midterm C or B is due cause for shame and humiliation. The point here is only a reminder that these matters have more complexity than we realize at first thought.

Old professionals say they are just as consistently respectful. The issue is never whether disrespect is justifiable, but only when and how much disrespect is needed to get the job done and fulfill their solemn duty. They'll concede the possibility of their being wrong on the facts, but their confidence has the strength and size of their enormous collective experience.

They say (in so many words):

> If new professionals' sensibilities are so offended by the conduct we commend, if they honestly feel that such treatment is beyond the pale of what military proficiency can justify, we must respectfully submit that they are not entitled to risk our nation's survival just to suit their sensitivities, so to them we say "Suck it up or get out"—unless we're given good reason for deferring to a sensibility so contrary to our near two century honored traditions, and still longer traditions of respected allies. We rest with the challenge to convince us that the limits of disrespect you lay down don't compromise our security, or, if they do, they are nonetheless limits that reasonable social contractors would unanimously demand despite their compromising their security.[5]

Some of military professionalism's finest minds have been enthralled by (their understanding of) Kant's conception of the call of duty and the demands of respect. They conscientiously live by it and devote themselves to instilling this attitude in their students and their other subordinates. They may get queasy from a hasty reading of occasional Kant comments,[6] and then reassured by finding nothing they cannot reconcile with their own training practices.

However, officers who suppose Pure Reason alone can identify the specific conduct respect demands should read beyond the *Grundlegung* and consider how many of the Master's specific judgments on the matter they approve, and how many they are appalled or amused by. Apparently, though his contemporary armies allowed more brutality and servility then our own old guard could stomach, Kant wasn't moved to criticize it. Military Kantians may fairly insist that commitment

---

5   To sharpen the conflict, the dialectic in the text conflates distinct issues: What specific trait(s) in an officer maximize his professional proficiency? What regimen most effectively induces that trait. Regimen relaxation derived significantly from an altered assessment of the optimal leadership and managerial traits, traits better developed by regimen relaxation. The text collapses the different ways demands of respect enter and impact these issues.

6   Some moral sweating may be induced by passages like the third prescription of "Toward Perpetual Peace" that standing armies be abolished "in time"—and some stomach knotting at its clause saying that being hired to kill or be killed "seems to involve" using people as mere means. Still, Kant does not issue an unequivocal categorical condemnation of military service. Most pertinent here, Kant's comments *directly* on the condition of freedom within the military structure provoke no worries about our current practices, except, perhaps, at the margins: e.g., some current constraints on an officer's public political speech seem to restrict the broad use of "public reason" by officers advocated in "What is Enlightenment?".

to Kantian principles entails no commitment to Kant's application of them in every case. What commitments are entailed remain to be explained.

Consider: However much honest consideration is given to the feelings and wishes of a slave, what can be the character of respect of any of his master's actions as long as the master assumes himself entitled to own and control the slave as chattel? What role can the principle of respect play in military morality beyond that of a side-constraint on the principle of maximizing military proficiency setting some upper-bound on permissible acts elsewhere deemed disrespectful? If in fact that is its current role, how is the quality of respect of any individual action to be assessed in a world of human relationships whose power structure, practices and policies are fixed and certified by this ethos? Can there be any defensible, operational criteria for determining the upper bound of permissibly inflicted pain or humiliation in general or in some situations, or is the determination ultimately, irredeemably arbitrary, a function of a superior's sensibilities?

Those who violate or criticize the new standards are accused of sadism, savagery, cruelty. They retort with accusations of the opposite vice: the new professionals are egregiously soft-hearted moral cowards caving in to a corrupted civilian culture, so corrupted that its respect for people's rights and liberties now entitles everyone to talk and act in ways previously regarded scandalously disrespectful. It is a culture so corrupted that its respect for women now obliges the military to jeopardize the unit cohesion and good order and discipline indispensable for combat proficiency just to the satisfy some girls' whims to play macho man. Kantians can parry that, plausibly claiming that their accommodations to cultural shifts are principled, prompted not by political expedience, but by respect for each of the great mass of recruits and plebes and their socially sanctioned conceptions of proper respect.

Assessing aspersions of ignoble motivations is a mug's game. My own sense of current military professionalism is colored by an absence of evidence of some sudden massive conversion to Kantianism. I've rarely caught officers consulting Kantian texts when they aren't teaching an ethics class. Instead I see officers imbued with the spirit of professionalism ready to guide their lives by the findings of science, including the currently dominant theories of social science. Looking at their leadership texts, it seems that the dominant motivation for the new professionals comes from their being convinced that social science has demonstrated that leadership respect down the line is absolutely essential for securing the respect up the line absolutely essential for military managers and leaders to operate effectively. But, once more, causal conjectures here are bottomless pits of controversy, and as guides for the future their value gets madly exaggerated.

The fact beyond dispute and indisputably important is that our leaders-to-be are being taught to develop and strengthen habits of respect in every direction, down the line, up it, and horizontally, just because this respect contributes to military proficiency. The texts may have a passage or two hinting at some other rationale, but the dominant message drowning out all others is that our officers must value and enforce respect for persons because of its military utility.

Meanwhile, the rationale for requiring respect future leaders find in their ethics course Kant readings is a paradigm of impenetrable philosophical obscurity. Among the rare and precious certainties is that Kantian respect is not predicated on its managerial utility. It seems likely, if not apodictic, that a respect so motivated ultimately regards its objects as mere means to organizational ends.

Whys

What is the motivation for our military service academies? Like many of its allies, America's expenditures for developing the character of its military officers dwarf the budgets for enhancing anyone else's virtuousness. Aside from scattered occasional efforts by local governments at lower school levels, our political and secular civilian institutions generally expend little real time and money empowering the conscience of its citizenry or its civilian professionals. There's no end to ways governmental and other public institutions, intentionally or not, influence everyone's moral thinking, but mostly it is training, indoctrination, much of it subliminal, not education. Little of it is intellectually demanding; little aspires to upgrade capacities for moral understanding and deliberation. Of the pittance we spend on training our police (our paramilitary defenders against violent domestic threats), the least fraction goes toward training its managers (lieutenants, captains, chiefs), and the education of their character rarely approaches the perfunctory semester of professional ethics sometimes mandated at nongovernmental professional schools. Our community leaves the edification of moral character to its extra-governmental institutions and agencies, which do little to take up the slack.

Meanwhile, we build and comfortably equip three large Bachelor-of-Science granting schools for the Army, Navy and Air Force—and two smaller ones for the Coast Guard and Merchant Marine, which I'll have less in mind. We tax ourselves to pay for the plant, equipment, all operating expenses, the costs of labor (management, faculty, and staff), and all the raw materials: the cadets and midshipmen who receive (tax free) schooling, food, shelter, amusements, miscellaneous amenities, and a stipend to boot. By a conservative accounting, we're investing beyond a billion dollars per annum making that raw material into the managers of our means of killing masses of people.[7]

---

7   The figures from the "Annual Report to GAO; Office of Institutional Research, U.S. Naval Academy" are: for 2003, costs per USNA midshipman: $291,289; per USAFA cadet: $346,652; per USMA cadet $383,042. With approximately 4200 enrolled at each academy, the four year totals are: USNA—$1,223,413,800; USAFA—$1,455,938,400; USMA—$1,608,785,600. Yearly overall total: $1,072,034,400. Why does it cost us over 20 percent more to produce Air Force officers than Navy/Marine officers? and over 33 percent more for Army officers than Navy/Marine officers? Nice questions for which I have yet

What's it all for? Not primarily to produce leaders equipped with exquisite technical expertise. Our federal military academies are unlike professional or trade schools for dentistry, computer programming, and the like. Cadets and midshipmen endure relentless, rigorous physical conditioning and mindless chores galore while their course content differs little from that for Reserve Officers' Training Corps (ROTC) students at civilian colleges, who are commissioned like academy graduates at a fraction of taxpayer expense. Most of the technical knowledge required for commissioning is transmitted as well in a dozen weeks of Officer Candidate School (OCS). As with police lieutenants and captains, a military officer's expertise is acquired mostly post-commissioning, on the job, in the "internship" and "residency" of junior officership, and subsequent training programs, war colleges and the like.

The military trappings of America's academies are mainly ambience, mimicked at private military academies, high school and college. The martial programs and practices are mechanisms meant to mold character. The academies' chartered mission, mandated by Congress, is to produce, not military officers *simpliciter*, but specifically officers of high moral character. Their graduates have inhabited 24/7 for 47 months a total institution (meant to be) calibrated for that mission. The closest counterparts to all this are some sect-supported seminaries and monasteries training intercessors with the higher powers. Our interests in the saintliness of our military leaders are more mundane. What are they?

One legitimate interest is self-protection. Any nation has reason to fear its military turning against it. However low the likelihood here, the possibility has been realized too often in human history ever to be prudently ignored. A society's armed forces are its *de facto* ultimate power with the might of brute physical domination and demolition. Whatever the laws and political structure, whatever the other operative forces in a society, ultimately its health and very existence are at the mercy of those commanding its military personnel and equipment. Nothing stands between their power and the usurpation or destruction of the state. More commonly, like a foreign army or fleet, a state's military may, without seizing control of the state, be beyond its control and act with impunity in small matters or large. At minimum, as happens here, a nation's military is one of many competing centers of power, each prone to perceive its own interests as coincident with the nation's interests and to distort the nation's priorities accordingly. Against all these threats, a state's last line of defense – its defense against its own defense force—is the honor and humility of its military leaders.

Also, and now more than ever, America is vulnerable to the moral failings of its military commanders, whose injustice, indifference, impatience or intolerance

---

discovered no sensible answers. Caveat: The 2004 DoD commissioned study by the Tench Francis School of Business, *Comparative Analysis of ROTC, OCS and Service Academies as Commissioning Sources*, notes that such numbers, and others reported in the study and cited below, are problematic.

toward other peoples would secure us deep enmity and shame, shredding the last remnants of our leadership and moral authority. Here self-interest commends what justice commands. We'd be derelict in our relations with other peoples if we made no effort to protect them from the power we bestow on our officers, especially when we ramp up the frequency and intrusiveness of our officers' roles in their lives. The moral training of our military leaders is a minimum gesture of respect for another people after exacting from them legal immunity for crimes against them our service people might commit.

We have legitimate interests in the protection of our world from ourselves. Our defense policy has been intent on maintaining "full spectrum dominance". Our unmatched military superiority is an inherently dangerous reality. We prefer to think of it as a force for peace and justice, but it cannot be that without being available as a force for belligerence and injustice. We have too much power and too much pride in it and too little fear of its exercise. We desperately need devices to keep from unduly indulging in violence to have our way in the world. One such device is demanding that our officers get some intellectually serious schooling in moral reasoning and understanding. As I told our ethics students: "This might seem a perilous, counter-productive policy, for such studies equip and encourage officers to consider the justice and justifiability of any armed conflict their nation orders them to wage, and this means they may question the justifiability of their obedience and service. Actually, it is a bulwark of a free, democratic society that its military leaders have an enlightened conscience. The more dominant our military becomes, the more significant this safeguard becomes for our nation and the world."[8] Only politicians bent on mischief could have anything to fear from empowering our military conscience with the analytical tools for evaluating its basic values and principles. Any attempt to abort this new mission of our service academies should be seen as a sign that some despotism is in the works.

Moral education of our military leaders serves much of our citizenry individually, as well as members of the collectivity. The nation entrusts its military officers with near absolute subordination of fellow adult citizens, a totalistic control not countenanced in the secular, civilian world outside our prisons. Military subordinates have the vulnerability of captives, for however voluntary their entrance into service, their options for exiting are minimal, costly and can be closed at the government's pleasure. Also, military personnel lose most of the civilian employee recourse to the courts.

The control is massive, and so are the numbers controlled. Even at (relative) peace our armed forces are huge and their turnover is high. In war they may include any number of us, our friends and family. Nowhere else in a functioning democracy are so many legally competent, law-abiding citizens so much at the mercy of the moral sense of their superiors.

---

8   Introduction to the chapter on *jus ad bellum* in the USNA course text *Ethics for Military Leaders*, Pearson Custom Publishers, Boston, 2002.

A further way grooming our officers' character serves the national interest is that their—and thus our—military success depends mightily on their character. Strong character is generally crucial for effective leadership in any field, and especially in the military, for warfare tests character like no other common human activity. The respect, trust, loyalty, and devotion of the troops depends on their perception of their leaders' character—as does the respect and trust of our allies and our enemies. The effectiveness of military operations depends on the former; the need for military operations on the latter.

Evidence

When the academies hawk themselves to civilians holding the purse strings, they address our democracy, where everyone knows the political costs of a politician's questioning the value of our officer corps being filled with fair minded, decent human beings we'd happily have as neighbors. When our elected purchasing agents want to be resold on the whole academy enterprise, they want some justification for the immense extra expense of educating officers in the academies instead of ROTC, OCS and other possible paths of ascension.[9]

Academy advocates cannot convincingly claim that the products of other routes to commissioning are not and cannot be as virtuous. I once informally polled USNA officers of the highest ranks whether they would be able to identify an officer's ascension path based solely on their sense of the individual's character. None thought they could. Despite this, none wavered in his/her faith either in the academies as molders of character or in themselves as judges of character. They may acknowledge their fallibility about the effects of specific programs and policies, but they resist conceding that, if enhancement of moral virtue is the aim, the whole academy experience could well be for naught.

Faith in the efficacy of academy character education withers, I'm told, in JAGS after years prosecuting and defending transgressions by officers—committed at much the same rate whatever the commissioning history. One senior military academy clinician privately opines that the academies' principal effect on personality

---

9   Just as this book's manuscript was readied for delivery to the publisher, the internet was filling with reactions to a Thomas E. Ricks' column, "Why We Should Get Rid of West Point," *Washington Post*, April 16, 2009 <http://www.washingtonpost.com/wp- dyn/content/article/2009/04/16/AR2009041603483.html>. Ricks argues, like others before, that, compared to ROTC and OCS, all the academies are woefully cost-ineffective producers of officers. Reader reactions, pro and con, heated and humorous, are rich with anecdotes, and some new data is coming to light as I write. I learned of the Tench Francis study cited above and below from a response to Ricks' critics by Bruce Fleming, a USNA civilian professor notorious for unflattering publications about his employer, yet previously unknown to me.   http://ricks.foreignpolicy.com/posts/2009/04/27/usna_prof_to_usma_flack_ricks_is_ basically_right .

is infantilization due to lost independence and decreased range of responsibility. (Such regression soon enough evaporates after graduation and assumption of "real world" responsibilities.) The anecdotal evidence is not encouraging.

Neither is the only credible relevant research, the 2006 USMA review of a recent decade stretch of Army officer records of separation for misconduct sorted by sources of commission. The findings are not well known. Official announcements cherry pick the evidence. The probability of an unprodded publication of the raw data is not high. The numbers say that West Point graduates have somewhat better misconduct records than officers from the non-collegiate OCS path, but not significantly better than officers from all other sources combined, and not at all better than the most comparable group, full scholarship ROTC. (Reluctance to release the research has been premised on statistical circumspection: the sample size, some 50,000 records, has been declared too small to be probative. Defenders of their own research have been dealt with predictably.)

Despite discouraging data, faith in the academy system stays robust in some quarters. Perhaps faith in the efficacy of the military regimen as molder of moral character is akin to faith in the unique efficacy of capital punishment as a deterrent of crime, and of torture as an elicitor of information. Such beliefs are notoriously popular and powerful. They have been for ages before there was evidence that could explain and justify any certainty. Passionate certainty motivates searches for evidence to justify itself. People are certain because they want to feel certain because they need their world to be normatively ordered, a world they can make sense of, where things are as they should be, and doing good things, like respecting people, pays, especially when it's deserved, and doing bad things to the bad people deserving it is necessary to get the best results.

We live our lives and run our world on pet hunches. We've had little better to go on. Now things grow more dire. Our common sense conception of character is being subjected to unnerving critiques deriving from recent empirical and analytical studies.[10] We're getting better and better reasons to worry that we are all far more clueless or flat out mistaken about these matters than we dare imagine. Currently, while faith in the academies as moral character factories might not be wholly misplaced, confidence in that costly system is not warranted by any facsimile of scientifically respectable evidence.

The academies are to be commended for recently recognizing this, and taking the first baby steps toward remedying it. Are they prepared to recognize the magnitude of the task they've set themselves? Are they willing to commit themselves to pursue seriously the creation of intellectually respectable measures of character? The task is tantamount to a Manhattan Project in psychology and

---

10   See John M. Doris' *Lack of Character* (Cambridge, 2002). Doris and his allies may be exaggerating the philosophical and moral significance of some socio-psychological research. See John Sabini and Maury Silver, "Lack of Character? Situationism Critiqued," *Ethics* 115 (April 2005) for criticism and a bibliography of a growing debate that aspiring molders of character better ponder carefully.

ethics—and in this case it's not unlikely that the military may learn lots it doesn't want to hear—so optimism for the near term looks ludicrous.

My own native pessimism was reinforced during my last act as ethics advisor dissuading the USNA leadership from committing to a perfectly preposterous "character assessment measure" promoted by a three-year special subcommittee (2/3 clueless how to evaluate any such animal, but pressed by an impatient Superintendent for results). Sparks of optimism survive when the High Command listens to reason. Despair settles in when the organizational mindset hampers its mission. Despite—or because of—all the mind-numbing encomia of character, military minds seem to suffer some diminished capacity for grasping the challenges of the epistemology of character assessment.[11]

Though obvious, it is too rarely noted that the difficulties of measuring character and its development differ considerably, in degree and kind, depending on the trait. To take a pointed instance, when assessing the utility of officers studying moral reasoning, in the academies or elsewhere, the first question must be what traits it is likely to influence. Having Marines muddle through moral theories is often abruptly dismissed as worthless, patently irrelevant to the military's mission. All bridges from such refined cerebration to enhanced vaunted military virtues (courage, discipline, loyalty, honor, integrity, selflessness, perseverance) are all too rickety. The payoff of a proper intro ethics course is looked for in the wrong places.

Evidently, the disvaluation of instruction in moral reasoning betokens the disvaluation, endemic in the military, of humility. The benefits of participation in well regulated Socratic battles, though less regular than the effects of sunshine on seeds, are frequent and manifest. Competent ethics instructors live on the common, dramatic occasions when it comes as a revelation to some students that their moral beliefs are not mere opinions invulnerable to all contradiction, that they are subject to and at the mercy of reasoning that literally *compels* assent or at least respect, and that their embarrassment by a compelling argument opposing their beliefs is only compounded by dismissively declaring, "Well, that's just your opinion." Retreat to that redoubt is not an option, not when the argument's premises match your own beliefs, and its inferences run the same rails as your own rationality. The longer you brazenly resist, the more humbling the surrender when you've spent

---

11   Despite yearly teaching a couple classes about Aristotle on virtue, officers don't balk at research proposals declaring that virtues are *abilities*, and failures to act virtuously are due solely to a deficiency of moral courage. They listen respectfully to "experts" selling assessments of academy character development programs using the same kind of tests used for assessing academic programs. They do not readily appreciate the import of the few basic certainties: e.g., propensities and abilities are metaphysically and epistemologically disparate things; virtues are peculiar propensities: behavior in one situation apparently exhibiting a virtue is an unreliable predictor of the person's passing a "test" of that virtue in some other kind of situation. A perspicuous specification of virtue propensities eludes us.

your last clip. Experiencing that a time or two tends to leave lasting, measurable effects on a person's openness to other people's "opinions."[12]

Another testable benefit: education in moral reasoning enhances skills leaders need for explaining the reasonableness of their decisions to superiors, peers and subordinates, and therewith securing the respect, trust and confidence requisite for effective leadership.[13]

Some military leaders display such skills and propensities. They are open to the idea of a character assessment project. They see that they command an unmatched laboratory for longitudinal studies, from academy to retirement. The potential boon for civilian society doesn't excite them. Their conception of the profit for the military is inchoate so their enthusiasm is tempered. Presently they seem ambivalent, less from skepticism of success, and more from a reluctance to recognize fully that without an answer to the question of how to measure character, reason can never control practice or be truly practical. Without a reliable measure of results, talk of ends and means is idle uplift.

ROI

Despite an undistinguished record for instilling righteousness, no service chief dare abandon the academies and alienate their proud alumni, who dominate the senior staff and top ranks throughout the services. The academies' official *raison d'etre* has resided in that very circumstance. The academy superintendents' favorite power-pointed apologia is that academy graduates tend to stay in service longer than officers of other ascensions, and fill the highest ranks at a greater rate. The higher the rank, the higher the percent of academy alumni. Officer retention rates constantly fluctuate for all kinds of reasons, but the academies' relative

---

12   Academy leadership textbooks do commend due humility, but it ranks way down the list of traits regularly emphasized. Hopes of our military's appreciating the military value of "a degree of intellectual humility" would be more encouraged if its current golden boy could manage a tad more enthusiasm than: "not at all a bad quality in those who may be charged in the future with some very weighty responsibilities" (David H. Petraeus, "Beyond the Cloister," http://www.the-american-interest.com/article.cfm?piece=290). Actually, in context his backhanded understatement is plainly tamping down the preachiness of his message about a matter he thinks of great importance.

13   A disposition to consider the opposing opinions of others, and an ability to prevail in open debate that encourages the disposition are relatively readily measured (compared to traits like courage, honesty, integrity, justice). Factoring for influences is challenging. We may reasonably assume, but cannot readily demonstrate, that these benefits are affected less by the institutional setting of instruction and more by the instruction's quality (an attribute not easily measured apart from such effects). Still, a fair conjecture is that the better civilian schools whose philosophy faculty's PhD training enhances the necessary (but not sufficient) Socratic skills for teaching moral reasoning may have an edge over military schools where fewer ethics instructors have near as much essential training.

success remains the highest. Amortize the training investment over a career and the academies appear to have a comfortably high Return on Investment (ROI). Or so it is said.

The superintendents' case for cost-effectiveness had better be good. The academies would be extravagant failures if they produced first-rate ensigns and lieutenants without thereby producing first-rate career officers serving 20-30 years and becoming captains, admirals, colonels or generals. Recent analyses of the data suggest that the superintendents' case is getting steadily less compelling, so it now convinces few but the converted.[14]

Obviously, whatever the raw numbers regarding retention and rank, their explanation must recognize diverse factors. One such is self-selection. Those willing to serve a short term to finance a college education and not needing a total subsidy might see ROTC as the best deal, while someone eager for or open to a military career may be more amenable to the rigors and privations of academy life. Also, old boy networks are unlikely to have a lesser role in the military than elsewhere. And more than likely the politics of retention and promotion is aggravated by our military's policy of requiring steady promotion for retention. (One officer, upon becoming a Navy Captain, was counseled by his superior: "This is the last promotion you'll receive based on merit." Readers will have their own hunches how much of that is dismissible exaggeration betraying disgruntlement.)[15]

All the statistical niceties of ROI analysis may be a sideshow. No analysis can be politically decisive when so many intangibles merit consideration and

---

14   Turgay Demirel concluded that "the magnitude differences in retention between the five major commissioning sources often are not large. Moreover, the direction of the retention effect often varies across the services for each commissioning program" ("Abstract," *A Statistical Analysis of Officer Retention in the U.S. Military*, Master's thesis, Naval Postgraduate School, Monterey, CA, 2002). Later, Zafer Kizikaya concluded that, for those commissioned in the period 1981-2001, USMA "graduates have the lowest retention rates, whereas OCS graduates have the highest retention rates." Yet, USMA "graduates are more likely to be promoted to Lieutenant Colonel than those from other sources" ("Abstract," *An Analysis of the Effect of Commissioning Sources on Retention and Promotion of U.S. Army Officers*, Master's thesis, Naval Postgraduate School, Monterey, CA, 2004). The 2004 Tench Francis study cited above mentions many of the obstacles to forming a meaningful ROI measure for comparing the academies with ROTC and OCS, but provides some of the pertinent data, including evidence that the advantage of academy graduates in attaining the general/flag officer ranks has diminished. See also <http://www.truthout.org/article/west-point-grads-exit-service-high-rate> for a 2007 news report on the sharp drop in USMA graduate retention rates. After their five year commitment, 35 percent of the classes of 2000 and 2001 got out.

15   Other factors affecting promotion may be surprising. Ibrahim Korkmaz found that "commissioning source has significant strong effect on survival rates with Naval Academy graduates have [sic] a better survival rate than other commissioning sources" ("Abstract," *Analysis of the Survival Patterns of United States Naval Officers*, Naval Postgraduate School, Monterey, CA, 2005).

the prospects for agreement on a metric are so grim. Anyway, whether or not it's factored into the ROI, one consideration will swamp all others. Grant the high likelihood that ROTC and OCS and other options could be sufficiently developed to produce all the needed fully proficient officers. We'll never really know since it is not going to happen. Until all the world's lions lie with its lambs, we are not going to suffer a national trauma of losing the academies, and work through a shaky time regaining our level of confidence in our officers and our whole military.

I sense that many Americans—and foreigners too—would *feel* threatened by shuttering the academies: it would assault the national and international certainty of the professionalism of this military. The prestige of those schools is self-perpetuating. What we want from our military (and our police) is security. What we want even more is a feeling of security. We want to be feeling comforted when we think about our military. Our nation justifiably enjoys its confidence in its professionalized military. We don't much doubt that ROTC and OCS grads are sufficiently competent, but, in my experience, even the proud ROTC and OCS grads commonly share the civilians' sense that the academies are the true font of our military's professionalism. If we knew how to price America's—and its allies' and enemies'—confidence in this military's professionalism we might conclude that at a billion a year the academies are a bargain.[16]

Commitment

Whatever their success, the intent of the academies is explicit. The official "purpose" of USNA: *To provide the Naval Service with leaders of character who will serve the nation in peace and war.* Its stated "mission": *To provide graduates who are dedicated to a career of naval service....* The Navy's "core values" make it emphatic: *Honor, Courage, Commitment.* Each service branch and academy has its own motto, mission statement, core values, or the like, but every item is saluted at all. In response to the precipitous drop in officer retention in previous decades, the West Point mission statement was revised last decade by its new Superintendent to further emphasize this goal: "to educate, train, and *inspire* the corps of cadets for a career as an officer in the United States Army."

What the nation wants from these schools sits oddly with what the students want. Students aren't being enticed by intimations that their peculiar post-secondary education will induce an abiding penchant to remain till pension time in the military. I have yet to meet any midshipmen (current or graduate) who say they welcomed the privations of their undergraduate years in the hope that this route to a commission would secure them a perduring proclivity for military life. Predictably, their motivations are all over the map. Some come with career uncertainties and

---

16 This analysis may supply the needed missing premises for the conclusion of Robert L. Goldich, *The DoD Service Academies: Issues for Congress*, Washington, DC: Congressional Research Service, Library of Congress, February 6, 1997.

hopes that they'll like the regimen well enough to be more settled of mind. Some don't come that way, but come away glad the academy had that effect. Many come with clenched intent to be a careerist, with no need for the academy to encourage the ambition, other than not discouraging it. They'd head for ROTC or OCS if the academies hadn't picked them—or didn't exist. Taxpayers might wonder whether their money is wasted on them.

Tax dollars may seem more misspent on the many midshipmen and cadets who come with no inclination to pursue a military career, and never share the nation's goals for their academy attendance. No such motivation is required of them. No commitment to service is made until the third year, and a mere five year obligation may suffice. No disposition for dedication to the service is demanded for academy admission or commissioning. The services dare not do more than encourage career ambitions for fear of losing too many of the most promising candidates. Among our best and brightest, there is no surplus of interest in a military career—and we dare not let any but our best and brightest command so much power.

The academies continue to attract a comfortably high caliber of students. The minimum physical requirements are unthinkable at any other college. Academy entrants are the swiftest and strongest, the most physically fit and athletic of any freshmen class and the differential grows over four years. They are hardly just jocks. No school admissions process more stringently scrutinizes applicant character. However crude our indicia of character, it's a safe bet that academy students on average have more strength of character and altruism than any other student body. So while they don't rank highest for pure intellect (average SAT's 1300-1350), among all the able-bodied, earnest and decent young men and women in our land, they are an exceptionally bright lot.[17]

Demanding more passion for service from prospective (or actual) officers would be pointless and counterproductive. An adequate devotion to duty need not be a love of duty, a yearning for its continuance. Absent a surplus of credible candidates, efficiency prefers aptitude over proclivity. Wasting some dollars training gifted prospects who'll never want a career from it costs less than settling for ambitious second-rate talent. Demanding career commitment is impracticable. Encouraging it is necessary and unobjectionable, within limits.

---

17   They'd be still brighter if our academies shed the penchants of civilian schools. How exactly the academies' mission is furthered by recruiting athletes is not obvious when the academic admission scores of almost half of them are in the lower 30 percent of their class, a predictor of a lower graduation rate. (Data reported in GAO-03-1000, "Military Education: DOD Needs to Enhance Performance Goals and Measures to Improve Oversight of Military Academies," released September 10, 2003.)

Glorification

The military's self-valorization is among the more audible and visible contrasts between professionalism in the military and elsewhere. Our military's exaltation of a military career and glorification of warriors and particularly their commanders are deliberately beyond what other professions would dare. (The deliberateness is manifested in exaltations of such exaltation, praising the praising, honoring the honoring). A service career is valued as noble, and so are the aspiration and dedication to it. Any honest workman regards his work as honorable, in the minimal sense of being respectable, not dishonorable. The warrior ethos aggressively glorifies warrior work, regarding it honorable in the most robust sense of being a noble calling, worthy of honoring with the highest honors of the nation—a nation grateful for its men and women willing to risk limb and life, saving it from oppression, or conquering others, winning wealth, power, and glory for the whole nation. No other profession is more celebrated or bears such an exalted self-conception. The most estimable of dentists, teachers, accountants and attorneys get no ticker tape parade, and don't dream of professional exploits deserving one.

Professionalism elsewhere does not urge practitioners to bethink themselves a breed apart. The best respected doctors and teachers get off the pedestals their clients keep putting under their feet. They create a human relationship fit for open, honest communication. Here the consistency of the military ethos with our civic culture gets strained.

Our civilian-military relations are notoriously subject to tensions, mutual suspicions, and sharp conflicts of values and ideals. The strains can have diverse sources. The military's legal and political subordination entails some kind of respect for the basic principles and values of the civic culture it serves, but the mission it is assigned drives it to develop and enforce a profoundly different ethos that proudly promotes pride in itself, its values and standards. There are real sources of real oppositions, and real obstacles to mutual comprehension. Conflicts are commonly misconceived in counter-productive terms of military versus civilian when actually the alleged disagreements may appear within one or both sides as well as between them. Both sides can be victims of stereotypes of their opponents and themselves by supposing that some belief or attitude is an essential fixture of a perspective when actually military professionalism is not committed to that belief or attitude, and civilian culture is not committed to its opposite. Some military professionals insist that the military conceive itself as subject to "higher" standards than civilians, a conception suggesting some competition and moral superiority that some civilians think ominous and arrogant—and some military professionals deride.[18]

---

18 The dialectical options are endless, when, for example, many military personnel and civilians insist that our founding documents are products of their current conception of Christianity rather than expressions of nonsectarian Enlightenment principles.

The ROI on our military and civilian practices of glorification of military service and of commitment and dedication to that service must certainly be huge. We'd be radically confounded—we could not know what to believe about human motivation—if we somehow discovered that all of our cheering has no tendency to raise the likelihood that some of us will be willing to have their brains blown out just so the rest of us remain brained.

But, stopping there aborts the ROI. No human activity is totally riskless and costless. Yet an ROI "measurement" of the risks and costs of all our glorification of military service now sounds near oxymoronic. We are profoundly fractionated in our attitudes about the military and its glorification. Many civilians feel certain that a republican liberal culture is imperiled by the glorification of the warrior typical of other cultures. (Never mind that the certainty certainly exceeds anyone's ability to specify the kinds and degrees of excessive glorification and consequent kinds of costs and benefits and persuasively measure them and the risks.) While measurement is beyond us, it still seems reasonable to worry whether our indiscriminate honoring of devotion to dubious purposes carries more terrible risks and costs than we're willing to admit.

Just what social status of the military is consistent with the evolving liberal egalitarianism of our democratic tradition is up for grabs. This whole subject is made more puzzling, and maybe paradoxical, because we cannot evaluate our activity of evaluating and glorifying the military in ROI terms alone. We are not really glorifying if we are doing so only because of a belief in its utility. The glorifiers must and do suppose that the service, and dedication, and glorifying have some significant value apart from keeping them safer. What could that value be?

It seems to be an intrinsic value in one respect: Its value seems independent of any effect on the quality of job performance. Many of the most dedicated may be incompetent, while others who wish they were elsewhere may perform impeccably. Yet, dedication is not an unconditional good. Its value varies with the value of its object. And also with the person's motivations and character. Dedication to the US Marine Corps may be an admirable trait when possessed by someone of good character. In the lives of the vicious and brutal there may be nothing in their dedication to esteem or respect. The dedication is unworthy of encouragement unless subordinate to a dedication to serving one's country, a commitment to substantial selflessness for the sake of one's own people, or the like. There's reason to doubt that a military organization can be in itself a legitimating object of dedication that makes dedication to it commendable apart from a dedication to some intrinsic good.[19]

Presumably the glorification of military service is due to the basic, supreme value it serves along with the great risks and costs of the service. All that transfers to the glorification of dedication to the service. Professionals generally respect

---

19   This may be entailed by the moral precariousness of the military, See Chapter 7 herein.

dedication to their profession; their glorifications of it are low key. Our military's need of dedication is like no other. The job of a standing armed force is to stay on the job. Its job to secure our safety, now, next Tuesday, and perpetually. That is not the performance of some action like a surgical operation or a lecture. We want a standing army to just stand there and stay put. The job of its personnel is to be dedicated.

Our civic culture's core values are threatened when our glorification of the military suggests some disparagement of dedication to other forms of community service. And while some amongst us might wish it otherwise, our nation cannot officially stigmatize a life lacking any such dedication, a life markedly more spontaneous. Such lives may be lived badly and wasted, as may lives of unflagging dedication. A nation may properly encourage a longing to serve it with a lifetime in the military. It may honor the service and the longing, but our best traditions don't derogate citizens devoid of any wish for membership in the nation's military. No eagerness for such service is necessary for being a good citizen. Suffice that citizens be willing to serve when the nation needs them. Society and its state may wish to encourage more, but penalizing its lack is antithetical to the individualism this nation prizes.

A deficiency or absence of dedication is not readily regarded a vice. Dedication is not perseverance, a trait whose potential for contribution to job performance is evident, and whose absence can be costly. Motivations like dedication and pride don't improve job performance like other virtues. It's rather that pride motivates the production of its justification; ambitions and aspirations are themselves means to their own attainment. Yet, again, the drive to have a distinguished career does not strictly correlate with success. When job performance is faultless, faulting someone's dedicational deficiencies seems senseless, and perhaps self-defeating. And when the absence of a trait is not regarded a vice, regarding the trait as a virtue is subject to instabilities.

Propaganda?

The academies are tasked with commissioning a high rate of their Plebes, and thus with nurturing and fostering a passion for commitment and dedication to military service. Elsewhere, conceptions of respect set some limits to the methods and means of persuasion. So there's room for worry whether and when the academies' control over the informational environment may fail to fully respect the autonomy of the students making life choices.

Armed combat calls for extreme selflessness, a willingness to die for comrades and countrymen. The academies need and want to nurture this. They call upon students by appealing to their love of country, loyalty to their mates, sense of duty, their personal honor and other selfless springs of virtue to motivate conduct endangering the self. Yet, students willing to shed their life's blood in the line of duty can get resentful and rebellious when made to sacrifice some hours to the gnawing boredom of the ceaseless, omnipresent character training they're subjected to. To pleas that they selflessly submit themselves to hours of torment listening to prattling about the beauty of selflessness, they might listen obediently, but incredulously. Instead they are told to value this training for its contribution to their character development. In turn, the character development is to be valued for its contribution to their career.

Students swim in a steady stream of stories of the utility of virtue for victory and career advancement. They are taught the 1001 ways that leaders and mangers benefit by respecting subordinates. The constant refrain (rarely sung by philosophically trained faculty, military or civilian) is that success as officers and leaders comes from character, particularly integrity, the pole star of a constellation of moral virtues validating trust and vindicating obedience. Moral virtues (and the training developing them) are valued for their contributions to an officer's proficiency, and thus to professional success; their contribution to the military's proficiency is assumed, but left in the background.

That sales pitch is popular—echoed at business schools and elsewhere—and, not coincidentally, simplistic. It is so pervasive even among leaders who better know better as to merit a few paragraph excursus into the heart of daylight.

In the absence of any objective, operational measures of character, its correlations with anything else are moot. Currently our evidence is a rag bag of anecdotes. On that basis, while the moral virtues of military leaders appear to frequently and importantly affect their professional success, only blind or bad faith would infer that nice leaders *always* finish first and nasty ones last. Elsewhere sometimes a John Wooden wins; sometimes a Bobby Knight; sometimes a Leonard Bernstein leads his troops to musical success; other times Toscanini-like tyrants triumph. Bradleys, Marshalls and like models of military rectitude reap victories and honors, and so do monsters of horrific cruelty toward the enemy or subordinates or anyone in their path.

The ancient idea that virtue is essential for happiness has some truth, but it is not that a leader deficient in moral rectitude must be disadvantaged in mortal combat. Common sense says that different leaders succeed in different circumstances. In some, good character is a great asset; in others, priceless. But, sometimes vices are assets. Vanity has its costs, and is specially liable to be lethal in the military, yet the rank, renown, and charisma of a Patton or MacArthur are often more consequences of vanity than causes of it. (Vanity amongst the cleverest philosophers is no less endemic.)

The virtue-success equation must be complex, varying with the virtue and the circumstances. Physical courage is called for and displayed on the front lines; valor is less tested in senior strategists continents away from the fray today. Circumstances call on specific virtues, and virtues call for specific rewards: compassion and cooperativeness don't occasion the same awe and respect as bravery or garner the most coveted medals. A virtue's rewards have variant contingencies; the risks run vary with the vice. The tests of integrity, courage, truthfulness, and loyalty are *relatively* uncontroversial once the bare empirical facts are known, while the tests of justice are liable to more variant interpretations and evaluations, so the just man's rewards are more subject to luck. Academy catechism says that integrity is the key virtue of military executives: their leadership rests on it, so the organization must value it, and tend to reward it. The same cannot be said about justice, not as confidently and convincingly. Accordingly, though not denied, it is less said at the academies. The trouble is: integrity without justice may win honors and admiration while its ethical value is suspect or nil.

When what we really care about is simply victory, a success specified without moral notions, the officers and traits we promote come with all kinds of vices. Where and how ethical virtues have a role in professional success depends mainly on how much we really admire the nobility of those traits, not just their utility, and how well we secure their utility by institutional and cultural constraints, incentives and sanctions.

Often the best sanctions seem natural by being effects of extra-institutional norms or rules adopted for other reasons. Leadership by instilling respect and trust rather than raw fear may meet more success when the troops come from an egalitarian culture inhospitable to servility. Also, forswearing conscription encourages an institutional culture valorizing ethical leadership. Moral concern for the welfare of subordinates may wane when their service is voluntary, but political pressure waxes, for the ranks must be filled. When service jobs compete in a free market of employment, enlistment and reenlistment are jeopardized by maltreatment of subordinates. This is among the best, if less cited, reasons for all-volunteer armed forces.[20] Another is that abjuring conscription may brake resorts to military force to attain a nation's ends.[21] Among the most heinous and resented mistreatments of subordinates is commanding them to use violence against other people for an unworthy or dubious cause. (The ever popular idea that universal conscription would make America more pacific defies history and horse sense.) Here and elsewhere the reward rate for virtue reflects the fairness of background conditions.

Any post-adolescent who denies such patent truisms risks being suspected of dishonesty by many mature adults. Science suggests an alternative hypothesis. Anthropology tells us that notions of immanent justice structure primitive people's perception of reality. Piagetian developmental research adds that infantile convictions of the regularity of virtue's worldly success commonly persist and permeate the thinking of well-educated young adults. It does seem that, despite all their professed cynicism, cadets and midshipmen generally profess or betray some such simple faith in a straight line dependence of effective officership on good character. Many return to preach the word to later classes with evident conviction.

---

20   See Erik Eckholm, "As Recruiting Suffers, Military Reins In Abuses at Boot Camp," *New York Times*, July 26, 2005 <http://www.nytimes.com/2005/07/26/national/26training.html>.

21   *Ibid.*

Perhaps faith in the perfect utility of virtue is a necessary ladder, best thrown away later. Evidence of damage done by this conviction tends to be equivocal. Still, insofar as PMEE is owned and operated by officers whose conception of its mission relevance is predicated on this juvenile hope, some anxieties about PMEE's intellectual and moral integrity might be appropriate. There are at least two causes of concern here.

First, trust in the academies' honesty is tested by moralizing that tends to pretend that the sanctions for moral failings are natural and inevitable, when that is rarely true anywhere and less so in the military, where formal and informal norms of secrecy and loyalty present formidable obstacles to the exposure of wrongdoing and effective enforcement. What's inevitable is that the virtue-reward relation in the military is prone to perversion by politics and public relations. Academy moralizing is mocked by the reality of pervasive hypocrisy—by Pentagon and political leaders' fabricating a heroic death for Cpl. Pat Tillman, and doing nothing (or damn little) to discourage the media glorification of the misadventures of Pfc. Jessica Lynch, while still doing near nothing to encourage the national recognition and glorification due the awesome, humbling heroism of CWO Hugh Thompson at My Lai. Add on to this our nation's doing near nothing to dishonor and punish "our boys" who commit military atrocities (e.g., bombing civilian water facilities and disabled enemy soldiers) while screaming "war crime" at the least infraction by any enemy (e.g., broadcasting POW photos.) Compounding it further, the enemy war criminals we go after are, rightly, the leadership, while our own war criminals we prosecute (successfully or at all) are the lowest ranked involved. All this makes an exquisite recipe nourishing cynicism or self-deception.

The academies' treatment of such matters is nearly as discouraging as it is encouraging—and it is stupendously encouraging. Our academies deserve to be publicly honored and glorified for honoring and glorifying Hugh Thompson, and requiring its future officer to contemplate the horror of My Lai – and commanding a gunship to kill the next fellow American who tries adding to the horror. The academies are among the rare places in this military and this nation where Thompson gets some bits of his due recognition; this is one of the many ways the moral tenor of the academies surpasses the rest of the military culture and our public culture. But, this denial of Thompson's due elsewhere is not dwelt upon at the academies. The institutional moral courage gets strained when talk turns to the treatment our government and our military have given to members of our military whose conduct causes them some embarrassment. Students are not much made to ponder Thompson's fate at the hands of Congress, the DoD and down the line—or the fate of the officers responsible for the massacre. Students are not discouraged from it, but neither are they encouraged to consider the incidents and patterns of injustice by politicians, Pentagon, and public, befalling our blackest sheep, and whistleblowers and moral heroes who embarrass our nation and its military. However understandable and justifiable, it is dispiriting to observe a pattern of avoiding full discussion of the dispiriting realities of the career to which these students are to commit themselves.

Character

The other worry about all the attention on the profits of virtue is a worry about the operative morality of military professionalism. If we are aiming to nurture *moral* virtue, do we need to inculcate a faith that we make our fighting forces more effective by denying their managers the option of flogging insubordinate subordinates? Shouldn't our leaders-to-be instead be learning to be willing to accept the consequences of abjuring cruelty and callousness? Shouldn't the "take away" be that brutality is not a legitimate leadership style, however effective?[22]

Absolutely. And not necessarily. There's no impropriety in our military impressing upon its future leaders that respecting subordinates is necessary for their respecting the leader. There's no impropriety in a leader being moved to be respectful by the fact of its utility. But, first, what that motivates is only the respect necessary to receive the respect necessary for mission accomplishment. Determining the bounds of the respect thus required is beyond the capacity of current social science. And, second, implicit in that, it matters mightily what motivational system that reason fits into and where.

Most people are moved by much the same reasons. We differ mainly in the ordering and prioritizing of our motives. Military professionalism may root itself in some contractualist self-conception premised on equal respect and mutual consent to impose a maximization of military proficiency where necessary for survival. Where and how respect constrains maximization is debatable. Instead, a military professional might be a Sidgwickian esoteric rule consequentialist whose secret deepest principle is military proficiency maximization, which motivates an organization to institutionalize a public morality in which respect constrains the maximizing principle—but is constrained by the deeper principle when pushed to the wall. And, if the empirical assumptions are right, another military professional might be an egoist officer who profits by running his life according to any of the above possibilities.

These contrasting structures of principles and reasons may come to similar judgments about specific actions, but the character of persons depends profoundly on the structuring of their motivations, and the content of their most basic reasons and dominant principles.

The character of military professionalism is most fully expressed in the character PMEE promotes. The character the academies aspire to inspire is more specific and peculiar than a set of ethical virtues we all have reason to want in

---

22   That lesson needn't be a simplistic absolutism banning exceptional acts in exceptional circumstances. Military honor might not be tarnished by resort to drastic punishments to keep some crew of brutish conscripts in line sufficiently for mission accomplishment. If we want officers of truly high moral character, we've got to habituate them to complex, nuanced reasoning, not sound-bite moral slogans. This is hard enough to teach anywhere. Teaching it in the military is harder for reasons that make the teaching more important.

any fellow member of our community. Even coupled with technical proficiency, the moral virtues of a decent human being don't suffice for competence, let alone excellence, as a military leader. In the military, some traits like hardiness become vital; for leaders, still other traits like decisiveness are crucial. The distinctively military virtues include higher degrees of toughness (physical and emotional), self-confidence, and earnestness. The toughness risks running to callousness, the self-confidence is liable to arrogant imperiousness, and the earnestness is a susceptibility to sanctimoniousness. (A ready sense of absurdity is an asset in military life, but is not officially classified a virtue.)

Yet, again, our military ethos is supposed to be consistent with our civic culture and to depart from it only in its context-appropriate accentuations. The character of military professionals is to be, I take it, a compromise, wherein distinctively military traits are substantially constrained by a civilian enlightenment ethos – in evolving ways and degrees. Finding the right balance is challenging. Our prized virtues, traits and ideals can collide.

Discipline

USNA declares that its mission must "*... imbue [academy students] with the highest ideals of duty, honor and loyalty.*" Actually, not every ideal of duty, honor and loyalty inspires a dedication to military service. The ethos the academies aim to instill (what the military considers "the highest ideals") is supposed to inspire such dedication. An ethos is more than universal ethical principles and values.

USNA further specifies its mission to be: *To inspire and develop outstanding young men and women to become ... officers with knowledge, character, and discipline.* Discipline is itself a character trait. This double counting of discipline expresses the military's distinctive conception of the best character.

"Discipline" is a noun naming a trait presumed to be developed by an activity named by the verb. Civilians value the trait as a form of self-control, a capacity for staying focused, unfazed by distractions, impervious to impulse. The military values that too, but its emphasis has long been on fixed habits of obedience and the automaticity of compliance with commands.

The name of the activity developing the trait is sometimes synonymous with "punish". The activity is normally impermissible unless performed by someone entitled to control its object. It is a stern regimen difficult to maintain outside a closely controlled environment. All of the distinctive features of the whole military regimen, and thus the whole academy regimen appear to be premised on the assumption that the primary trait, throughout the troops, essential for military proficiency, that the military can much control, is discipline. The prioritization of discipline is the academy's fundamental contrast with civilian colleges.

The regimen has long been liable to influences by the military value of other traits (especially loyalty), but any reform imperiling discipline is suspect. The recent relaxation of the regime may indicate that the trait is now less valued, its value less absolutely dominant. It may indicate instead or in addition a reconception of that trait.

The academies tout their regimen as contributing to an officer's character, not just the trait of discipline, but the whole complex of desired character traits: justice, honesty, integrity, etc. Upon reflection, this seems *prima facie* implausible. I suggest that they have inherited an honored traditional regimen well-enough designed to maximize discipline, with a well-enough documented record of success. They must promote other traits contributing to military proficiency, but just how this regimen would further the development of most moral virtues is a mystery, while the potential for retarding the development of some prized traits seems evident.

The newly softened regimen may increase the proficiency of the resulting discipline, but however softened it is a form of behavioral conditioning designed to effect a reflexive response to a stimulus. Discipline is not conscientiousness, a disposition to be moved by the call of duty. Discipline responds directly to a command; the sacredness of duty is out of sight. This disposition is unlike the propensities we commonly consider moral virtues, and the differences seem morally significant. Paradigm moral virtues like justice, honesty, self-control and courage seem to be dispositions regulated by some kind of practical wisdom which finely adjusts behavior to respond to situational variables affecting the contextual significance of specific actions.

The hey-day of Skinnerian behaviorism is long past. The extravagance of its claims of the pedagogical powers of behavioral conditioning is widely recognized. If there be a causal chain from the blunt conditioning to the fine modulations of a moral virtue, the links remain opaque or invisible.

The military wants to avoid instilling habits imperiling military proficiency— like compliance with commands so automatic that the agent is incapable of intelligently responding to an evident catastrophe. The fine-tuning of discipline to get just the right balance of situationally appropriate automaticity and situationally appropriate circumspection has yet to be mastered by our learning theories. The possibilities for collisions of competing dispositions here are not remote hypotheticals. And the problems of installing the right dispositions are compounded by our pervasive disagreements in particular cases as to just which conduct is proper, optimal or acceptable. Those disagreements are nowhere more prevalent than in the contexts of questioning the propriety of questioning authority.

Liberation

The academies evidence an admirable interest in promoting liberated thought—up to a point. The academies make efforts to avoid producing "good Prussian soldiers" who robotically render unthinking obedience. They want officers to be thoughtful followers because they want thoughtful leaders, capable of independent, critical judgment.

There is authentic concern that what is billed as a philosophy course toward a baccalaureate degree not be a bully pulpit for indoctrination into the conventional code: "the Navy (Army/Air Force) way." Rather than teaching the right answers and testing for recall, the intent is to improve the students' powers of thoughtfulness, and perhaps their propensity for thoughtfulness of some intellectual sophistication. They teach future leaders to listen with some open-mindedness to dissenting opinions of subordinates, and to question authority—when appropriate. They don't want officers who park their conscience when they don a uniform. They have students study M.L. King's "Letter from a Birmingham Jail" advocating civil disobedience. They teach that obedience to an illegal order is itself illegal, and that an officer retains the ultimate moral responsibility for his/her obeying an immoral order, and that refusal to obey may be morally appropriate or required.

The motivation for liberating thought is, of course, to improve military proficiency. The academies teach that training for proficiency at routine procedures is insufficient preparation for officers, and that rigidly authoritarian systems risk suffering significant and sometimes calamitous inefficiencies. That rationale is fine as far as it goes, but it stands alone, unchecked, and that is consequential because teaching pious platitudes takes no thought or courage. The devil is in the details of what, when, how much questioning is appropriate or allowable, and whether refusal of an order is required. Such matters tend to be controversial. The military settles such controversies by considerations of military proficiency.

The wisdom of the new enlightened leadership style is readily illustrated with stories of superiors operating with misconceptions of plain fact or disregard of black letter law. The wisdom of welcoming a subordinate's questioning one's values or basic principles may be less obvious. That practice is less warmly recommended.

What is recommended and practiced is a standing presumption, for factual and value judgments alike, that a superior's decision is to be trusted and acted upon. With all the bold extolling of independence of thought, in practice officers bethink themselves required to presume that their superiors (civilian and military) work with the best information available and would not be deliberately commanding anything illegal or immoral. Some such presumption could be sound. It becomes willful naiveté when (as happens even at the highest ranks) the presumption is rendered indefeasible via such popular supplementary suppositions as that the leadership must have classified information justifying decisions and policies which appear unwise, unjust or irresponsible by unprejudiced study of public information.

Such supporting presumptions may be made more palatable by weakening the claim of infallibility and necessity ("they *must* know"), and acknowledging the real possibility of competing, unflattering explanations of a leader's decision. The epistemic grounds for such acknowledgment are conceded. There's no scandal in teaching that soldiers and sailors have done some horrible things following orders of their military or civilian leaders. Many academy instructors (more frequently but far from exclusively civilians) would admit that the ratio of righteous warring by this or any powerful democracy is not encouraging: it is not patently better than the ratio of right choices by leaders in other domains, where professionals don't encourage habits of blinkered confidence in their leadership. Midshipmen are warned against indulging themselves in delusional patriotism. They read the wisdom of Admiral James Stockdale, wrought from brutal experience, that POW's nurtured on patriotic myth are especially vulnerable to being turned by being disabused of their historical naiveté.

So much for their sense of the past. Understandably, academy leaders do not invite the inductive leap to the present. They have seemed unprepared and unwilling to openly grapple with the issues of the integrity of PMEE at a national military academy under a regime acting with evident contempt for the principles of *jus ad bellum* and *jus in bello* taught in their military ethics textbooks. When coupled with the regime's evident contempt for its highest commanders, PMEE can become mission impossible.

I know more than a few academy officers and instructors privately disapproved of our invasion of Iraq in various ways and degrees. They were outraged or exasperated or depressed—and that was before being shamed, agonized by obscene prison interrogations by the Army they had dedicated their lives to. Even among those sympathetic with the Bush Crusade (before learning of the intelligence fiasco or fraud) their bellicosity hadn't the politicos' enthusiastic pitch. Overall, whether for the invasion or against, their responses to 9/11 were markedly more tempered and measured—enough so that I began ruing the civilian control over our military, an attitude I'd never have imagined my ever entertaining.

However, the faculty's mature, educated misgivings were not as freely or forcefully aired as at secular civilian colleges and universities, and at most all but our more dogmatic religious schools. That was hardly because their worries could go without saying. Not when, in the commons room of the USNA Professional Development Division (housing the Department of Leadership, Ethics and Law), the TV stayed tuned to a rabid FOX News. And not when the students, whose acculturation is a work in progress, are far more prone to whoop it up with the politicians and the revenge-ridden public they come from.

The most depressing and hopeful moment of my academy stay was a Western Lit class in March, 2003 diverted to responding to earnest student requests to help them comprehend how any reasonable, decent American could possibly oppose our up-coming invasion of Iraq. The hopeful part is that their incomprehension of so many of their countrymen really worried them. These future military leaders are teachable, reachable, and more open to rigorous independent reasoning than prevalent stereotypes predict. In one USMA military ethics class I've heard of, 80 percent of the papers argued, unprompted, that our Iraq invasion violated *jus ad bellum* principles.

Yet, informed public debate on any issue of such intense, immediate concern is, if not quite censored, not encouraged, as doubtless it will be when the issues are safely past and innocuously academic. Frank conversations with USNA leaders disclosed unembarrassed fears that serious debate on issues touching the students' current or likely imminent decisions might end in "bad" choices.

That attitude is alien to other secular colleges and professional schools. There, such an occasion, when students are primed by intense personal involvement to dig deep into questions of immense complexity would likely be greeted as a supreme "teachable moment." When better to fully engage students intellectually, emotionally, morally, as whole persons? At intellectually serious schools, an instructor, however confident in his/her own convictions, is pedagogically obliged to challenge students to wrestle with responsible opposed ideas. And after all, when it comes to moral education and character development, what point could there be to a study of principles and the past if it is not to be brought to bear on a student's own present decisions?

But then, other schools do not have a comparable investment in their students. They do not run any comparable risk of losing it all in a single decision that defeats the institution's essential mission and its responsibilities to the citizenry. Other school administrators are not nearly so properly susceptible to paternalism. Given the totality and intimacy of academy leadership control over the lives of people they care about, staying their natural parental dispositions is an act of heroism.

Academy ethics education programs could not blithely ignore the 800 lb. gorilla looming over their shoulders. Thanks to its compliant military, the government had triumphed over a sizeable (crippled) monster, and did not take kindly to any tarnishing of its glory. Academy instructors might be discreetly close-mouthed about the caricature of leadership role-modeled by their Commander-in-Chief. But academy ethics (and law) instructors can't well finesse questions about their government's official military policy and its (re)conception of the basic principles of *jus ad bellum, jus in bello* and *jus post bellum*, policies whose implementation looms as the lot of their students. How is a coherent explanation of the military's professional ethos to proceed when its basic principles are being violated, clipped, shaved and/or explicitly (if not publicly) contradicted by its current leaders? That hypothetical is an "academic question" with a vengeance. It has not been asked with the urgency it merits.

Quite apart from the occasional, circumstantial, external political pressures, the interplay of moral principles, military rules and policies, and pedagogical goals poses endless nice moral and pedagogical challenges for PMEE. For example, many a moral issue is ill-suited for academy ethics courses because the military has answered the question. There are sensible institutional rules that need to be impressed upon students since so many outstanding, upstanding young Americans enter the academies with scary assumptions. From Day 1 as Plebes onward they are told a few thousand times that all lying within the military is *verboten*. They don't dare dispute that, yet in six or so sophomore ethics classes I had polled, never less than 50 percent and often almost 80 percent thought it fine for the military to paternalistically lie to the press and Congress ("They can't handle the truth" or be trusted with it.) Getting through to student skeptics and cynics that the Navy *really* condemns categorically lying in those contexts is beyond the most talented civilian instructor. It takes a trusted Navy Captain or Admiral to give the official policy credence. Delivering such important messages is wasted time in a philosophy course. Of course philosophical questions can still be asked here, but to what pedagogical end? Military professionalism encourages independent thought, but officers are not encouraged to think lying to Congress a live option, a proper object of deliberation any time one is called to the Capitol.[23]

Philosophy

One pervasive constraint, perhaps the greatest handicap PMEE labors under, is the fault, not of the military or its ethos or external pressures, but of philosophers. The available intellectual resources for PMEE seem to me in a sorry state. Compared to other areas of applied ethics, the literature of military ethics has been intellectually underwhelming, despite having originated centuries earlier. The available relevant theories, concepts, distinctions, analyses, arguments and counter-arguments thus far are not exemplars of philosophical depth, rigor, insight or sophistication. I see little hope for their utility as a guide for professionals perplexed by serious moral dilemmas not resolvable by applications of moral common sense. (All the dilemmas derive from common sense; untying the knots takes an uncommonly nimble mind.)

Our ethical theories are all written within and about civilian society. They are preoccupied with the opposition of self and other, I versus everyone else. The military cannot sponsor that perspective. It subordinates the self, and legitimates only oppositions relating to military affiliation—the others versus my nation, my corps, my ship, crew, mates, comrades. Military affiliations are moral bonds, assigned, not chosen. Loyalties with your comrade, squad, ship, service, nation are axioms of practical reasoning. An officer's daily moral dilemmas are conflicts, not of Prudence versus Justice (or Morality in general) but of Loyalty vs Justice or Honesty or some other impartial virtue. On many matters of special concern for PMEE, much of the best work is quite recent and remains to be tested. Meanwhile academy instructors must be forgiven their fumbling attempts to navigate students through the moral reefs when esteemed ethicists supply charts calling to mind 14th century cartography.

---

23   The distribution of labor within academy PMEE that might seem somewhat suspicious may result from reasonable curricular preferences or inattention. The core philosophy courses on ethics devote significant time to virtues and character traits like honesty, loyalty, justice and courage, whose valuations in the military are more similar to than different from civilian valuations. Inculcation of the values, ideals and virtues that are far more distinctively military virtues and prized traits—like discipline, commitment, toughness, leadership traits, etc.—are left to other academy programs. Such matters are not subjected to philosophical reflection. They might be vindicated by such reflection, but I've sensed no interest in putting them to the test.

There is a pressing need for morally thoughtful military professionals with substantial intellectual abilities—the officers who, hopefully, attain the highest ranks—to join with ethical theorists and start reconsidering matters of military ethics with greater seriousness, openness, and sustained reflection. We're seeing a new wave of rigorous, scholarly assaults on the simplistic absolutism of prevailing dogma. Writings like those in this volume and others are presently but a ripple lapping the distant shores of academia, rarely reaching the mainland of the military and mass media. That's how intellectual movements always begin, including the ones that eventually drive social and political revolutions. Noticed or not, the worrisome truth is that those academic arguments are not readily rebutted and dismissed. They have in fact already demolished all the old defenses walled with bluff and bluster. Immediate refortification is a strategic imperative. Right now, the armory of the professional military conscience is exposed, its last bulwark a faith increasingly threatened with becoming blatantly delusional.

Competence

The failings in PMEE are not philosophers' alone. Though rarer than in the public at large, some active officers, in the academies as well as outside, have a tenuous grasp of the basic ideas of Jeffersonian liberalism. With some, the intellectual grip is sufficiently tight, but their sympathies lie elsewhere.[24] With others, the sympathies are sincere enough, but they haven't much taste or talent for critical analysis of basic values and principles.

USNA has lagged behind its sister academies because its core ethics course, the prime opportunity for "free" thought interrupting indoctrination, has never been turned over to instructors versed in this intellectually daunting subject. Instead, senior officers, most with hardly more preparation than their students, remain in close control, ill-trained and ill-disposed to lead their charges in thinking through departures from right-think more radical than center-left Democrats. For all their very considerable native intelligence, they are under-equipped for much rigorous, dispassionate re-examination of their profession's moral axioms. The explanation for this may be more crass than sinister: in the judgment of some well-placed

---

24   That comes out in the still too frequent incidents of military officers, including academy administrators, allowing their religious convictions to color their commands or the esprit they aim to instill. The 2004-2007 reports of coercive evangelizing at USAFA are exceptional mainly in the notoriety they achieved. Even among the more thoughtful leaders, there linger hankerings for greater "spirituality" in the military and its academies. Their reassurances that they mean some nonsectarian notion of spirituality lose credibility when they prove incapable of articulating a conception inoffensive to nonbelievers. Their attitude is reminiscent of Dwight D. Eisenhower's: "Our government makes no sense unless it is founded on a deeply felt religious faith—and I don't care what it is."

senior officers, the academy has run the course on the cheap. Penny-wise, pound-foolish economizing imperils the whole mission.

The native intelligence of such instructors is ample (though likely below the self-assessments of successful careerists), but intelligence comes in many kinds, many not helpful here, and some talent is needed, and more knowledge than any instructor's summer training course can provide. Only occasionally do any have near the tiny training expected of officer ethics instructors at USMA and USAFA. USNA's tendency to discount this and suppose that years of personal experience as a commander making momentous decisions will (more than?) compensate for a lack of book-learning is itself evidence of ignorance of the subject matter and its intellectual demands: a case of not knowing what you don't know.

Take one pervasive deficiency especially threatening at a military school. Far more than at secular civilian schools, academy ethics courses are rightly concerned that their encouragement of critical thought about fundamental principles not encourage the spread of moral relativism or subjectivism from the culture to the campus. With its responsibility for life and death, the military's mood is too grave, too earnest (too much given to sanctimoniousness) to brook indulgence in any attenuated sense of righteousness, or doubts of the reality of duty or the sanctity of honor. And mere belief in there being right answers isn't enough. Our military wants its personnel to believe that the answers it supplies are right, or, in any case, what comes to the same, those answers are to be acted upon.

But to belay the students' (justifiable or excusable) suspicions of being graded on giving the moral answers matching their instructors' beliefs, they are reassured over and over that "there are no right or wrong answers here." The trouble is, to say that (and worse, to make a mantra of it) is to leave the students baffled how there could be any value in their moral reasoning course: How could reasoning be improved when all conclusions are equally good? Warning neophyte instructors against self-defeating reassurances is easy enough, but insufficient, for this is a philosophically delicate matter. Considerable sophistication is needed to keep the intelligibility and credibility of moral objectivism afloat while piloting 20 plus hours of moral debates through treacherous minefields of reasonable moral disagreement trailing translucent tripwires.

The problems here get depressingly resolved in the academy extracurricular character development programs which are supposed to complement the required curricular ethics course taught, or at least overseen, by philosophically trained instructors. At all the academies, responsibility for the extracurricular programs is given to earnest officers having minimal philosophical sophistication and thus prey to the attractions of popularized instructional materials by patently second- and third-rate ethicists—moral cookbooks with nifty mnemonic aids, short order recipes a 10 year old can follow, indigestible distortions of moral concepts, obliterations of crucial distinctions, etc. Here the reassurances that no answer is right or wrong constantly risk exposure as fraudulent by the instructors' not-so-subtle steering of discussion toward a preferred conclusion.

Some of this is rectifiable by sponsoring further faculty education. The benefits might well be substantial. They are likely to be limited. Liberating the moral and conceptual imagination of a mind that's made the grade with ten, twenty, thirty or more years of habituated rigidities is a Herculean task. That mindset is not designed for teaching reasoning about the matters most threatening for military professionals. In class and out, senior officers of impeccable integrity, fully deserving all the respect due their rank, who elsewhere may display estimable intellectual agility, commonly become dogmatic (and testy) about simplistic moral absolutes. They may obdurately refuse to reconsider the legalistic rule that, when faced with a directive they deem morally unconscionable, officers must first exhaust official channels, and failing that, then the sole legitimate alternatives are compliance or resignation. They resist contemplating circumstances where compliance is morally impossible and resignation is morally irresponsible—where it's just not good enough to just walk away.

Our academies exhibit astonishing moral seriousness and fearlessness in making their students ponder the propriety of the German generals' attempted assassination of Hitler. Too often the exercise is wasted, for their mentors seem not so much flummoxed as incapable of wrapping their minds around the conundrum. Commanders may prefer to believe that they have no real need to consider seriously such circumstances. Perhaps, God willing, unless they play with abstract theory, it would do them no good to think of such things. Would that they could rest confident that God is on our side, now and forever.

The academies repeatedly display surprising boldness in the questions they make students consider, but the boldness gets vitiated and the surprise turns to disappointment, when instructors rely on the dodgy answers. Academy teaching stresses that, unlike an enlistee who swears to obey the chief executive, midshipmen, cadets and officers vow to uphold and defend the Constitution. So, it's alleged, their allegiance is to the Constitution, not to a chief executive's orders that may conflict with it. Serious moral thought does not end there. When the government will not recognize any such conflict is this legalism any better than a transparent fig leaf? Within the academies and without, it seems too little considered (perhaps it's too dispiriting) that the price of the purity and completeness of our officers' *de jure* political neutrality is their being *de jure* and *de facto* pawns of the political party led by their Commander-in-Chief.

Was it really a live option for a general or admiral to refuse to direct his troops to participate in the invasion of Iraq (Grenada, Panama, whatever) on the grounds of the illegality of the chief executive's order? The premises of such refusals cannot but be controversial, but they needn't be unreasonable or mistaken. Yet, however reasonable the claim in theory, does it matter when in fact no Supreme Court would dare question an executive directive to use American troops against another people—unless perhaps the directive blatantly contravened some contemporaneous Congressional limitation of military action? Short of that, while a subsequent Court might reverse it, no Supreme Court would stand alone against a current Presidential military adventure. (Expecting more moral integrity from our military than from our courts is symptomatic of psychotic political naïveté.)

Consider a case straddling the border between *jus ad bellum* and *jus in bello*: Could U.S. Air Force Major Hal Knight have successfully defended disobeying his secretly delivered orders from Nixon/Kissinger (to execute the illegal bombing of Cambodia without the knowledge of the Strategic Air Command) on the grounds that the orders were not a Constitutionally authorized exercise of executive power? More to the point: Would it have been reasonable for Knight to stake his career on the hope that he would prevail in the Courts? Perhaps he could have harbored some hope that after (long after) the war a Court might vindicate him, but is an unfounded hope of eventual cold comfort enough to sustain a sense of dishonor in getting along by going along?

Knight faced a 2 x 3 decision matrix. I've seen each of Knight's six options find sincere defenders in a room of 30 plus morally earnest senior U.S. Naval and Marine officers. To my mind, such disunity and confusion are healthy, hopeful symptoms of the progress of military professionalism. Midshipmen are made to mull over this matrix. Debates amongst themselves are encouraged, but they are not made privy to their mentors' disarray. On the contrary, I saw no effort to have midshipmen directly observe the moral disarray among senior officers on this matter or any other. What I saw looked like an unspoken policy of muffling such exhibitions and maintaining some illusion of a uniform understanding and acceptance of this military's moral code.

Honesty

Military professionalism subserves military proficiency, so it permits and promotes independent thought only insofar as a departure from uniform thought contributes to military proficiency. That holds across the academy. Academy leaders worry about heresy. They especially worry about the prevalence of student accusations of institutional hypocrisy. They appreciate that nothing so undermines their efforts at ethos inculcation than the rife, frank student cynicism fed by perceptions of inconsistencies in the regulations, or their applications, or between official preachments and actual practice. The leaders strive for a single, consistent message delivered, in word and deed, by every staff member up and down the line, civilian and military.

The goal may be worthy. Its attainment is a fantasy when self-deception reigns. The hardest thing is to recognize, let alone appreciate, that the higher the standard, the lower the tolerance for shortfall, the more likely that the standard setter, like everyone else, will trip up and fall short, or seem to do so in some eyes—and also the more likely he won't see it. The standards we avow are the damnedest things. They're sure to bite us in our but's. We don't know how to formulate fool proof rules, particularly moral ones. We keep finding new exceptions, or making them, "but" by "but." Whatever we may think, we cannot survey all that they imply. We don't see everywhere they'll take us, and least of all how it will look to others. The more rigorist we are, the more we resist apologizing for running afoul of our own rules, and resist acknowledging that we've done anything of the sort. We're aided and abetted in persuading ourselves and others by the endless options for alternative interpretation and rationalization supplied by logic and language. Meanwhile that supplier works against us by providing unanticipated possibilities of "misinterpretations" of our actions and intentions.

No school matches the academies' concern with fidelity, truthfulness, honesty. No civilian organization is as insistent about it as the military with its demands for automatic, absolute trust up and down every command chain. Dishonesty and distrust in the military can be fatal, disastrous. Of course, since the military has vital secrets to keep, and enemies to deceive, and Presidential politics to serve, and so on, military leaders must deal with all sorts of dicey questions about candor, not all of which are neatly solved by silence. Of more immediate interest to the future officers it trains are the conundrums about candor at the academies.

The costs of dishonesty in its ranks understandably dispose the military to insist on honesty where civilians regard the matter as more morally ambiguous— or not really the heavy-duty moral issue the academies make of it. The academies have great difficulty (and mostly don't try) avoiding being moralistic when their real concern is with "good order and discipline" and what they consider the proper functioning of the organization. They create an intensely regimented life, with all kinds of petty rules and restrictions inconceivable at civilian schools. There may be good enough reason for all or most of it, even though infractions are generally utterly harmless actions in themselves and their natural consequences. And there may be reason enough for the academies to demand not only compliance with the regulations, however arbitrary they be, but also complete truthfulness about any noncompliance, whether by a student or by any classmate. The stage is thus set for dramas, played again and again, between the institution and its students, who are naturally appalled by the prospect of ratting on classmates and close friends for their harmless peccadilloes. To their imperfectly acculturated minds, the higher-ups are demanding full disclosure about matters of no importance were it not for the rules, despite the searing breach of loyalty and the consequences of betrayal. (Even minor infractions can have decidedly unpleasant sanctions, including, if repeated, expulsion.) To the authoritarian mind, the only conflict is between a higher loyalty to the institution, the whole over any of its parts vs. a misplaced loyalty to the miscreant, who cannot be a real friend, a truly loyal classmate, when he puts you in a position where you must lie to protect him. (At other times and places the authority's attitude is called blaming the victim.)

When an institution raises the standards this high, it invites charges of hypocrisy, for bullshit from bureaucrats is inevitably as routine here as elsewhere. As at other schools, whether addressing students or staff, Deans and other officials regularly avoid frank representations of the real reasons for their decisions when those reasons are unpopular or embarrassing. No doubt their flexibility with the truth is often well-meaning: being upfront can be painful, even brutal, and to little good effect. Elsewhere we welcome the costs of the conventional facades, where all but the most naïve know (and know that each other knows) that what is said is other than truth unvarnished. But those conventions have heavier costs in a culture of highly moralized truth telling. (So does grade inflation in classrooms and in fitness reports in the fleet.) The rampant cynicism of cadets and midshipmen about such matters is infamous and unmatched at any civilian school I've heard of.

As elsewhere, officials often avoid outright lies by evasion, stealth, subterfuge and secrecy. Far more than elsewhere, the academies have felt needs and real powers to keep truth from coming to light. The usual concerns about institutional repute are magnified in the military, where whistle-blowing risks being taken for a breach of national security and bad-mouthing sounds downright unpatriotic. Our military academies are, like no other, the schools of this nation, so their PR anxieties rim paranoia. (The fretting becomes comedic at the academy imperiled by proximity to Capitol Hill and the national press corps.) As elsewhere, some institutional self-protectiveness may be reasonable and defensible. It bears special risks and costs when constrained candor must be reconciled with denying cadets and midshipmen any right to stay silent to protect the mates with whom mutual loyalty is a must.

Humility

Among the more ironic instances of institutional looseness with the truth is the puffery, deemed A-OK, indeed *de rigueur* from the CNO down to Associate Deans, of proclaiming the Naval Academy to be, not merely fit and proper schooling for future officers, nor merely very good, but nothing short of the very finest college education in this or any nation. School officials everywhere indulge in exaggerations, but none I've heard in my many semesters and campuses comes close to the self-congratulatory excesses of the naval leadership. They seem captive to a fragile vanity, terrified that, unless the school's excellence in every dimension is unmatched, its graduates—and Naval service and nation—could not be properly proud of the school. USMA and USAFA, I gather, exercise no greater modesty.

Meanwhile, faculty (who weren't educated at the academy) are not so self-deluded to bethink themselves stellar, or any better than competent and respectable. (Predictably, studies akin to weapons engineering have more exceptional faculty.) Rarely are academy instructors besieged by offers from research universities like Stanford or elite small college like Haverford. Some have competent judges say nice things about their work, but seldom are words like "world class" used of them by the very best in their field. They take pride in their teaching without delusions of their upper level classes being marvels of erudition and acuity. Their pedagogical strengths and shortcomings are well suited for their students' needs and capabilities. They know the intellectual quality of what they give their students isn't world class, and so neither is what the students give back. What else could be expected when the native talents of the students, while well above national norms, are like those of their faculty: few have the raw brainpower of their peers at Cal Tech? What else could be expected when traits other than intelligence are, quite properly, weighted more in academy admissions, and (the flip side of that) when brilliant high schoolers are generally bright enough to know that the academies are not where you go if your priorities are primarily intellectual? Exam periods excepted, academy libraries are lonely halls.

Some lapses from strict veracity about themselves might be excused as of a piece with the hyperbolic bravado befitting a profession where finishing less than first is fatal. That excuse looks lame when the leaders behave as though they actually believed their public boasts, when they roll out their defenses (a favorite being that classes at elite schools are taught by graduate students, not the prestigious professors)—reasoning inducing slack-jawed wonderment at whom these leaders spend their days talking to if they don't know or don't care when they insult their audience's intelligence.[25] (Authoritarian organizations are always at risk of having institutional authority kidnap epistemic authority.)

How can anyone with the acuity of senior military officers believe that the intellectual vitality of student life at our premier civilian schools could be attained and maintained after laying on the entire student body all of the academies' required hours of physical training and military activity, from marching to shoe shining and daily room cleaning? How can one imagine that that miracle could be managed with a student body whose native intellect measures at the low end of the brighter student bodies, and a faculty of little intellectual distinction? Those questions are serious, not rhetorical.[26]

---

25 Just for starters, for those entirely ignorant of such matters: (I) The academies are properly compared, not to public universities with 30,000-50,000 plus students, but to respected colleges with 3,000-5,000 students where graduate student teachers are exceptional, and (II) the grad student teaching assistants at respected research universities generally (1) teach only one of the weekly three hours of classes, (2) have more interest in, talent for, and training in their subject matter than many academy officer instructors (who rarely have more than the M.A. training many grad student teachers have, and often lack the undergraduate major in their subject normally needed for graduate admission), (3) are not burdened by responsibilities unrelated to their teaching remotely as massive as academy officer instructors'.

26 Many respondents to Ricks (*op. cit.*) ridicule him for referring to Gen. David Petraeus while likening West Point to a community college. They are all cock-sure that the Petraeus Princeton graduate degree after his West Point studies is proof positive of West Point's academic excellence. Their certainty bespeaks ignorance of Petraeus' perceptions (*op. cit.*) What reads as the most heartfelt part of a heartfelt essay promoting the value of civilian graduate studies for military officers is his report of the humbling responses (e.g., D) the Princeton professors gave the first papers of this top West Point scholar, who'd just won the "white briefcase" as first of some thousand students at Army's Command and General Staff College. His morality tale of learning some intellectual humility sits prominently in an essay meriting required reading at the academies and elsewhere. Readers

My own (decidedly unidiosyncratic) sense is that academy leaders indulge in too much mutual back-slapping and institutionalized self-delusion. It's not a coincidence that those in charge are academy alums with no personal experience of civilian undergraduate education, and usually no more than a year or so at a civilian graduate school. Mostly they are clueless what it's like to spend years of semesters with a teacher or three of truly world-class brilliance. (ROTC graduates of civilian schools are scarce above academy middle management.) Their efforts to remedy their nescience compete with self-protective proclivities and policies like foregoing external peer review for faculty retention, promotion and tenure. When a Provost confidently insists that they (unlike other schools?) need no such data, one can only bite one's tongue to keep from disingenuously asking: But, but sir, how would it hurt to get this extra, inexpensive, independent info? This admiral gets testy when pressed.[27]

All this puffery may be hardly more heinous than the local hamburger shack billing itself as the home of the best burgers in town, or the nation, or the cosmos. Still, our academies boast of being houses of the highest standards of honor, so it would be fitting and proper if they settled for less extravagant boosterisms. They cannot compete with Miami in football or Chicago in economics, but they have no need to. The academies do not, as whole institutions, compete against civilian schools, no more than Walla Walla vies with Wharton. The bald truth about these schools is plenty to be proud of. The undergraduate education is better than civilian professors might expect. It could be better still, and the nation would do well to support it. That's not going to happen if the academies aren't more honest with themselves and the public.

If they are to be duly proud of the integrity and honesty they aspire to inspire in their graduates, it behooves them to embody those virtues even at the cost of

---

may conjecture that other lessons were learned as well. Petraeus writes more diplomatically than I need to, yet candidly for someone in his position: e.g.,

> Being part of a wide-open culture of discovery can be a very stimulating, challenging experience for those of us who attended West Point, which (tongue in cheek) we felt represented 150 years of tradition unhampered by progress. Of course, West Point has changed enormously over the years and it is a true national treasure, but despite the varied curriculum and experiences it provides, it is not an institution that puts creativity, individuality and discovery before all else.

27 Some 60 years ago, Adm. James L. Holloway III—who authored the Holloway Plan that transformed Naval education, then served as USNA Superintendent and later as CNO – dreamt of making what had been a military trade school into "MIT on the Severn" (the river by the campus). USNA is rightly proud of its leagues of academic and cultural progress by its "Academic Revolution" and "Professional Revolution" of the 1960's and subsequent efforts. No one is well served when Holloway's successors now run this ship under the Bush-era banner: "Mission Accomplished." (See Todd A. Forney, *The Midshipman Culture and Educational Reform: The U.S. Naval Academy: 1946-76*, University of Delaware Press, 2004; H. Michael Gelfand, *Sea Change at Annapolis: The United States Naval Academy, 1949–2000*, University of North Carolina Press, 2006.)

due humility in their other accomplishments. If there was ever a time and place for a people to resist the deadliest sins of pride and vanity, it is now and here, in this nation and its military. There is no better place than the academies to begin teaching those virtues so unnatural for warriors: modesty and humility about one's wisdom, goodness, powers and value.[28]

---

28   Though not a large or random sample, it is worth reporting that vet respondents to Ricks (*op. cit.*) reporting personal experience preponderantly favor fresh academy graduates over their ROTC peers as better prepared to be junior officers. Few report differences of competence persisting among senior officers sorted by commissioning path. Differences in character are seldom mentioned, with one notable exception. Repeatedly, academy graduates are alleged to be hampered as young officers by a snobbish attitude of superiority.

Index

Abu Ghraib 7
academies and colleges, military 18, 159-
    60, 164-6, 182-3, 194n26 *see also*
    education (military), PME, PMEE,
    U.S. military academies
adversarial review 54
Afghanistan
    just war 20, 22, 136
    opposition to war in 21
    pre-emptive strikes against 52
    Russian invasion of 26, 64
aggression 18, 24, 41, 109, 137, 138 *see
    also* defense
ahistorical approach 36, 138-40
al Qaeda 52, 96, 105 *see also* terror/
    terrorism
Albright, Madeleine 63
American Philosophical Association 41n15
Amin, Idi 25, 53, 70-71
analytic philosophy 35, 36n7n
Anderson, Kenneth 98n15
Annan, Kofi 69
Annapolis *see* U.S. Naval Academy
Anscombe, Elizabeth 35n6, 78n2, 95n7
applied ethics 4, 35-6
Aquinas, St. Thomas 4, 15, 41
Arguing About War (Walzer) 33, 34-5
aristocracy 18, 143-4, 150n15
Aristotle 7, 170n11, 52
arms trade 64
atrocities 180 *see also* massacres
Augustine, St. 6, 15, 141
Austin, J.L. 35n6
authoritarianism 143-4, 151, 158, 160,
    161, 183-4, 192, 194 *see also*
    obedience, totalitarian
authority
    epistemic/intellectual 36n8, 143, 194
    legitimate 42-54
    moral 42, 60n1, 167

political/institutional 26, 36n8, 42-54,
    72, 101, 110, 118-21, 139, 142-49,
    156-8, 183-4, 192, 194
autonomy
    individual 54n35, 119, 138, 147, 150,
        156, 177
    political 55, 58, 63, 146, 161 *see also*
        integrity (political), sovereignty
    see also Enlightenment, independence
        (intellectual and political),
        individualism, liberation
        (intellectual and political)

Bangladesh 25
Boer War 19
bomb
    atomic/nuclear 27-8, 95-6, 102, 106,
        109-10
    Cambodia 25, 71, 191
    Dresden 100
    Germany 100, 102-3, 106
    Iraq 27-9,
    Israel 29, 52
    Japan 24, 95-6, 102, 106, 109-10,
        141n10
    see also targets, weapons of mass
        destruction
Bosnia 23, 53
bravery 16, 178
British Empire 66
Brough, Michael W. 122n41
Buchanan, Allen 55
Bush doctrine 3, 50
Bush, George H.W. 19-20, 25n13, 67n15
Bush, George W. 27, 28-9, 30, 46, 47-8,
    50, 185, 186, 195n27
business 35n6, 36n7, 161, 178

calamity ethics 94, 100, 102-5

Cambodia 25, 71, 191
Camus, Albert 23, 24
Carter, Jimmy 43n19, 64
casuistry 19, 36, 40
Catholic moral philosophy 6, 34, 36n7,
    37n9, 38n11
    pre-emptive war 44
    U.S. Catholic Bishops 39n13, 43n19
    see also Anscombe, Aquinas,
        Augustine, casuistry, Double
        Effect, Hehir, Salamanca, Suarez,
        Vitoria
character 1, 9, 181-2
    academy admissions 174
    development 177-8, 189
    effect of military academies on 168-71,
        183
    importance of officer character 165-8
    measurement of 170-71, 174, 178
    mission of military academies 1, 165-6,
        182
    see also virtue
Chechnya 70
Cheney, Richard (Dick) 28, 48
children 105
Chile 30
China 58, 59, 62, 65
Christianity 15-16, 41n15, 175n18 *see also*
    Catholic moral philosophy
Christopher, Paul 108, 110n10, 111, 119
civil disobedience 48-9, 54, 184 *see also*
    vigilantism
civilian
    casualties 19, 20, 24, 61, 71, 72-3, 97-
        8, 141n10
    control of military 116, 142-43, 145-7,
        149-50, 152, 158, 165, 185
    education *see* education (civilian)
    professions *see* professions/
        professionalism (civilian)
    relations with military 175
    responsibility for war 103-5, 115-6
    see also Double Effect, non-combatant,
        targets, terror/terrorism
classical just war discourse 40-46, 54
closure 25
COIN *see* counterinsurgency
Cold War 30, 34, 65

collateral damage 20, 97-8 *see also*
    civilian (casualties), Double Effect,
    intentionality, non-combatants,
    targets
collective security 40-41, 47, 57, 58
collectivism 6, 46, 51, 59, 60, 73, 125,133,
    158 *see also* individualism
colonial conquest 16, 41, 136
combatants
    distinguished from non-combatants 4,
        99, 101, 123
    Invincible Ignorance 6, 107-17
    responsibility for warfare *see* moral
        singularity of military
    risks of humanitarian intervention 61
    targeting of *see* Double Effect
        (Doctrine of)
    see also moral equality of combatants,
        moral singularity of warriors,
        warrior
compliance-based discourse 35-6
conscience
    civilian 7, 43n21, 65, 143, 155-6
    military 21, 43n21, 110n10, 141, 143,
        167, 188
    see also conscientious objection,
        conscientiousness
conscientious objection 6, 140, 141, 155-7,
    159, 167, 184, 188, 190
conscientiousness 137, 153, 163, 168
conscription 179
consequentialism 94, 125, 126, 181 *see*
    also utilitarianism
constabulary 41, 44, 53-55 *see also* law
    enforcement, police
Cook, Martin L. 43n19
cosmopolitanism 50, 55, 142, 155
counterinsurgency (COIN) 39, 63-4
courage 178
Czechoslovakia 30

Darfur 40n14
DCE *see* Distinguished Chair in Ethics
DDE *see* Double Effect, Doctrine of
dedication 176-7
defense 18, 46, 47, 62
    anticipatory 41, 44
    elasticity of term 135-7

rival discourses 40-41
U.N. Charter 47n28
dehumanization of the enemy 122n41
Demirel, Turgay 172n14
democracy 18, 20, 22, 25, 27, 49n29, 54,
 104, 115, 116-9, 127 143, 145,
 146, 150-51, 153, 155, 161, 167,
 168,176, 185
deontology *see* Kantian ethics
Department of Defense (DoD) 9, 136, 159,
 161, 180
discipline 7, 50, 120, 150n15, 152, 162,
 164, 170, 182-3
Distinguished Chair in Ethics (DCE) 2-3,
 8-11, 159, 170
DoD *see* Department of Defense
Dominican Republic 30
Doris, John M. 169n10
Double Effect, Doctrine of (DDE) 4-5,
 18, 36
 critique of 71-91, 98-99
 see also intentionality
Dresden 100
Du Bois, W.E.B. 114n20
duty 182, 183, 189
Dworkin, Ronald 93-4

EAC *see* Ethics Across the Curriculum
East Timor 23, 25, 64-5
education
 civilian *see* universities and colleges
 military *see* academies and colleges
 (military), PME, PMEE, OCS,
 ROTC, U.S. military academies
 of police 166
 profession 154, 175
 professionalism, importance for 143-4,
 159
 see also character (development),
 educators, indoctrination, *jus in
 disciplina bellica*, training
educators
 civilian 193-5
 military 193-5
 profession 134, 154, 175
egalitarian/egalitarianism 140, 142, 144,
 150n15, 152, 154-5, 176, 179
Eisenhower, Dwight D. 188n24

Elshtain, Jean Bethke 41n15
ending of war 24-6 *see also jus post bellum*
enlightenment/Enlightenment 8-9, 140,
 142-4, 147, 150, 154, 158-
 9, 160-61, 175n18, 182 *see
 also* autonomy (individual),
 cosmopolitanism, egalitarian,
 independence, individualism
 (individuality), liberalism, Kantian
 ethics, liberation, privacy, respect,
 universal (principles)
esprit de corps 150, 155
Estlund, David 127n53
ethicist 9, 10, 133, 141, 153, 159n1, 187,
 189 *see also* Distinguished Chair
 in Ethics
Ethics Across the Curriculum (EAC) 2, 8
ethnic cleansing 23, 30
ethos ix, 9, 134, 136n5, 146-8, 150, 159-
 60, 175, 182, 186-7, 191
 ambivalence 139, 147
 civilian warrior 145
 collectivization 148-58 *see also*
 uniformity
 Enlightenment 143-4, 159
 obedience and loyalty 157
 professionalization 144-5
 warrior 149-50
Evans, Gareth 40n14
executioners 126-7, 137n7

failed states 66
Feyerabend, Paul 37
Fish, Stanley 21n9
Fleming, Bruce 168n9
formal justice 111-12, 115n22
France 30, 66, 69, 71
full spectrum dominance 167
Fussell, Paul 95-6

Gaza 70
genocide 40n14
geopolitics 63, 65-6, 69, 142
Germany 24, 109, 115, 190
 Allied bombing of 100, 102-3, 106
 civilian responsibility 104
 Rommel, Erwin 114

glorification of military 146-7, 149, 156, 175-7, 180
Grotius, Hugo 16, 42
Guantanamo 7
Guatemala 30
Gulf War (1991) 19-20, 22, 24-5, 27, 61, 97-8

Habermas, Jürgen 54
Habsburg Empire 66
Haditha 7
Haiti 52, 71
Hamandiya 7
Hamas 105
harm prevention 104, 105, 106
Hartle, Anthony 18n6
hazing 161-2
Hehir, Brian 34, 35
Hiroshima 95-6, 102
Hitler, Adolf 104, 109, 190
Holloway, Adm. James L. III 195n27
honesty 162, 163, 164, 171n13, 175, 180, 183, 186-7, 191-3, 195-6
honor 175, 182, 189 *see* glorification
human rights
    constabulary action 41, 53
    promotion of 64
    rival just war discourses 34
    violations of 58, 69
    Westphalian paradigm 45
humanitarian intervention 4, 23, 25-6, 30, 39-40, 43-54, 57-73, 135
    reasons against 56-65
    reasons for 65-71
Hume, David 33, 39n12
humiliation 162, 164
humility 8, 110, 127n53, 166, 170, 171n12, 193-6
Hungary 30

ideal 16, 57, 58, 108. 114, 133, 147, 154, 161, 175, 182, 187,
identification, self and group ix, 58, 59, 66, 68, 133-4, 136, 149 *see also* collectivism, individualism
Ignatieff, Michael 48, 49n29, 54, 55n38
independence
    intellectual 7, 183-7, 191

political 57, 59, 66-7, 70, 72, 145, 151, 154
    see also autonomy, liberation
individualism (vs. collectivism) 46, 55, 133-4, 138, 142, 157, 159, 177 *see also* collectivism
individualism/individuality 59, 142, 150, 177, 195n26
indoctrination 1, 99, 138, 150-51, 158, 165, 184 *see also* discipline, independence (intellectual), liberation (intellectual), propaganda
Indonesia 64-5
integrity
    personal 144, 170, 171n13, 178-80, 183, 185, 190, 191
    political/territorial 34, 45, 47n28, 57
intentionality 4, 5, 36n7, 49-51, 54, 63, 77-91, 94-106, 113-4, 192 *see also* Double Effect, permissibility
international relations
    legalist/Westphalian paradigm 34-5, 46
internationalism 48-9
intervention 18, 34
    humanitarian *see* humanitarian intervention
    multinational 69-70
    non-intervention 68-9
intrusion 149-51 *see also* collectivism, identification (individual)
Invincible Ignorance 6, 107-17
Iran 30, 61
Iraq
    Gulf War (1991) 20, 24-5, 27-9, 52, 61, 67, 97-8
    Iraq War II (2003) 3, 4, 7, 26-31, 34-5, 40-41, 48-9, 52, 71-3, 97, 136, 180, 185-6, 190
    opposition to 43n19, 119n32, 185-6
    U.S. military academies 2, 119n32, 185-6
Israel 29, 53, 105

Japan 24, 95-6, 102, 106, 109-10, 136,140-41
Jewish political theory 38n11

Johnson, James Turner 37-8, 39n13,
    41n15, 43n19
Johnson, Samuel 16n3
jus ad bellum ix, 4, 5, 15-32, 33-55, 57-73,
    87n11,185-6
    just war, criteria for 44-46 *see also*
        just cause, last resort, legitimacy
        (authority), reasonable hope
        of success, right intention,
        proportionality, publicity
    responsibility for compliance with *see*
        responsibility
    see also humanitarian intervention
        (reasons against/reasons for), pre-
        emptive war, preventive war
jus ad pacem 54n34
jus ante bellum ix, 9-10
jus in bello ix, 4, 5, 7, 19, 23, 31, 93-
    106, 107-29, 122-3, 140-41,
    180, 185-6 *see also* collateral
    damage, Double Effect, moral
    equality of combatants, moral
    singularity of warrior, non-
    combatants, punishment (aggressor
    combatants), targets
jus in disciplina bellica ix, 10
jus post bellum ix, 30, 124, 186 *see also*
    ending of war
Just and Unjust Wars (Walzer) 3, 6, 34, 35,
    38n11, 95n7, 133
just cause 16, 18, 41-43, 54, 62, 96,
    113n17, 139 *see also* punishment
just war theory (JWT) ix, 3-4, 6, 8-10,
    15-32, 33-55, 77, 87-9, 93-106,
    107-29, 138-41, 185-86, 191
    application of *see* Afghanistan, Gulf
        War, humanitarian intervention,
        Iraq War, Vietnam, World War II
    history of 3-4, 15-22, 33-46
    methodology of *see* methodological
        anarchy
    subjects and principles of *see jus ad
        bellum, jus ante bellum, jus in
        bello, jus in disciplina bellica, jus
        post bellum*
    treatment at U.S. military academies
        185-6, 191
justice 16-17, 19, 20-21, 22, 96

combatants' responsibility 6, 108-12,
    115-16, 117-19, 123-4, 126, 127-8
    comparative 43n19
    formal 111-12, 115n22
    Gulf War 25
    humanitarian intervention 58, 59, 60, 63
    Iraq war 27, 28
    legal profession 121-2
    loyalty conflict with 157, 187
    moral precariousness 138
    occasional compliance with principles
        of 136
    tests of 178-9
    universalist principles of 138-9
    victors' 108, 110
    vigilante 47, 49-51, 53
JWT *see* just war theory

Kamm, Frances 78n4, 82n6
Kant, Immanuel 7, 9, 54, 97n13, 104n20,
    161, 163-4, 165
Kantian ethics 94, 98, 100, 101, 102-3,
    104, 160, 163-5
Kiesling, John Brady 119n32
Kilner, Peter 122n41
King, M.L. 184
Kizikaya, Zafer 172n14
Knight, Major Hal 191
Korkmaz, Ibrahim 172n15
Kosovo 48, 53, 61, 66, 67
    just war 20, 22
    massacres 23
    Rambouillet accord 62-3
    risk-free war making 23, 24
Kurds 30, 63-4, 67, 70
Kuwait 25, 61, 109

last resort 43n19
law, enforcement 28, 46n, 49, 54-5, 101,
    123, 126-7, 135n4, 139n8 *see also*
    constabulary, police
law, international
    ending of war 24
    failure to enforce 28, 50-51, 53
    institutional reform 54-5
    just war theory 16
    legal right to kill 140n10
    legalist paradigm 44, 47-8

non-intervention 68, 69
pre-emptive war 44, 46-7
preventive war 40, 45
rival discourses of just war tradition
    33-4, 35, 37n9, 39n13
sources of 51-2
U.S. violation of 46-8, 52
vigilantism 49, 51, 53
see also United Nations
law/legal profession 121-2, 124-5, 126, 137-8
leadership 171, 179, 183, 184-5
    textbooks 160, 164
Lebanon 66
Lee, Robert E. 114n20
legalist paradigm 34-5, 40, 44, 45, 47-8
legitimacy 25, 33
    government 67-8 *see* authority
        (legitimate)
    Iraq war 34-5
    legal versus moral 34
liberal/liberalism 142, 150n15, 188
liberation
    intellectual 4, 6, 8, 183-7, 191
    political 17, 26, 62
    see also independence
logic of community 120
loyalty 142, 151, 153-7, 178, 180, 187, 192
Lucas, George R., Jr. 3-4, 33-55, 118n31
Lynch, Pfc. Jessica 180

Machiavellianism 16, 17
Marxism 17
massacres
    East Timor 64-5
    humanitarian intervention 30, 58, 65,
        66, 71
    My Lai 18, 180
    risk-free intervention 23
McMahan, Jeff 43n20, 111n11, 115n21,
        123, 124n46, 125n49, 133-4, 141-2
McPherson, Lionel K. 120n36
media 8, 20, 137, 157, 180, 185, 186, 193
    profession\journalism 36n7
medicine\medical profession 4, 7 35n6,
        36n7, 43n21, 81-4, 104, 110n10,
        116, 148, 151, 152, 155, 175
meritocracy 144

methodological anarchy 37-9, 54 *see also*
    Catholic moral philosophy, classical
    just war discourse, compliance-
    based discourse, legalist paradigm,
Mill, John Stuart 45
Miller, Richard W. 4, 57-73
mission creep 136n5
moral equality of combatants 5-6, 9,
    107-29, 133-4, 139-42, 157 *see
    also* Invincible Ignorance, moral
    singularity
moral errors 11, 45
moral philosophy 34, 35 *see also* applied
    ethics, Catholic moral philosophy,
    Kantian ethics
moral precariousness of military (warrior)
    8, 139-42, 153
moral reasoning
    analytical approach to 36n7
    humanitarian intervention 71
    justification of military vs. civilian
        professions 133-7
    military education 2, 167, 170-71, 189
    military professionalism 144, 145, 152
    moral singularity 141-2
    Walzer's approach to 35
    see also applied ethics, calamity
        ethics, casuistry, consequentialism,
        deontology, methodological
        anarchy
moral singularity 5, 9, 133-58
    cultural and political conditioning 139-
        40, 142-3, 158 *see* Enlightenment
    of military professionalism 9, 133-58
    of professional warriors, 147, 157-8
    of war 5
    of warriors 139-42
    see also just cause, moral equality of
        combatants, moral precariousness,
        responsibility
Morris, Herbert 94n5
Moynihan, Daniel Patrick 64-5
Murphy, Jeffrie 94
My Lai massacre 18, 180

Nagasaki 95-6, 102
Nagel, Thomas 94-5, 100n17

national interest 17, 136, 141n10, 156, 168
national security 135-7 *see also* defense
NATO *see* North Atlantic Treaty
    Organization
Nazi 30, 114, 115, 117, 127
9/11 terrorist attacks 101n18, 185
non-combatants18, 93-106
    calamity ethics 102-5
    combatant distinction 4-5, 99, 101, 123
    Double Effect Doctrine 77
    harm minimization 87, 88, 89, 99
    immunity 21, 22, 43n19
    see also civilians, targets
North, Lt. Col. Oliver 1
North Atlantic Treaty Organization
    (NATO) 24, 53, 61, 62-3, 71
Nozick, Robert 125
nuclear weapons 27, 28
Nuremburg 108, 110, 137n6, 153
Nyerere, Julius 53

oath of military allegiance 154, 155, 156
obedience 115, 118-21, 147, 151-3, 157-8,
    167, 178, 182-4 *see also* civil
    disobedience, conscientiousness,
    discipline, duty
OCS *see* Officer Candidate School
offensive war 41 *see also* aggression
Officer Candidate School (OCS) 166, 168,
    169, 172n14, 173, 174
officers
    alternative ascension paths *see* Officer
      Candidate School, Reserve Officer
      Training Corps
    education *see* education (military)
    military ethics 188
    obedience 114-15, 157, 184
      misconduct rates 169
    public conduct 146
    religious convictions 188n24
    resignations 119n32, 157, 190
    respect 160, 164-5
    retention and promotion 171-3
    see also aristocracy, leadership
O'Neill, Onora 54
organizational imperatives 143-5, 151-152,
    158, 159-60

Ottoman Empire 65

pacifism 15, 16, 21, 33
Pakistan 59, 69
Panama 52
paramilitary 135n4, 165
patriotism 58, 59, 61, 66, 107n2
    delusional 185
    military allegiance 154, 155, 156-7
    soldiers 99
peace 15, 43n19
Pearl Harbor 140-41
permissibility 77-91
Perry, John 50n31
Petraeus, Gen. David H. 171n12, 194n26
philosophy 1, 8, 9, 34, 35, 142, 187-8
    see also American Philosophical
      Association, analytic philosophy,
      applied ethics, Catholic moral
      philosophy, Marxism, moral
      philosophy, politics (theory)
PME *see* Professional Military Education
PMEE *see* Professional Military Ethics
    Education
Poland 109
police 2, 61, 101, 122, 126-7, 135n4,
    136n5, 139n8, 165-6, 173 *see also*
    constabulary, law enforcement
politics
    conscientious objection 157
    decoupling of military from 145-7
    humanitarian intervention 59
    left wing 17-18, 21
    military involvement *see* civilian
      control of military
    military professionalism 145
    theory *see* Just War Theory, realism
    U.S. military *see* U.S. Congress
    U.S. military academies 1, 10
Powell, Colin 48
POWs *see* prisoners of war
pre-emptive war 28-9, 34, 46
    rival discourses 41, 44
    as violation of international law 46-7,
      52, 53
    wild west analogy 50n31
Presidential authority 190-91

press *see* media
preventive war 34, 46, 137
    Iraq war as 29, 40-41
    rival discourses 39, 40-41, 45
pride 146, 147, 177
principle 10, 21, 31, 33-4, 60, 67, 71, 102-
    5, 133-4, 139-44, 160-65, 180-82,
    184-6, 188-9
    calamity ethics 102-5
    critical vs. deliberative use of 84-7, 90
    Enlightenment 142-4
    geopolitical 48-9, *see also* Just War
        Theory
    military 6, 9, 133-4, 161-5, 188-9 *see*
        organizational imperatives
    moral 84-7, 89-91 *see also*
        consequentialism, Double
        Effect, Kantian ethics, universal
        (principle), utilitarianism
    organizational *see* organizational
        imperatives
prisoners of war (POWs) 18, 185 *see*
    also non-combatants, punishment
    (aggressor combatants)
profession/professionals/professionalism ix
    autonomy of *see* autonomy (personal)
    civilian 121, 134-8, 140-46, 148,
        150-55, 165 *see also* business,
        education (profession), ethicist,
        executioner, law/legal profession,
        media (profession), medicine/
        medical profession, police, religion
        (clergy)
    dynamic nature of 150n15
    ethos of 143-5, 159 *see* virtues
    education, importance of
    ends/goals and means/practice *see*
        moral precariousness
    Enlightenment influences 142-145
    militarization of 145
    military ix, 9-10, 18, 61, 107n4, 111,
        133-58, 159-96 *see also* civilian
        (control of military), moral
        singularity of military
Professional Military Education (PME)
    ix, 6-7, 10, 144, 159 *see also*
    education (military), profession

(military), Professional Military
    Ethics Education, professionalism
    (military), U.S. military academies
Professional Military Ethics Education
    (PMEE) ix, 1-2, 6-10, 143-5,
    149, 159-96 *see also* education
    (military), profession (military),
    U.S. military academies,
    professionalism (military), U.S.
    military academies
professionalization 144-6, 148, 150n15
promises 84, 85-7
promotions, officer 172
propaganda 137, 177-80
proportionality 5, 18, 43n19, 87
public conduct 146
publicity, principle of 54
Pufendorf, Samuel von 16
punishment 24, 94n5, 100, 162, 169, 182
    aggressor combatants 122-5, 138-9,
        141, 180, 181
    just cause for war 41, 42, 51

Rambouillet accord 62-3
Rawls, John 54, 97, 99, 102, 103
realism
    moral 189
    political 16-7
reasonable hope of success 43n19
regime change 25, 33, 41
    Iraq 29-30
    as violation of international law 52, 53
Reiman, Jeffrey 5, 93-106
religion 15, 44, 151
    cause for war 15-6, 45, 59 *see also*
        Westphalia
    Christianity 15-16, 41n15, 175n18
    clergy 4, 15, 148, 151-2, 166
    Enlightenment, relation to 142
    Just War Theory 3, 17, 36n7 *see*
        also Catholic moral philosophy,
        theological discourses
    proselytizing in military 150-51,
        188n24
Reserve Officers' Training Corps (ROTC)
    166, 168, 169, 172-3, 174, 195,
    196n28

respect 160-65, 168, 179, 181
responsibility
   of civilians for war 103-5, 115-6
   combatant, imposed risk to 60
   of combatants for military service *see*
      moral singularity of military
   divested by civilian control of military
      116, 120 142-43, 145-7, 149-50,
      152, 158, 165, 185
   divested by ignorance *see* Invincible
      Ignorance
   Invincible Ignorance 107-17
   legal 123-5
   natural moral sentiments regarding 139
   of political and military leaders for war
      22, 99, 103, 110, 116, 190
   post-war 26
   professional 133
   significance of intentionality 98-9
Return on Investment (ROI) 171-3, 176
Ricks, Thomas E. 168n9, 194n26, 196n28
right authority *see* legitimacy (authority)
right intention 5, 43n19, 87n11
rights 93-4, 140n10, 157 *see also* human
      rights
risk
   humanitarian intervention 60-63
   risk-free war making 23-4
Rodin, David 46n26, 137n6
ROI *see* Return on Investment
Rommel, Erwin 114, 123-4
ROTC *see* Reserve Officers' Training Corps
rule of law 55, 120
Rumsfeld, Donald 48
Russia 26, 30, 65
Rwanda 23, 25, 40n14, 69

Sabini, John 169n10
Saddam Hussein 24, 27-8, 30, 60, 71, 109
Salamanca, University of 16
Sandinistas 62
scale-sensitivity 94, 100, 104, 105
Scanlon, T.M. 5, 36n7, 77-91
Schoonhoven, Richard 5-6, 9, 107-29, 133-
      4, 141-2
Schroeder, Gerhard 31
Schwarzkopf, Norman 9
secessionist rebellion 66-7

self-defense *see* defense
self-determination *see* autonomy
   foreign imposed government 25
   humanitarian intervention 57, 58-60,
      65, 66-7, 69
   legalist paradigm 45
Serbia 24, 61, 62-3, 71
Shue, Henry 42n18, 45, 55n38
Sierra Leone 23
Silver, Maury 169n10
skills 6, 134-5, 136n5, 138, 145, 148
slavery 114n20
Somalia 60, 66
sovereignty 16, 34, 42
   distributed 44
   Enlightenment principles 142
   humanitarian intervention 57, 65
   legalist paradigm 45
Spain
   colonial conquest 16, 41
   Franco dictatorship 59
state
   logic of community 120
   monopoly over use of force 121
   moral equality of combatants 125-6
   rise of the modern 16
Stockdale, Admiral James 185
strict liability 105n21
Suarez, Francisco 41, 43
Sudan 40n14, 52
superpower rivalry 44
Syria 66

Tanzania 25, 53, 70-71
targets 4-5, 93-106
   Double Effect Doctrine 77, 88-9
   Gulf War 20
   long-range targeting 23
Taylor, Kenneth 50n31
Taylor, Gen. Maxwell 108, 110, 126
territorial integrity 34, 45, 47n28, 57
terror/terrorism
   bombing 83, 88-91
   terrorism 18, 21-3, 27, 49-53, 63, 72,
      98, 101n 18, 103, 106, 137, 185
   war against terrorism/war on terror 2,
      22, 39, 46
   see also al Qaeda, Hamas

theological discourses 34, 40, 41, 44 *see also* Catholic moral philosophy, classical just war discourse
Thompson, CWO Hugh 1, 180
Thomson, Judith Jarvis 35n6, 82-3, 84, 87-8, 89
thoughtfulness 183-7
Tibet 62
Tillman, Cpl. Pat 180
torture 64, 122-3, 169
totalitarian 143, 146, 147, 150
training
    behavioral conditioning 185
    character development 1, 177-8, 189
    harsh 161, 162, 163
    police 165
    see also Professional Military Education
Truman, Harry 96, 109-10
trust 156, 168, 178, 179, 192
Turkey 63-4, 70
tyranny 58, 68

Uganda 25, 53, 70-71
uniformity, military culture of 9, 149, 152, 156 *see also* independence (intellectual), individualism (individuality), liberation (intellectual), resignation
unilateralism 46-7, 49, 54
United Nations (U.N.)
    Charter of 40-41, 47, 52, 55
    humanitarian intervention 69-70
    Iraq war 48
    Iraq weapons inspections 27, 28, 29
    non-intervention 68
    weakness of 55
U.S. Air Force Academy (USAFA) 1-2, 159, 193
    religious proselytizing 188n24
    see also U.S. military academies
U.S. Congress 1, 8, 47-8, 110,166, 168, 180, 187, 190
U.S. military ix, 1, 6-10, 18-20, 133-58, 159-96
U.S. military academies 1-3, 6-8, 9-10, 18, 159-96
    commitment 173-4
    competence of instructors 188-90, 195
    discipline 182-3
    effect on character development 168-71
    expenditure on 165
    honesty 191-3
    humility 193-6
    hypocrisy 180, 191, 192
    leadership 160, 164
    liberated thought 183-7
    philosophy 187-8
    propaganda 137, 177-80
    purpose and mission 173, 182
    reasons for 165-8
    Return on Investment 171-3
    student motivations 173-4
    virtue 177-80
    see also education (military), Professional Military Education, Professional Military Ethics Education
U.S. Military Academy (USMA) 1-2, 159, 193
    cadet evaluation of Iraq war 185
    comparative rate of graduate misconduct 169
    graduate retention rates 172n14
    revised mission statement 173
    Ricks' controversy 168n9, 194n26
    see also U.S. military academies
U.S. Naval Academy (USNA) 1-2, 7, 159, 168, 185-6, 195n27
    character assessment measure 170
    DCE position 2, 8, 9
    graduate retention rates 172n15
    instructors 188
    see also U.S. military academies
USAFA *see* U.S. Air Force Academy
USMA *see* U.S. Military Academy
USNA *see* U.S. Naval Academy
universal
    phenomena 55, 57, 65, 108, 109, 114, 179
    principles 55, 109, 112, 138-40, 142, 152, 154, 156, 182
universities and colleges, civilian 3, 18, 152
    religious 16, 17, 166, 185

secular 165, 185-6, 189, 193-5
utilitarianism 94, 100, 101, 102, 103 see
    also consequentialism

vanity 178, 193, 196
vengeance 49, 60, 61, 67, 139, 185
victors' justice 108, 110
Vietnam 8, 17-20, 25, 36, 71, 136, 161 see
    also My Lai
vigilantism 4, 41, 47, 49-55
violence 17, 34, 51, 58, 60, 62, 65-72, 105,
    134-6, 165, 179
virtue 16, 26, 59, 99, 149, 170n11, 177-80,
    181-2, 183, 187n23, 195-6
    relation to success 175-80
    see *also* bravery, character, conscience,
        courage, dedication, discipline,
        honesty, honor, humility, integrity,
        justice, leadership, loyalty,
        obedience, patriotism, pride,
        respect, vanity
Vitoria, Francisco de
    combatants and justice of war 115n21,
        117-19, 121, 126-7, 128
    constabulary action 41, 44, 53
    just war theory 15, 16, 41
    unjust wars 116n23

Walzer, Michael 3-4, 6, 15-32
    critique of 46n26

jus ad bellum 46, 48, 103
jus in bello 95-97, 99, 102-3, 123
just war theory 3-4, 6, 33-38
    legalist paradigm 44
    on Rommel 123-4
    self-determination 60n1
    war between political entities 100
    see *also* moral equality of combatants
war colleges see academies and colleges,
    military
war crimes 7, 18, 180 see *also* atrocity,
    Nuremburg, torture
warrior see combatants, identification,
    moral singularity
Wasserstrom, Richard 97n12
weapons of mass destruction 27, 28, 29, 30
    see *also* bombs (atomic/nuclear)
Wertheimer, Roger ix, 1-11, 77n1, 93n1,
    107n1, 110n9, 113n15, 114n19,
    123n43, 124, 125, 133-58, 159-96
West Bank 70
West Point see U.S. Military Academy
Westphalia, Treaty of 42, 44-46, 142
wild west analogy 50
Williams, Bernard 35n6
women 164
World War II 24, 25, 102, 140-41 see *also*
    bombs (atomic) (Germany) (Japan)

Zupan, Daniel 107n1, 118n31, 120-21